Chinese Religion

Also available from Continuum:

Christianity as a World Religion, Sebastian Kim and Kirsteen Kim

An Introduction to the Phenomenology of Religion, James Cox

An Introduction to Religion and Literature, Mark Knight

An Introduction to Religious and Spiritual Experience, Marianne Rankin

The Study of Religion, George D. Chryssides and Ron Geaves

Religious Diversity in the UK, Paul Weller

Sacred Scriptures, Joan Price

Chinese Religion

A Contextual Approach

Xinzhong Yao and Yanxia Zhao

continuum

Continuum International Publishing Group
The Tower Building   80 Maiden Lane
11 York Road   Suite 704
London SE1 7NX   New York, NY 10038

www.continuumbooks.com

British Library Cataloguing-in-Publication Data
A catalogue record for this book is available from the British Library.

ISBN: HB: 978-1-8470-6475-2
      PB: 978-1-8470-6476-9

Library of Congress Cataloging-in-Publication Data
A catalog record for this book is available from the Library of Congress.

Typeset by Newgen Imaging Systems Pvt Ltd, Chennai, India
Printed and bound in Great Britain by CPI Antony Rowe Ltd, Chippenham, Wiltshire

Contents

List of Figures

Preface

It is difficult to give a clear definition as to what Chinese religion is, if by this we mean a single tradition. Traditionally, Chinese religion is associated with the three institutional doctrines: Confucianism (*ru*), Daoism (*dao*) and Buddhism (*fo*). But this has long been regarded as an inaccurate and out-of-date paradigm. The reason for the difficulty in defining it this way is that Chinese religion is both syncretic and multidimensional: on the one hand, it attempts (successfully in many senses) to construct a holistic world view; but on the other hand, it is diverse in its expressions of the view. In addition, Chinese religion is composed of more strands and traditions than what the three have covered. What we mean by 'Chinese religion' in this book is thus not confined to the three traditions; rather it refers to the religious ideas, beliefs and practices of the Chinese people, which developed in history, are continually pursued and practised in today's personal and communal life, and have therefore become an important part of the Chinese way of life. To present a coherent treatment of Chinese religion, this book will concentrate on the religious way of the Han Chinese, while excluding the faiths and spiritual practices of the minority nationalities of P. R. China and indigenous religious cultures in Southwest and Northwest China. Nor will it deal in any substantial depth with the 'imported religions' such as Islam and Christianity, although both have, in varying degrees, integrated with Han Chinese culture; in particular the latter has been widely accepted and practised by the Han Chinese.

Religious ideas and beliefs never exist in a vacuum; they are an element of a particular culture, interwoven and interactive with other elements of that culture and tradition. Nor are religious behaviour and practice simply out of individuals' instincts or preferences. They are, implicitly or explicitly, motivated by spiritual beliefs (faith), strengthened by philosophical reasoning (doctrine) and manifested through communal performances (ritual and rites). Religious belief and practice are formed or shaped in life experiences, followed and modified in cultural circumstances, and reformed or renovated along with social changes. Chinese religion in this sense can be said to be an essential part of Chinese culture and history, a constantly flowing current in the lives of individuals, families, communities and societies. Taking these into account, this book explores Chinese religion in its general and specific cultural settings, and investigate the ideas, understandings, choices and behaviours that are typical of the Chinese way of life; in other words, it examines Chinese religion within its contexts.

The main contexts in which we attempt to examine our subject matter are historical, linguistic and cultural. The Chinese believe that all trees must have their root and all rivers their fountainhead. By the same token, they also believe that most religious ideas and beliefs come from history, and can be fully understood only by referring them back to the historical background and circumstances. It is for this reason that we trace the key ideas and practices to their origins and follow their evolution in history. To help the reader to appreciate the historical contexts of these ideas and practices, we have produced a timeline in which major religious events and figures are placed in Chinese history and in the contexts of world religions.

Language is another factor that affects our understanding and interpretation. Chinese language has rich etymological and pragmatic meanings which as interpretative tools facilitate the acceptance or rejection of particular beliefs or practices. It is necessary therefore for us to examine the key terms against their linguistic origins, and to take into account their historical and contemporary applications in special language contexts. For many Chinese characters, it is often difficult, if not totally impossible, to find an exact match in English. In order not to diverge too far away from the original meanings, we will not only provide transliterations for Chinese terms, phrases, names and key text titles, but also append two glossaries with transliterations, original characters and the possible or closest English counterparts or meanings. In transliteration we will follow the *pinyin* system, while retaining other spellings such as the Wade-Giles only if they are used in quotations.

Above all, religion is part of culture and must be understood in its cultural context. A significant part of Chinese beliefs and practices are phenomenologically meaningful only in relation to their cultural background and expectation. This view underlies the structure of the book, with chapters devoted to cultural origins, the family and the state. Beliefs and practices are treated as cultural events or phenomena, and examined through their cultural bearings and impacts on personal and social life.

The main point this book intends to establish is that Chinese religion is a special way of life, which, with all its cultural and theoretical paradoxes, has been accepted and practised by the Chinese for hundreds of years, and the core of which may well continue to be so in the foreseeable future. This central theme is dealt with through thematic discussion in chapters, by which we intend the discourse to be informative, contextual and, occasionally, 'apologetic', in the sense that not only 'objective' observations but also views from the standpoint of a cultural and linguistic insider are presented and examined.

The idea and motivation for this book has largely grown out of our experience in teaching the course, *Chinese Religion and Culture*, during the past 20 years. Presented as a concise but sufficiently in-depth monograph, this book is intended to exercise a cultural journey into the various aspects and layers of the Chinese way of life, as demonstrated in its history, religion, literature and philosophy. Its primary objective is to integrate the examination of historical materials and the critical analysis of contemporary evidence, and to equip readers with the tools necessary for understanding the particular views held by the Chinese concerning the universe, the spiritual and the material world as well as communal and personal life. It will also seek to answer questions concerning why and how the Chinese, ancient and contemporary, pursue their spiritual practices in a particular way, strongly emphasizing the impact and effect of moral teachings that have been closely relating religious practices with personal, familial, communal and political life, and persistently searching for ways of harmonizing the human and the divine sphere. It is also our intention that by going through this book readers will be able to reach a balanced examination of religious beliefs and practices in contexts, to increase their awareness of and acquaintance with cultural modes of religious living that may be different from the ones they are already familiar with. The questions listed at the end of each chapter are intended to facilitate further reflection and discussion, either in the classroom or as topics and titles for courseworks.

There are already a number of books concerning Chinese religions. Some of them deal with issues at an advanced level and are pitched at scholarly research; some are intended for more general reading; while others are more 'history-loaded', examining religions in China mainly as historical traditions. This book will draw on these books but seek a thematic approach and examine important themes in religion; it attempts to strike a balance between history and contemporary times, between texts and practical applications, and between classical scholarship and newly discovered evidence and material. This book seeks to guide readers through the most important and complex concepts and the associated source materials while introducing them to the continuing, contemporary debates and interpretations of ideas, concepts and practices in China and beyond.

Contextualization is the chief characteristic defining this book. Apart from this, it also has other features. First, instead of a full account of religious history in China, it takes history as the source of the beliefs and practices that are still meaningful and applicable today. Therefore our approach is historical only in the sense that history is taken as a background to providing an explanation for particular ideas, beliefs and practices. Secondly, although intended as a comprehensive introduction, this book goes only as far as it can cover. It focuses its attention on the most important dimensions that have become part and parcel of the way of life for the Chinese, rather than delving into too many details of the established traditions. Therefore our readers will not find detailed discussion on doctrinal speculations or on specific ritual arrangements, because it is not our purpose to provide a manual for professional religionists. What we try to do is to engage in-depth examinations of ideas and beliefs, informing the typical way of life in China and providing an account of what the Chinese believe, how they maintain and practise these beliefs and why they hold on to them in their daily life. Thirdly, while in terms of history and theoretic narratives what it investigates, examines and explores would be applicable to all Chinese people in mainland China, Taiwan, Hong Kong as well as Chinese communities in other regions, it gives priority to the consideration of the mainland as far as the modern relevance of religion is concerned. It deals with the social context and political implication of religion and presents evidence that contemporary religious life in the Chinese mainland is not so peculiar that it has totally severed its connection with historical and cultural contexts. This way it provides a concise account of the religious life in contemporary China which is a continuation of the past and still reflects, in a general sense, the cultural expectations of being a Chinese.

Parts of the book have drawn on the published articles or book chapters by the authors; for example, Chapter 2 draws much material from the article published in a Chinese journal ('Zongjiao and religion', in *Xuehai*, No. 1, 2004, pp. 87–95); the chapter on religion in history has made use of the materials from the *Cambridge Illustrated History of Religion*, edited by John Bowker (Cambridge University Press, 2002, pp. 110–143), and the statistics on contemporary Chinese beliefs and practices are taken from the book entitled *Religious Experience in Contemporary China* (Cardiff: University of Wales Press, 2007). The authors wish to thank the publishers and editors of these books and journals for permitting us to reuse them in this book. In the process of writing, Carol Russell-Williams, Nick McFarlane, Thomas Jansen and Marian Mac Polin each read a number of the chapters of the manuscript and made a good effort to improve its language. Some of their comments or suggestions have been taken and incorporated into the manuscript. Mr Sun Zhongbo of Tianlong has generously provided a number of photos as illustrations to religious beliefs and practices in China. To them we owe sincere thanks. We would also like to thank Tom Crick, the Editorial Assistant for Humanities at Continuum for his patience, encouragement and all necessary assistance, which has made it possible for us to submit the manuscript in time for publication.

A Timeline for Chinese Religion

Chinese history	Major events in Chinese religion	Major events in World religions
Neolithic Age: (5000–2000BCE): **Myth and Legend:** Three Sovereigns (Fuxi; Divine Farmer; Yellow Emperor) and Five Emperors	• Potteries painted with the sun, moon and stars • Bronze masks, birds, trees • coloured Goddess Head, pregnant woman statues • Pottery and stone made penises	• Egypt: predynastic burials; Pharoah Hhufu's great pyramid of Cheops • Near East: Cylinder Seal with watergod, birdman and deities • India: female figurines, burial potteries
Three Dynasties: (?2205 BCE–221 BCE) –Xia Dynasty (?2205–?1600 BCE) –Shang Dynasty (?1600–?1045 BCE) –Zhou Dynasty (?1045–249 BCE) Spring and Autumn Period (770–476 BCE) Warring States Period (475–221 BCE)	• Natural spirit worship; royal ancestor worship; *Shangdi* • The oracle bones inscriptions • Daoism: Laozi (?600 BCE) and Zhuangzi (?369–?286 BCE) • Confucianism: Confucius (551–479 BCE), Mengzi (?372–?289 BCE) and Xunzi (?313– ?238 BCE) • Mohism: Mozi (?479–?438 BCE) • School of Yin-Yang and Five Elements: Zouyan (?305– ?240 BCE)	• Judaism: divine covenant between the God of ancient Israelites and Abraham (2000 BCE) • Zoroastrianism: Zarathushtra (1000 BCE) in Persia • Buddhism: Gautama Buddha (tr.560–490 BCE) • Jainism: Vardhamana in East India (d.420)
Qin Dynasty (221–206 BCE)	• First Imperial *Feng Shan* sacrifices (219 BCE) • Burning books and burying Confucian scholars (213 BCE)	
Han Dynasty (206BCE–220) Former Han (206BCE–8CE) Later Han Dynasty (25–220)	• Huang-Lao Daoism and prescription masters (*fang shi*) • Dong Zhongshu (?179–104 BCE) and Confucianism as the state orthodoxy • Zhang Ling and Five Bushels of Rice Daoism; Great Peace Daoism and Yellow Turban rebellion; Zhang Lu's theocratic state (191–215)	• Christianity: Jesus Christ • Confucianism was introduced to Vietnam, Korea and Japan • Buddhism entered China

(Continued)

Chinese history	Major events in Chinese religion	Major events in World religions
Wei-Jin Dynasties (220–420) Three Kingdoms (221–264) Wei (220–265) Jin (265–420) Dynasties	• Mysterious Learning (Neo-Daoism) • Ge Hong (283–343) and the *Bao Puzi* • Buddhist commentaries on *Zhuangzi* • Translation of Buddhist sutras and Buddhist adaptation to Chinese culture	Christian Church became the state religion of the Roman Empire
Southern and Northern Dynasties (386–581)	• New Heavenly Master Daoism: Kou Qianzhi (365–448); Daoist scriptures published • Lu Xiujing (406–477) and Ling Bao Daoism • Buddhist sculpture works at Yun-Gang and Longmen caves • Debates between the three religions; alternative suppressions of Daoism or Buddhism	Buddhism was introduced to Korea, Vietnam, Japan
Sui Dynasty (581–618) **Tang Dynasty (618–907)**	• Buddhist schools established: Three Treatises, Huayan, Tiantai, Weishi, Chan, Pure Land, etc. • Daoism promoted as the royal family religion • Xuan zang (?602–664) travelled to India • Court debates among the Three Religions • Emperor Wu (r.840–846) suppression of Buddhism and other foreign religions (840–2)	• Roman Catholicism • Islam and Mohammed (570–632) • Nestorians, Manicheism and Islam entered China
Song Dynasty (960–1279) Northern Song (960–1126) Southern Song Dynasty (1127–1279)	• Buddhist and Daoist cannons compiled • Neo-Confucian Renaissance: Zhou Dunyi (1017–1073); Zhang Zai (1020–1077); School of Principle: Zhu Xi (1130–1200); School of Mind: Lu Jiuyuan (1139–1193) • Perfect Truth (Quanzhen) Daoism: Wang Zhe (1112–1170), Qiu Chuji (1148–1227)	• 1095–1258: Christian Crusades • Further expansion of Islam and Islamic states • Mongols sack Baghdad • Mongols embrace Buddhism

Chinese history	Major events in Chinese religion	Major events in World religions
Yuan Dynasty (1260–1368)	Confucian 'Four Books' and civil service examinations Millenarian beliefs in *Maitreya* or *Mile* and the White Lotus Religion developed into anti-Yuan movements	Black Death epidemics devastated Europe Hundreds of Jewish communities were destroyed by violence
Ming Dynasty (1368–1644)	• White Lotus Society proscribed • Wang Shouren (1472–1529) and Idealistic Confucianism • Matteo Ricci (1522–1610) in China	• Sikhism: Shri Guru Nanak Dev Ji (1500 CE) • Protestantism: Christian Church Reformation
Qing Dynasty (1644–1911)	• Taiping Kingdom of Heaven movement (1850–1864) • Boxer rebellion (1900) • Kang Youwei (1858–1927) and the Confucian religion	• Bahá'í Faith (1800s) • First Jewish synagogue in Berlin • James Legge's translations of Confucian classics into English
Republic of China (1912–)	• Confucianism was separated from education and the cult of Confucius in public school was abolished in1912 • May Fourth Movement (1919) and anti-traditional ideologies	• Taisho edition of Buddhist Cannon (1924–1929)
People's Republic of China (1949–)	• Modern New Confucians: Xiong Shili (1885–1968), Liang Suming (1893–1988) • Cult of Mao Zedong (1893–1976) • Cultural Revolution (1966–1976) and destruction of traditions and religions • New religious policies from 1982 onwards; Religious institutions restored and popular religions flourish	• Religious fundamentalism • Nazism and persecution of Jews • 'Liberation theology' in South America • Postmodernism and interfaith dialogue • Debates on the 'Conflict of Civilizations' • 2001: 9/11 terrorist attack on the USA • Wars in Iraq and Afghanistan

Setting the Context

A major questionnaire survey of religious experience carried out among the Han Chinese in 2005, resulted in a significant outcome for our understanding of Chinese religion. One question in particular yielded a fascinating result where participants were asked to identify themselves as (1) religious; (2) non-religious; (3) anti-religious (firm atheist), irrespective of their attendance at churches or temples. Of the 3,193 samples, 8.7 per cent chose the first, 52.3 per cent the second, 26.1 per cent the third and the rest were undecided or did not know. Statistically, these figures seem to suggest that the Chinese are in no sense a religious people. Nevertheless, when coming to other questions regarding religious beliefs and practices, we have found that their answers are far from clear cut. For example, 27.4 per cent said that, in the past year they had paid homage to or worshipped Buddhas or Boddhisattvas; 21.6 per cent had prayed to the God of Fortune; 12.5 per cent to other spirits, while 28.6 per cent said that they felt comforted or empowered through these religious activities (Yao and Badham, 2007:30–31).

These facts demonstrate that in China the line between the religious and the non-religious is not clearly drawn. The demarcation between one faith and others that is so important in other cultures tends to be blurred and frequently ignored in a Chinese cultural context. In this sense, we may say that Chinese religion cannot be studied with any credibility without a full understanding of Chinese culture. The question of what is meant by 'religious' in China would not thus be adequately answered except in its cultural, social and historical context.

For many people who have some knowledge of China, it may be evident that various religious groups were active in society and are still distinguishable from each other by their commitments and practices. Among these, there are traditionally four so-called indigenous religious systems: Confucianism that venerates Heaven (*Tian*), the ultimate power which controls the human world; Daoism that calls for the return to the Dao in order to be one with the ultimate Way; Buddhism that propagates the true nature of reincarnation and paths to enlightenment; and folk-religion in which ancestor worship and animistic cults are crucial and essential for current and future fortune or misfortune. In more recent times, imported religions such as Islam and Christianity have gone far beyond their traditional boundaries to penetrate the heart and mind of mainstream Chinese people, and thus have increasingly become part and parcel of being 'Chinese' for a large portion of the population.

However, to examine all the streams and branches of these religious traditions at one and same time is beyond the scope of this book. Instead, we intend to explore the common themes that run through different religious belief and practice systems which can be explicitly or implicitly called 'Chinese', not only manifesting the general features of Chinese culture and society, but also expressing its philosophical world views and practical way of life. In other words, we are seeking to analyse the religious dimension of Chinese culture in order to identify those elements which are uniquely Chinese, and to investigate religious faiths and practices in a typical Chinese cultural context to reveal how they are perceived, followed and why they are pursued.

China and Chinese culture

Geographically, contemporary China is a land embracing a vast territory. At one extreme, 'When the Northeast China hits the depth of winter, the Hainan Island in the south is still in its summer', while at the other, 'when fishermen living by the East China sea sail out to work in the morning, herdsmen on the Pamir Highlands are still sound asleep at midnight' (Overseas Chinese Affairs Office of the State Council, 2007:7). Demographically China embraces more than 50 different nationalities and ethnic groups most of which have seamlessly intermingled in one way or another through thousands of years of conflict, penetration and merging. Of these nationality groups, however, the Han is the single largest, making up 91.59 per cent of the total Chinese population according to China's fifth national census of November 2000. What we refer to as 'China' in this book is nevertheless a cultural concept; namely, a cultural China that distinguishes itself from other world civilizations. Cultural China is defined not only by its territory and nationality but more importantly by its history, language, customs, religion, philosophy and way of life.

Identity is an important element of culture and is at the same time perhaps part of what culture is. 'Culture' has been used in a variety of ways to express quite different things, ranging from materialistic perspectives such as architecture and agricultural skills to political and social structure, such as governmental regimes and clan networks. In a narrow sense, it refers to a system of artistic and intellectual representations, or a collective system of the arts and other manifestations of human intellectual achievements, but it can also be equated with an entire social, moral and political order. More specifically, culture is defined as 'a historically transmitted pattern of meanings embodied in symbols, a system of inherited conceptions expressed in symbolic forms by means of which men communicate, perpetuate, and develop their knowledge about and attitudes toward life' (Geertz, 1975:89). In this book, however, 'culture' is primarily used in the sense of the distinctive features, characteristic of a particular way of life, including (but not confined to) ethical, religious, educational and communal ideas and ideals which define the meaning and value of life (Bol, 1992:1). In brief, the term 'Chinese culture' is here used to denote the essence of what it means to be 'Chinese' and manifest the features of the 'Chinese way of life' in its formation, evolution and transformation.

Chinese culture in this sense defines how the Chinese lead their lives, materially, socially and spiritually. This culture was formed and changed through history and within particular social contexts, and has been manifested in a myriad of ways. The divergence of cultural expression in China reflects both the co-existence of different ways of life, and within it, the historical conditions that determined and shaped these ways of life. Do all these different expressions of life experience and spiritual pursuits have something common? Do they contain a number of key themes that run through all of them, as fundamental principles that have put them together as one holistic unit? If they do, then how can we distil these common themes out of various subcultures and define them as the underlying principles for what is meant to be 'Chinese'?

Diversity goes hand in hand with convergence in a complex cultural system. How to understand the relationship between divergence and convergence is therefore the first task for us to undertake in order to grasp the defining features of Chinese culture. In the same way as for all other world cultures, Chinese culture is distinguished not only by its richness in variety and diversity but also through its convergence and consistency as demonstrated both throughout history and in contemporary times.

This harmonization of diversity and convergence was only gradually achieved over a long period of history. Culturally, China was originally confined to the small area of the Yellow River Valley, and became distinctive when agricultural culture began to replace the nomadic. The interchange between the culture that thrived from the Yellow River Valley and that of others that initially developed separately gave rise to a particular culture system that cultivated a pious consciousness of a supreme being, or cosmic power, of the importance of ancestors for the well-being of living people, and of interactive relationships between the human and the spiritual world. The rise of this culture marks the beginnings of Chinese religion, language and philosophy.

Scholars have commonly regarded the initiators and bearers of this particular history, language and philosophy as being of purely Han Chinese origin, a people living in and along the middle Yellow River Valley. However, recent archaeological discoveries have essentially refuted this view, pointing to historical multi-origins during the Neolithic era (around 7,000–2,000 BCE). Here there were different artefacts of the Yangshao Culture, represented by colourful hand-made pottery during the period from 7,000 to 4,000 BCE in the upper and middle Yellow River Basin, and Houli-Longshan Culture represented by pottery-wheel produced black pottery, during the period from 6,500 to 2,000 BCE, in the lower Yellow River Basin. At the same time, other artefacts were found which were very unlikely to be related to the Yellow River culture, such as the Hongshan Culture in the northeast Liaoning province, represented by colourful potteries, the female goddess temple, sacrificial altars and jade items, around 3,500 BCE (Bu Gong, 2007:89), and the south-west ancient Shu Culture (as discovered at the two sacrificial pits in Sanxingdui that are full of colour potteries, jades and bronze masks) around 2,800 to 800 BCE (Fan Yi, 1998:12).

Although we are as yet unable to confirm exactly how these cultures of different origins contacted one another and eventually merged, we can sketch a rough picture in which many different branches of the Neolithic culture interacted to form finally 'the culture of the centre' (*zhongyuan wenhua*), which was then gradually spread to other parts of the East Asian mainland. The mutual influence and penetration between the central and 'border cultures' was substantial and transformative, and the expansion of China itself eventually in turn brought about the expansion of its culture. On the one hand, each of the cultural groups grew up in specific natural and social conditions, accumulating rich reservoirs of social and spiritual experience which resulted in a distinctive cultural identity. On the other, these identities were mutually changed by frequent encounters. Living conditions and experiences were thus formulated (and to a great extent continue to be formed) in intercultural contexts where both the Han and other peoples carry on their own traditions but at the same time absorb cultural nutrition from other traditions.

What then followed was a long history in which the Han culture not only strengthened its own cultural sphere, but also gradually spread to other parts of China and became accepted by their peoples. This expansion was not achieved, however, without a price. Like that of other civilizations, Chinese history is never static and social conditions are not always peaceful. Rather, the integration of different ethnic groups and cultures into a single cohesive whole was often accompanied by conflicts, invasions and wars. A number of massive migrations on a large scale were either orchestrated by the dynastic government (or were forced by civil wars), or were driven onwards by northern or Western invasions. In the process of these migrations, the Han people were dispersed from the central region to underdeveloped areas, and carried with them advanced technologies and sophisticated ideologies that were eventually embraced by the border peoples so much so that the borders became part of the central.

The 'transportation' of these skills and ideas to less advanced areas was an important step in the organic growth and expansion of the central culture. However, this is only one mode of cultural formation and it would without doubt be a mistake to conclude from this that the formation and expansion of Chinese culture is simply one dimensional. Peoples and cultures of border regions also significantly transformed those of the centre; their customs and cultures impacted, enriched and sometimes even imposed themselves upon that of the central zone. The reverse impact took different forms. For some it was gradual and natural, through communal contact, intermarriage and commercial trade; while for others, peoples from other regions came to central China through war, invasion and aggression, imposing their beliefs and practices upon the Han people, accepting as well as transforming the central culture.

Such cultural migrations not only created conflicts and clashes between traditions but also contributed to the amalgamation of different nationalities, religions and ways of life. In the processes of cultural exchange, the highly advanced central culture and civilization demonstrated its supreme ability to accommodate and to embrace new ideas and environment. Its way of life became the core of a unique cultural system and gradually came to constitute the mainstream of the Chinese way of life. Through thousands of years of encounters and mutual adoptions, divergent ethnic communities of different origins were gradually moulded into a unified whole with the distinctive Chinese style which is rightly termed *Chineseness* by Thompson (1996:xiii).

Chinese religion

Chinese religion is embedded in the Chinese way of life and draws its characteristics from cultural exchanges and clashes. In such intercultural contexts a typical Chinese world view was gradually formed, defining its attitudes towards the meaning and value of being human, towards the relationships between the human and the spiritual, towards life and death and towards community, the state and nature. While sufficiently coherent, in these attitudes we also find a clear diversity of spiritual and cultural expression from which, different traditions, schools and doctrines developed.

Believing in the interactive relationship between the ultimate power of *Tian* (Heaven) and humans, a group of educated people or specifically ritual masters (*ru*) came to elevate the transformative influence of education, self-cultivation, civil and religious rituals, and place confidence in the fact that by engaging in these activities humans could be purified and social order and harmony achieved. These people later became known as *ru jia* or Confucians, who regarded themselves as followers of the beliefs and teachings elaborated and expanded by Confucius (551–479 BCE), a towering figure in the intellectual and religious history of China (Yao, 2000:25). Daoism as a both mystic and naturalistic attitude was initially advocated by a group of people who were disappointed with the social reality at a time when the Chinese world began to disintegrate, the prime figures of which are known as Laozi (traditionally the sixth century BCE) and Zhuangzi (?369–?286 BCE). This elite group tended to lead a life of withdrawal and non-co-operation, believing that Dao (the Way) was more 'fundamental than any human rule or norm' (Sharma (ed.), 1993: 240–250). Daoism did not, however, develop into a full-blown religion with its own priesthood, monasteries and elaborated rituals until the first century CE. This coincided with the introduction of religious Buddhism from India and central Asia which initiated a long process of integration into Chinese social ideology and religious beliefs. In one sense the three traditions (Confucianism, Daoism and Buddhism) that originated and evolved independently of one another sustain the three dimensions of Chinese culture with clearly different doctrines and practices.

Apart from the three more or less clearly defined traditions, we have also a vast range of spiritual beliefs and practices such as ancestor worship, worship of various gods and spirits (for example, God of Earth (Tu di), one of the earliest indigenous gods in China, responsible for village and communal matters, see Figure 1.1), family rituals, animistic beliefs in all sorts of natural

Figure 1.1 A shrine for the God of Earth (Tu di)

and climate spirits and deities, and syncretic attitudes toward religious and non-religious teachings and activities. These indigenous religions were enormously enriched by absorbing ideas, rituals, beliefs and practices from all the three traditions, and at the same time frequently developed new orientations and movements. These religions do not normally have an institution, or a self-defined doctrine and a system of rituals. Although perhaps doctrinally unimportant, these beliefs and practices constitute the major part of the spiritual life among ordinary Chinese people and have significantly influenced all the dimensions of their lives. From different perspectives, this kind of religious beliefs and practices is named variously either as 'communal religion', or 'popular religion', or 'folk religion', but for reasons of simplicity, we shall simply term them 'folk-religions'.

A number of religions that are currently practised by the Chinese originated in the non-Chinese world and were then 'imported' to and spread in China, becoming gradually accepted to a lesser or greater degree by the people. The most significant of these religions is Buddhism. Throughout its long history in China, Buddhism was already totally sinologized and had become integrated into the social, communal and personal fabrics of China, woven into the Chinese way of life. What we mean here by 'imported religions' are those that command a following among the Chinese people but continue to retain their original religious characteristics. Some of these characteristics may have been accepted as part of the way of life, but the core of their teachings and practices are still regarded (at least by a significant portion of the people) as 'alien', in the sense that a clear boundary surrounding their faiths and worships is still visible, separating them from the rest of the population.

Among these religions, some have played an increasingly important role in shaping the way of life in contemporary China, while others are more or less confined to certain quarters of the land or certain groups of the people. Such indigenization is still in process, but its impact on shaping the mainstream way of life in China is nevertheless limited. Among these religions the most important two are Islam and Christianity. Islam itself was first brought to China in 651 and became popular among the northern peoples as well as southern port cities during the Tang and Song dynasties (618–1279). Today Muslims of main denominations are generically known in China as Hui, a minority nationality mostly concentrated in the north-west regions. Christianity had its first appearance in China in the seventh century in the form of Nestorianism, and fluctuated in popularity during its long history in China. Today its population comprises Protestants, Catholics and a small number of Orthodox Christians.

According to the official census provided by the 'Information Office of the State Council of People's Republic of China' in 1995, the syncretic practices of folk-religion which combined those of Buddhism, Daoism, Confucianism and folk-religions are popular among nearly 1billion people. Aside from this, Buddhism (primarily in its Mahayana form) as the largest 'institutional' religion has around 100 million followers, equivalent to 8 per cent of the total population. Christianity has a following of around 54 million or 4 per cent of the total population. Islam had followers of around 20 million, accounting for 1.5 per cent of the population. Apart from the bigger five 'groups' that have been recognized officially in the People's Republic of China as religions (Buddhism, Daoism, Protestantism, Catholicism and Islam), there are also a small number of followers of Hinduism, Dongbaism, new religions and sects such as *Xiantian jiao* (the Formerly Heaven Religion) and Qigong-related semi-religions such as *Falungong*. More new forms of religion are gaining in popularity in contemporary Chinese society, and take their shape through merging or integrating existing religious doctrines and new practices. In a survey carried out in 2006, approximately 300 million people are identified as religious believers, among whom 62 per cent are 26 to 39 in age, and largely from richer and educated backgrounds. This has contradicted previous surveys where the majority of religious believers were old, poor and illiterate, and has indicated that religion has become more influential for the young, comparatively rich and educated people (Zhuo, 2008:1).

Nevertheless, these figures are highly controversial and indeed most 'statistics' in terms of religious believers in China cannot be accurate in a real scientific sense. Apart from the social and political factors that influence our estimates of religious believers, there are also cultural reasons for the difficulty in determining the extent of religious membership. In both historical and contemporary times, definitions of religion are often too narrow to cover all of those who, although not consciously belonging to any defined religious organization, are 'religious' in their daily lives. The questionnaire survey among the Han Chinese in 2005 provides a strong evidence for this argument, for example, only 4.2 per cent of those surveyed claimed to be Buddhists (which translates into about 55 million Buddhists), but 18.2 per cent said that they had experienced the influence or control by Buddhas or Bodhisattvas in the past year; more than that, 27.4 per cent said that they had paid homage to, or worshipped Buddhas or Bodhisattvas; and 77.9 per cent said they agreed that there existed causational retribution, a fundamental Buddhist teaching concerning reincarnation (Yao and Badham, 2007:31).

All the above analyses thus point to a very different concept of religion in China from that familiar to the western world. While we will make this point more fully in the next Chapter, here we outline several aspects of Chinese culture that will shape this new understanding of Chinese religion.

The first of these aspects is the harmonious holism which is characteristic of Chinese culture. Under such holistic structures, all forms of Chinese religious expression tend to be syncretic, incorporating different, sometime even opposite, elements into one system. It is in this sense that we define Chinese religion as a single unit, rather than as many different denominations or strands. This unit contains both complementary and contrasting parts or elements, each of which is allocated a position that is unique and special, and each depending on the existence and operation of the others. All these elements can be likened to the pearls of the Buddhist Indra's net in which each, being 'an aspect of the whole', reflects and presupposes others (de Bary and Bloom, 1999:473). What differentiates the Chinese holism from Huayan Buddhism, however, is that in Chinese holism, parts are not permanent 'pearls' or 'atoms', eternal and unchangeable. Rather, they are in a constant process of growing, changing and transforming, which makes the whole an organic oneness.

Chinese culture is fundamentally ritualistic, synthesizing the moral and the religious. According to Bu Gong, this ritual system ran through all stages of Chinese cultural development, distinguishing Chinese civilization from all other cultures (Bu Gong, 2007: 3). This system originated from the primary ritual of sacrificing and burial developed during the Neolithic period, enriched in the bronze period (the Shang dynasty, c.1600–c.1045 BCE) and completed during the Zhou dynasty (c.1045–256 BCE). In this ritual system, religious rituals came to be adopted as moral, social and political norms, defining communal and political boundaries, and outlining collective and individual responsibilities. The religious and familial, social, political and educational dimensions were thus not separable in Chinese culture, and these dimensions together formed the whole of the Chinese life.

In this sense, cultural holism and religious syncretism have fundamentally cultivated and shaped an inclusive attitude towards religious matters. Unlike in other cultures, where different religious traditions are exclusively independent of each other, in Chinese culture following one religion does not necessarily mean the rejection or denial of others. The Chinese way of dealing with different cultural and religious tenets and practices is consistently inclusive: they find no contradiction in paying homage to the Buddha or the Bodhisattva in Buddhist temples, while at the same time living according to Daoist principles and participating family ancestor veneration rituals. Although in later times, different traditions were developed in terms of religious commitments and orientations (each having its own specific requirements and criteria for the faithful), the Chinese mindset on religion is primarily shaped and character-ized by this religious syncretism rather than denominationalism.

In this sense, the term 'Chinese religion' as used in this book should not be interpreted as implying the existence of only one religious system within Chinese culture. There were (and still are) many different ways of believing and practising, but all these different ways are rooted in and can be defined by culturally common themes and features. The motives and expectations of their beliefs and practices cannot be fully clarified except through a balanced inter-pretation of Chinese culture and society. Therefore different religious streams and strands have formed a culturally unitary single tradition in the sense that not only the ideas behind its practices are related to each other, but also the practices that are guided by the ideas are interconnected. From this perspec-tive, it is logically reasonable and justifiable to use a singular rather than plural term to define the religion of China.

'Three religions of China'

The most frequently used term to summarize Chinese religion is the one called *san jiao* or 'three doctrines' or 'three traditions' or 'three religions'. This model was dominant in all scholarly publications before the 1950s, and is still employed in a large number of contemporary introductions to Chinese history, culture and religion. Therefore, in the study of Chinese religion, we cannot shun the question about the three most influential ways of thinking and living: Confucianism, Daoism and Buddhism.

Implicitly or explicitly scholars have taken this paradigm as a basic structure, within which to categorize and assess religious ideas and behaviour in China (e.g. Soothill, 1929; Hans Küng and Julia Ching, 1990; Julia Ching, 1993; Ninian Smart, 1998; Joseph Adler, 2002). In many senses this paradigm provides us with a convenient catalogue to determine how religions existed, functioned and interacted in imperial China when Confucianism, Daoism and Buddhism were the three most influential ideological frameworks and social conventions, controlling and defining all the important aspects of the Chinese life, political, social, communal as well as spiritual.

The most important unifying feature of the 'three religion' paradigm is not that it recognizes the existence of three different religious/philosophical doctrines, but that it points to the context in which the three interacted and were mutually influenced, as Hans Küng has stated clearly: 'not only did the two main wisdom religions of Confucianism and Taoism become intertwined, they also absorbed a large number of Mahayana Buddhist influences – not, however, without giving them a deep Chinese coloring' (Hans Küng and Julia Ching, 1990: xvi).

Many scholars who embrace this paradigm have observed a clearly labour/functional division between them: Confucianism encouraged people to engage social and political activities, and elevated the significance of maintaining or reconstructing political and moral order through external social education and internal self-cultivation. A significant portion of historical Confucians considered these tasks to be their mission from Heaven as the ultimate spiritual power, and took great pains to work on these tasks throughout their lifetime. Daoist teachings were primarily concerned with the individualistic and naturalistic aspects of life, calling for the need to cultivate personal spiritual health and physical immortality rather than concerned with social and financial gains. Buddhism viewed life from the aspect of causational chain, highlighting the meaning and function of the merits and demerits that were accumulated in this life and how the attitudes and behaviour of this life would affect life hereafter.

The most famous European spokesman for the so-called labour division of the three religions is W. E. Soothill, who presents an unambiguous discussion of this concept in a book entitled *The Three Religions of China*: 'Two of them, the first and the last [Confucianism and Daoism], are indigenous. The other, Buddhism, while known in China before the Christian era, was not formally introduced until the first century A. D' (Soothill, 1929:1). It seemed clear to him that during the early part of the twentieth century, the three traditions represented three fundamental aspects of the Chinese way of life: Confucianism represented the politico-religious and moral side of national life, Daoism the ascetic, spiritualistic and magical side, while Buddhism the *vanitas vanitatum* of mundane existence and salvation for the life to come. However, in terms of spiritual quality, Soothill suggested that that all streams had degenerated in terms of spirituality: the cult of learned Confucians consisted chiefly of the officials and *literati*, as well as the cult of Confucius and his immediate disciples. The Daoists had the divinities and practices of a tradition which had already degenerated from a search after the absolute and the immortal into the pursuit of thaumaturgy and demonolatry and the practice in general of the magical side of pre-Confucian and pre-Laocian religion. The Buddhists also had their own objects of worship, especially for the dead (Soothill, 1929:17).

Dissatisfied with the perspective of a Christian missionary by which Chinese religions are catalogued, Thompson nevertheless employed, although much less explicitly, the 'three religion' paradigm to introduce traditional Chinese religion. For him, Confucianism was a state religion, and a *literati* tradition which took sainthood as the goal of personal salvation. Daoism he identified as a specialized religion with the following features: a nearly two thousand-year-old tradition of ordained priesthood; the accumulation of an enormous amount of esoteric texts comprehensible only to those with specialized competence; a grand liturgical tradition based on the ritual texts; a well-defined eremitic tradition, and many distinctive techniques conducive to the ultimate goal of transformation to transcendent immortality (Thompson, 1996:81). For him, Buddhism was an Indian originated tradition that had been transplanted into Chinese culture and society, with a particular feature of placing the monastery as the centre of religious life. The monasteries themselves were not only regarded as the home of Buddhist monks and nuns, but were also temples and places of worship for the people to honouring their deities (Thompson, 1996:107).

While admitting the convenience of cataloguing important religious institutions, we must also see the weaknesses and limitations of this paradigm. It would be counterproductive or even misleading should it be used to explore all the strata of religious life in China, either in the past or present. It has been repeatedly pointed out that identifying Chinese religion with the three religions of China, has 'caused the most important aspect of Chinese religiosity, the Popular Religion, to be ignored and neglected by Chinese and western scholars' (Pas, 1989:2). Apart from this obvious shortcoming, this paradigm has two more subtle but deeply misleading weaknesses. First, this paradigm tends to overemphasize the separation of the three. Indeed, there do exist some distinctive features separating the three ways of life from each other; there are, for example, some externally observable phenomena such as behaviour, clothing styles, rituals and musical instruments used in ceremonies, and so on, as well as other more doctrinal characteristics such as the nature and function of deities worshipped, and advocated paths towards final destinations. However, it is not appropriate if by this we divide them into three totally separable ways. More and more scholars have come to appreciate an underlying unity that since each of the three religions was 'the recipient of imperial recognition and favour', it would be therefore be more illuminative to consider them as 'three aspects of the established religion of the country', as Soothill states. From this perspective, 'there is much truth, then, in the Chinese saying that the three religions are one' (Soothill, 1929:4). Thus, the distinction between the three ways is meaningful only in the context of their oneness of nature: the majority of the Chinese people are sufficiently inclusive in their thinking to belong to all of three, in the sense that they follow the teachings of all three great traditions; they will therefore practise eclectically any of the doctrines which seem practicable at any one time.

Secondly, although the paradigm of 'three doctrines' does not necessarily exclude the mutual influence between them, the artificial separation of the three may overshadow their intensive and extensive interaction. In reality, the three religions mutually relate to and depend upon one another. They are 'syncretic' in the sense that they absorb useful teachings from each other and pragmatically apply the 'borrowed' tenets in their own way at particular times.

In this syncretic culture, the three religions are often interpreted as three teachings on the same Way, or three paths to the same goal: the difference between them is in 'form', but not in 'essence'. Each of the three teachings has been transformed over a long period of history into a particular part of the mainstream culture, and each has contributed in unique ways to the life of the Chinese people. Originally only one of many schools of thought competing for political favour and intellectual popularity, Confucianism had to wait for several hundred years before it was recognized by the imperial government as the supreme doctrine and became part of the state religion, shaping the operations of government, education, family, personal and communal life. As for Daoists, they were by nature against all ritualistic norms, either religious or political, and adopted an indifferent attitude towards life and death. They propagated a belief in a natural life, a life free of the worries and bondages of human-made disciplines. However, in due course, the teachings of this naturalistic school were transformed into a religious movement, aiming at longevity and immortality through ritual actions and religious devotions. This took place during the Later Han dynasty (25–220 CE), in the same time when, or immediately after, Buddhism was introduced and began to flourish. Buddhism brought to China different cultural elements from South Asia, and changed many aspects of Chinese attitudes and behaviours. At the same time, Buddhism was itself transformed by Chinese culture, and through its interaction with Confucianism and Daoism. Thus, from both historical and current perspectives, the three doctrines are in reality three dimensions of the Chinese heritage or indeed three aspects of Chinese life, rather than three opposing religions. In other words, the relation between them is more complementary than differentiating.

This mutually inclusive and complementary relationship remains apparent in contemporary China. As revealed by the questionnaire survey of 2005, many people had no sense of contradiction when visiting temples of different religious origins, and reported that they had simultaneously experienced the guidance of Buddhist powers, Daoist deities and Confucian 'Heaven'. The survey also demonstrated that homage was often paid to Buddhas, Daoist immortals and ancestors simultaneously (Yao and Badham, 2007:166). This data indicates that by nature Chinese culture does not encourage believers to claim an exclusive religious identity. Rather, it motivates people to select from each teaching, however doctrinally different, convenient methods to sort out life problems.

Other paradigms

Apart from this three religion model, there are a number of other paradigms which are popular with students and scholars when they come to conceptualize religious life in China. In the same way as the three religion paradigm, these paradigms have themselves arisen from specific philosophical methodologies, and therefore reflect particular views about how Chinese religion should be studied and catalogued. These paradigms are largely constructed out of a theoretical need to summarize particular features of Chinese life, and are therefore in general of historical value, or are probably convenient for us to outline religions in China. At the same time, we recognize that they are merely perspectives, and can equip us with nothing more than a lens that may or may not help us to look at actual situations clearly. Therefore we must not expect this kind of catalogue to be consistently conducive to our research; there are strengths as well as weaknesses in each of them, which can clarify or equally blur our vision were they applied blindly. For this reason we will not adopt or apply indiscriminately any of these paradigms in this book. Instead of looking at Chinese religion through these constructing lenses, we will take the view that Chinese religion is culturally holistic, and that it is above all a practical way of life in search of satisfaction for specific spiritual as well as material needs. It would first be helpful, however, if we briefly examine these prevailing paradigms, to determine in which aspects they can be useful and acceptable, and in which aspects they may be inappropriate and misleading.

Four strands

The first paradigm of Chinese religion that scholars frequently apply in their researches is an extended form of the three religion model; namely, the four religious strands in China. Many researchers have already observed that religious life in China reflects more than the three religions, and that the three religion paradigm does not fully encompass the richness and depth of its religious belief systems and ideologies. In reflecting on these complexities, a fourth element can be added to the three religions, by which a new paradigm is advanced. An early exponent of this paradigm was again Soothill who as cited earlier, while acknowledging that the two great religions (Confucianism and Daoism) originated from ancient roots, observed the existence of the third stratum prior to the arrival of Buddhism:

> The ideas promulgated by these two men [Confucius and Laozi] represent two different strata of the old religion . . . There was a third and prior stratum neither of them propagated, indeed out of which they sought to rise, namely, the old magical and spiritualistic animism which was the principal religion of the common people . . . This third, or magical form, which, strictly speaking, is neither Confucian or Laocian, but which has an admixture of both, together with a later intermixture of Buddhist ideas, is the prevalent religion of the common people. (Soothill, 1929: 9–10)

To ease the difficulty of defining these four religious strands in China, Fowler has done further work on this model, and has proposed a new phrase of the paradigm, which looks instead at four religious genres: 'China has embraced four religious genres from antiquity – Confucianism, which has been the dominant culture; Taoism; Buddhism, which infiltrated China at the beginning of the first millennium; and popular religion, the religion of the ordinary folk (Fowler, 2005:4). For Fowler, each of these has developed its own particular characteristics, while the cross-fertilization of beliefs and practices between all four has been prolific resulting almost in a fifth genre that may be termed as 'Chinese religion'.

The four religion or four genre 'paradigm' thus argues that each of the four religions/strands/genres functions in its own right, and that the four together form an overarching theme of Chinese religion. This paradigm effectively refutes the simplistic approach of the three religion model; it has instead pinpointed the location of popular beliefs and spiritual pursuits as the fertile soil in which religious life breeds. Nevertheless, there are two problems with this paradigm. First, in an attempt to characterize the four elements of religion in China, it confuses, rather than clarifies, the relationship between these four strands. For its proponents, the 'folk' element of Chinese religion has every right to become the fourth strand, and is therefore often treated as an independent religion. This is untrue, however, as folk-religion has never gained an independent position in China, neither in ancient times nor today; rather, its influence resembles a merging power penetrating all dimensions of social and familial life, functioning as a way of living which permeates the three more institutionalized traditions. In this interaction, folk-religion draws inspiration and doctrinal justification from Confucianism, Daoism and Buddhism; in turn it fuses the ideas and ideals of these three belief systems into common practice, often with intrinsic twists and thought-provoking transformation.

Secondly, the four-religion paradigm implies that the folk-religion represents the ancient and more indigenous belief systems in China, from which Confucianism and Daoism arose. However, methodologically, this classification is at best artificial. Folk-religion cannot be identified with the prime religion in China, out of which came all religious strands, including what we refer to as 'folk-religion'. In essence, there was no historical moment at which folk-religion existed independently. The relationship between folk-religion and the other three great religious strands is rather one of interaction and interpenetration of what is already embedded in each other. Each provides nutrition to the others, all impacting on each other, depending on each other and also supplementing and reinforcing each other; it will not be easy for us to separate out individual strands, nor will it be possible to clearly define any single strand if removed from the context in which they interact.

Two strata

Intellectually far more powerful than the four-religion model, the paradigm of the official and the popular religion has transformed the academic views of religion in China. This paradigm tends to divide Chinese religion into two strata: the official and the popular, each having its own specifics, which can then be totally differentiated from the other. This paradigm arose from the sociological and anthropological works on religion in the 1950s and 1960s, and has been applied to Chinese religions by a good number of distinguished scholars (for example, C. K. Yang) in their fieldwork and theoretical reconstruction of religious life in traditional China, which has been discussed in detail by Maurice Freedman in his article 'On the Sociological Study of Chinese Religion' (Freeman, 1974:19–41).

Thus, on the surface it seems justifiable to divide Chinese religion into two different fields, one official and the other popular, as the gap between them is so apparently obvious that exploration of each must be treated separately. The so-called official religion is said to have been created by the educated *elite* and sponsored by the imperial government, while the 'popular religion' is confined to the actual practices and beliefs of the common or ordinary people, often intermingled with folklore and local customs. In imperial China, Confucianism, Daoism and Buddhism were all institutionalized, adopted by dynastic governments albeit in alternation, and supported or rejected through various ways such as financial supporting, administrative controlling or military suppressing. They can be legitimately called 'official religions', in the sense that they enjoyed a limited or uncountable number of privileges which the state bestowed on them, and carried with special powers as endowed by a particular ruling class or political regime. The objects the 'official religion' worshipped were normally national, and the temples that were central to religious life were more likely built up, again by the imperial decrees, in all parts of the country. For such privileges the 'official religions' were expected, in return, to fulfil certain specific responsibilities. For example, they would be required to be consciously aligned with the government, assisting the ruling house to maintain rather than disrupt social order and harmony. In contrast, the popular or folk or communal religion (*minjian zongjiao* or *minjian xinyang*) does not in general enjoy such privileges. It would normally be sponsored by local communities, and in turn it serves their needs. Although under the strict oversight of various levels of the government, it was much freer in terms of which gods the people should or would like to worship, what kinds of rituals local communities must follow, and how the spiritual needs of the people should be met.

According to this paradigm, both the 'official religion' and the 'popular religion' cover a huge area, and there is a clear boundary separating the one from the other. Scholars endeavoured to capture the distinctive features of each, and provide different pairs of names for them; for instance, the great and the little tradition, or the elite and the peasants' culture (Redfield, 1956:70). By using such labels as 'the great' and 'the little', Redfield thus presents his view of the intellectual weight of each in the study of religion. C. K. Yang also makes use of a revised model of this kind to separate the two layers of religious life: the *institutional* religion and the *diffused* religion, suggesting that the two had quite different emphases and characteristics (Yang, 1961:294–340).

Although the religion sponsored by social and intellectual *elites* was different in certain aspects from that as practised by illiterate peasants. Or ordinary people, the opposition or separation between the *elite* and the popular religion should not be exaggerated. The line between that of the *elite* and that of the common people is not always easy to draw; the two aspects of Chinese religion are actually mutually penetrative and mutually dependent. In this sense Freeman's argument makes a great deal of sense: peasant culture and *elite* culture were not two different things, but present 'two versions of one religion that we may see as idiomatic translations of each other' (Freedman, 1979:366). The communication and mutual translation between them constituted the driving force of religious life in China, and frequently led to social and institutional changes that would fundamentally transform religious ideas and practices. The religious ideals of the *elite* provide insights and guiding principles for popular practices, while folk faiths and activities enrich those officially acknowledged religions, extend their boundaries and often soften the rigidity of religious ideologies upheld by the state. In historical China the two forms shared a common root, and nourished the same world view. They were both constructed by the concept of *yin-yang*, the five elements or 'agents', the mythological past, 'Heaven' and *qi* as the material power. To a great extent they also shared the same practices central to Chinese culture: ancestor worship, implicit or explicit animistic beliefs in natural deities, various forms of divination, cultivation of the vital force within, strict observation of the calendar, celebrations of civil and religious festivals, and *fengshui* or geomancy. The two so-called *elite* and popular religions are therefore more the two sides of one coin than two distinctive fields, and manifest more two different layers of religious life than two mutually opposite and separable religions. In this sense, it would be more damaging to our perspective on Chinese religion than help us gain insights of it if this paradigm were applied indiscriminately.

In short, the real meaning of Chinese religion lies in the interdependence and intertransformation not only between different religious strands, but also between different religious layers. They together constitute a unique religious culture in China.

The study of Chinese religion

There is already a rich body of scholarship on religious history and culture in China. A large number of books have been published either on its specific traditions or are of a comparative nature, and a variety of approaches have been taken in the study of religious complexities of China. Apart from general introductions to this field of exploration a number of books are devoted to the study of individual religious traditions. For example, on Confucianism there are *Transformations of the Confucian Way* (John H. Berthrong, 1998) and *An Introduction to Confucianism* (Xinzhong Yao, 2000); on Daoism there are *Taoism and Chinese Religion* (Henri Maspero, 1981); *Taoism: The Growth of a Religion* (Isabelle Robinet, 1997); on Buddhism there are *The Buddhist Conquest of China* (Erick Zürcher, 1972); *Buddhism in Chinese Society* (Jacques Gernet and Franciscus Verellen, 1998); on folk-religion there are *Religion in Chinese Society: A Study of Contemporary Social Functions of Religion and Some of Their Historical Factors* (C. K. Yang, 1961) and *The Sinister Way: The Divine and Demonic in Chinese Religious Culture* (Richard von Glahn, 2004).

There are also the historical as well as contemporary approaches. In the study of religion in Chinese history, we have, for example, *Mysticism and Kingship in China: The Heart of Chinese Wisdom* (Julia Ching, 1997) and *Religion and Society in Tang and Sung China* (Patricia Buckley Ebrey and Peter N. Gregory, 1993), while for contemporary studies there are *Religion in China Today* (Daniel Overmyer ed., 2003) and *Chinese Religions in Contemporary Societies* (James Miller, 2006).

Some books are based primarily on textual criticism and examination, while others are the results of sociological surveys and anthropological studies. For the former there are *Religious Experience and Lay Society in Tang China* (Glen Dudbridge, 2002), and *Daoist Identity: History, Lineage and Ritual* (Livia Kohn and Harold David Roth, 2002), while for the latter we have the *State, Market and Religions in Chinese Societies* (Fenggang Yang and Joseph B. Tamney, 2005) and *Religious Experience in Contemporary China* (Yao and Badham, 2007).

All these different approaches indicate, on the one hand, the complexity and diversity of Chinese religion, and on the other the multi-dimensional issues which religious life in China presents. Explorations can be from different perspectives involving a variety of methodologies that have developed in the past decades. Studies can be engaged with through phenomenological researching about its different aspects and different strata. Indeed dimensional studies of religion used to be favoured in a good number of leading scholars in religious studies (e.g., Frederick Streng, Eric Sharpe, Charles Glock). In this regard, Ninian Smart's seven-dimension paradigm would be a useful tool for us in observing and examining the characteristics of religious life in China. For Smart, all mature religions would have the following dimensions: (1) The Practical and Ritual dimension, (2) The Experiential and Emotional dimension, (3) The Narrative or Mythic dimension, (4) The Doctrinal and Philosophical dimension, (5) The Ethical and Legal dimension, (6) The Social and

Institutional dimension and (7) The Material dimension (Smart, 1998:11–12). It is our view that through a thorough study of these aspects or dimensions, we will be able to grasp how religion in China originated, evolved and functioned in the context of Chinese history, culture, language and philosophy, and how these different dimensions are related, interact, and how they together form an organic whole.

However, we are also clearly aware that it would not be possible for us to provide a comprehensive introduction to Chinese religion should we seek only to observe its different aspects and provide its primary material. The study of Chinese religion also requires philosophical reflection and hermeneutical interpretation, by which the unique characteristics of religious beliefs and practices can be revealed, presented or reconstructed. In so doing we must pay particular attention to the following dialectic relationships:

(1) *One and Many*: As we have repeatedly emphasized, Chinese religion is an organic whole that is composed of many different strands or parts. Any one of these can be appreciated only in its association with others, but at the same time the whole cannot be really presented unless we have clearly identified and clarified all of its important elements, dimensions and aspects. Therefore the understanding of one and the appreciation of many are conditional on each other.

(2) *Insider and Outsider*: In one sense, all religions are particular. Compared with other religious systems, Chinese religion has its own uniqueness, due to the particular contexts in which it operates. This means that we have to study it both within and without, both from the perspective of an enthusiastic insider and the point of view of a cool-minded outsider. A study of Chinese religion cannot be deep unless we put ourselves into the context. This insider experience is very important for us, because it can provide us with a perspective which cannot be gained outside of the field. However, it is not enough (and could be even dangerous) if Chinese religion is studied and examined by looking for things only an insider can see, because this approach would most likely lead to a biased view or distorted picture. To balance this, we must also see and investigate Chinese religion from the perspective of an outsider, namely studying Chinese religion in non-Chinese religious contexts. Chinese religion is itself part of the world's religions, possessing common features of a human spiritual perspective; it therefore can be and should be examined 'objectively'. By 'objective' we mean that religious texts must be subject to critical analysis, communal behaviour must be judged by constant standards and criteria, and spiritual experiences must be examined through sociologically and psychologically sound methods. It is our understanding that an insider approach that has lost its objectivity would lead to blindness, while an outsider approach that ignores the unique context of China would generate prejudice. Only by combining both approaches can a true vision be secured.

(3) *Theories and Practices:* Religious traditions contain theoretical and practical aspects, and the relation between theory and practice is never simple. Since the two aspects are sometimes in agreement and sometimes contradictory, it is clear that only through a study of both can we truly understand their agreements and explain their contradictions. Unfortunately some scholars tend to take only one of these as their approach, and produce self-contained but nevertheless one-sided studies. There might be many occasions on which we would find that what is said in books differs from what occurs in real life. For example, most Confucian, Daoist and Buddhist texts warn their believers not to indulge in the worship of gods, and encourage them to focus on internal cultivation and external diligence, while in reality, ancestor worship, cults of immortals and Buddhas are often employed as a necessary means to resolve spiritual and material difficulties or problems, and burning of incense and donating money to temples are regarded as an effective means of gaining divine blessings. If we only see one side of these complex situations we might well reach a wrong conclusion that Chinese people are either too philosophical to be spiritual or too superstitious to be counted as religious.

(4) *Religion and Culture*: Contemporary scholars tend to separate culture from religion and distinguish cultural studies from religious studies. In fact religion is part of culture, and culture is itself consolidated through religion. To study a religion is to study the people of this religion, including their culture, tradition, customs and language. In this book we will consciously place Chinese religion in its cultural contexts, and examine Chinese culture against its religious orientations.

(5) *Historical and Contemporary Studies:* A number of revolutions in the twentieth century attempted to cut the tie between historical and contemporary China, in which religion was blamed and persecuted, but the bond between historical and contemporary religion nevertheless remains strong. Contemporary religious life can be explained by looking at religious traditions, and new religious moments must be understood against the general background of religious history. On the other hand, religious beliefs and practices that arose from particular historical eras are also being carried on in a new context. Therefore instead of focusing on one or other of these shaping forces, our study of Chinese religion is to take both into consideration.

(6) *Concepts and Language*: Religious ideas and ideals are expressed through language, and different languages carry with them different cultural and philosophical values. To fully understand Chinese religion, we must carefully examine its key concepts in Chinese language, most of which cannot be simply rendered into one particular English word or phrase. Thus, although we use English terms or phrases to explain such concepts as religion, religious experience, religiosity, religious culture, spirituality, worship, cult, belief, myth, magic, Heaven and so on, we must bear in mind that their English connotations are not the same as those of the Chinese words themselves. It is not merely a language exercise to examine the cultural meanings and implications of the Chinese concepts; more

importantly, it is a cultural translation, from one religious system to another. This is, again, part of our hermeneutical efforts to make Chinese beliefs and practices meaningful not only for contemporary Chinese readers, but also for readers from other cultures and traditions.

Questions for discussion

1. What does 'cultural China' mean? How did Chinese culture evolve in the land of China?
2. How can a study of Chinese religion be associated with the study of Chinese history and culture?
3. What are the three religions of China? Why is it said that this paradigm is not an accurate catalogue of Chinese religions?
4. Why do some scholars prefer to use the four-religions or the four religious genres to replace the older paradigm of the three religions?
5. What do the terms 'official religion' and the 'popular religion' in China mean?
6. Why is it said that the paradigm of 'institutional religion' and 'diffused religion' could be misleading in the study of Chinese religion without being properly defined?
7. How can we apply phenomenology and hermeneutics to our study of Chinese religion?

2 Religion and *Zongjiao*

The *Chenjia Ci* (the Chen Clan Ancestral Temple) is a potent symbol of the multiplicity to which this term 'religion' refers. Located outside the old West Gate of Guangzhou city, the temple is the largest and best preserved example of ancient architecture in Guangdong province. Functioning both as a religious site and as a place for dealing with civil and communal matters, it serves to illustrate what religion was for the Chinese people. The erection of this 'ancestral temple' took place from 1888 through to 1894, funded by donations from members of the 'Chen clan' spread throughout 72 counties. Even by today's standards, its compound is huge, consisting of 19 buildings and 15,000 square metres in total. The design, structure and decoration are splendid, with delicately wrought paintings and numerous artistic features intended to display the virtues and values of traditional Chinese culture, religion and education.

The primary function of the temple at that time was to create a sacred place where members of the Chen clan could enshrine ancestral tablets and congregate to carry out their holy rites. Here all or most male descendants gathered to worship their ancestors at grand ceremonies which were held on specific days in both spring and autumn each year, in strict accordance with rulings laid down by Confucian rites. A second function was to act as a communication hub and decision-making centre for the clan, so that those members who were spread across the whole province would be able to gather, meet, consult and discuss matters not only about important clan businesses and individual families, but also matters concerning the clan and the government, and between the clan and other clans or communities. Yet a third function was to provide lodging or temporary residence for junior members of the clan who came from remote areas to the capital of the province, either to take part in the national or provincial civil service examinations or to study and prepare for such examinations. Apart from all these functions, it also acted as an arbitration court to solve disputes or conflicts between clan members, or between the clan and the outside community.

The fact that the Chen clan temple functioned in all these ways, acting as a religious site and as a place for dealing with civil and communal matters, is a telling example of what the term 'religion' meant for the Chinese people. The involvement of this ancestral forum in schooling and education for the clan juniors reveals to us the overriding civic characteristics of the 'religious organization' in traditional China. Interestingly, the temple is also known by another name – *Chenshi Shuyuan* (or the private school of the Chen Clan) – which reflects more accurately this civic dimension and purpose, especially after 1905 when the imperial examination system was abolished.

All these have illustrated again that 'religion' existed, and continues to exist, in a cultural context in China, which is very different from that of the West. It is significant here that there was no exact term to describe 'religion' in classical Chinese. It was only towards the end of the nineteenth century that a specific descriptor was coined by combining the two Chinese characters *zong* and *jiao,* in an attempt to capture something of the English word 'religion'. An exploration of these two characters, their meanings and implications is therefore a necessary step for us to gain an insight of what Chinese religion is.

'Religion' and Chinese religion

To what extent does the Chinese concept approximate to, and differ from, its English counterpart? To answer this question we need, on the one hand, to clarify definitions of 'religion' and, on the other, to pinpoint the original meanings and implications of '*zongjiao*' in the Chinese language and its cultural context.

No single definition of religion can satisfy all people at all times. There are a number of reasons for this. First, within a culturally indigenous community, it is difficult to apply one definition to all religious practices, primarily because of the social diversity where religious followers are often divided into different strata or sub-communities of the society, and the religion for one social group can be very different from that for another. Secondly, historical, economic and social changes have frequently made a once cherished conception of religion obscure or produced a new one following upon changed cultural situations and political conditions. Thirdly, different cultures or subcultures cultivate different perceptions and expectations of religion, sometimes overlapping and sometimes conflicting with each other. Scholars have thus long realized that one of the most difficult tasks in generating a commonly recognized definition comes from the diversity of religious traditions, a diversity that has been consciously or unconsciously generated in culturally derived self-identities and deliberately enhanced by politically motivated ideals. Geo-cultural distance frequently leads to differences in understanding what religion is. What is understood as religion in a traditional European community may well in consequence be far from the same as that perceived by the ancient Chinese. Fourthly, the concept of 'religion' itself defies specific definitions. Borrowing from the eighth century Chinese author Han Yu's (768–824) terminology, we can say that one of the reasons for the lack of a consensus in defining religion is at least partially because 'religion' as a category is not a 'definite name (*ding ming*)' but an 'empty position (*xu wei*)', a kind of basket that can be filled up with different contents by different people and by different eras (Han, 1997:120).

When expanding on Hans Blumenberg's defining of myth by its quality of significance, Gavin Flood suggests that 'Like the term "significance" itself, *religion* is resistant to definition, yet despite this problem there are forms of cultural life which are clearly identifiable as "religion" in contrast to other cultural practices' (Flood, 1999:42). It seems that a perception of religion is always associated with how to define and view these 'forms of cultural life'. 'Religion' in a typical English context refers to 'the belief in worship of a superhuman controlling power, especially a personal God or gods' and 'a particular system of faith and worship' (*Concise Oxford Dictionary*,

2008:1209). The Latin roots of religion reveal a number of implications or indications that are central to the understanding of religion in the West: '*religare*', for instance, means 'to bind back', while '*religio*' refers to 'obligation', 'reverence' and '*religere*' implies 'to re-read' and 'to ponder upon'.

Two fundamental meanings can be derived from the common uses and roots of the word 'religion': the bond between the superhuman and humans on the one hand, and the reflection upon that bond on the other. The former concerns the 'relationship' between the divine and the secular, often described and prescribed in the sacred texts of a religious tradition, while the latter involves how this relationship is understood or perceived, as elaborated by religious masters and scholars, and demonstrated in the practices of believers. The intellectual activities in these two areas have intensified the search for the meaning of 'religion', and resulted in a great number of definitions, attempting to capture its true essence. In a plain language, religion refers to the belief in and worship of a superhuman controlling power, especially a personal God or gods. For the general public, religion is a particular system of faith and worship sustained by intensive spiritual pursuits and other practices, referring to '*any beliefs which involve the acceptance of a sacred, trans-empirical realm and any behaviours designed to affect a person's relationship with that realm*' (Connolly, 1999:6–7). More sophistically religion is said to refer to a 'system of symbols which acts to establish powerful, pervasive and long-lasting moods and motivations in men by formulating conceptions of a general order of existence and clothing these conceptions with such an aura of factuality that the moods and motivations seem uniquely realistic' (Geertz, 1975:90).

Historically and culturally the Chinese 'forms of cultural life' differ from those of the West, and the Chinese perception of religion can be fully appreciated only in its conceptual and linguistic settings. The two Chinese characters *zongjiao*, with a combined original meaning of 'ancestral teaching' or 'pious doctrine', are used in contemporary times to refer to 'religion'. While this phrase was coined in the nineteenth century in this capacity, we must point out that as a compound of words it had already been used in a Buddhist biographical and anthological collection entitled *Jingde Chuandeng lu* or *The Records of the Lamp* compiled in the tenth century by Dao Yuan (1970:66) to refer to all Buddhist teachings: The Buddhists take what the Buddha taught as '*jiao*' and what his disciples taught as '*zong*'; hence in this context '*zongjiao*' equivalent to the doctrines of Buddhism. However, this is not what is meant by '*zongjiao*' today. Throughout the twentieth century, ordinary Chinese have tended to identify 'zongjiao' with all theistic and superstitious dimensions of 'religion', but for scholars, 'zongjiao' and 'religion' remain nevertheless significantly different.

Under the influence of Western rationalism and later Marxism, the dictionary meaning of zongjiao is said to be 'a social ideology and an imaginary reflection of the objective world which urges people to believe in God, ghosts, spirits and retribution for sin, and places hope on the so-called kingdom of Heaven or next life' (The Contemporary Chinese Dictionary, 2002:2554). For the majority of contemporary Chinese, zongjiao is primarily perceived as a superstructure consisting of superstitions, dogmas, rituals and institutions (Yu-lan Fung, 1961:3). Based on such an understanding, it is no surprise that many Chinese of an intellectual mind have made a conscious effort to disconnect their way of life from zongjiao. Instead, they tend to use xue (learning) or jia (family) to define, for example, Confucianism and Daoism, the two major streams of thought in traditional China.

Two questions have thus arisen from debates about whether 'zongjiao' can be identified with 'religion' as understood in the West. The first question comes from the fact that traditional China did not produce a concept of religion: if no such a word existed in classical Chinese, how then can we say that Chinese people could conceive of the contexts which this term connotes? To this debate, Julia Ching contributes a well-elaborated argument. For her, while in some cases the lack of a word or term signifies the lack of strength of a concept it represents, the non-existence of the term 'religion' in classical China does not however mean that no such phenomenon exists in China; rather this fact just shows how differently the Chinese and the Europeans understand religious matters (Ching, 1993:2).

The second question is concerned with the difference between 'religion' and 'zongjiao': if it is apparent that in its original meanings and implications, 'zongjiao' does not uphold typical 'religious' values, such as the bond between the human and the divine, how can we say the Chinese people are 'religious'? Such apparent differences between the Chinese way of life (primarily that of the Confucian elite) and Christianity as practised in Europe have led a number of twentieth century scholars (Chinese as well as Western) to the misleading conclusion that the Chinese are not a people of religion, because the primary concern for them is not transcendence of but involvement in human affairs. Based on this assumption, Max Weber, for example, made the following assertion: 'completely absent in Confucian ethic was any tension between nature and deity, between ethical demand and human shortcoming, consciousness of sin and need for salvation' (Weber, 1968:235). C. K. Yang quotes what Derk Bodde said about religion in China to illustrate this assumption:

> The Chinese have been less concerned with the world of the supernatural than with the worlds of nature and of man. They are not a people for whom religious ideas and activities constitute an all-important and absorbing part of life . . . It is ethics (especially Confucian ethics) that has provided the spiritual basis of Chinese civilization. (C. K. Yang, 1961:4)

This assumption and supporting arguments are in fact the echoes of the perspectives of earlier Chinese intellectuals who were susceptible to the influence of rationalism such as Hu Shi (1891–1962) who had already asserted that 'China is a country without religion and the Chinese are a people who are not bound by religious superstitions' (Yang, 1961:5).

The obvious contradiction between their assumption and the actual religious life in China highlights a real difference in their conceptions of 'religion' and '*zongjiao*'. To refute such a misleading contention as the Chinese are not religious, we must therefore first clarify the true meanings and references the Chinese take as religious. This requires us to investigate the original or primary implications of the characters that were typically used in traditional China to refer to what we may broadly view as religious dimensions.

Most key characters used today in China can be traced to their roots in the three confirmed writing systems before the adoption of more or less modern written Chinese during the Former Han dynasty (206 BCE–8 CE); namely, oracle bone inscriptions of the Shang dynasty (?1600–?1045 BCE); bronze inscriptions of the late Shang and early Zhou dynasty (?1045–249 BCE) and seal inscriptions of the Warring States period (475–221 BCE) and the Qin dynasty (221–206 BCE). In depicting and conceptualizing how ideas and ideals about this and next life could be distilled and pursued, and how religious institutions and organizations to enforce the beliefs and practices that were derived from these ideas could be established, the ancient Chinese came to produce a number of characters to describe and prescribe a wide range of spiritual activities which can be broadly termed as religious. Of these characters, *zong* and *jiao* are of a specific value, because they reveal to us how religion was understood in early China and how these understandings affected the subsequent Chinese conception of religion in later stages, in terms either of religious organizations and institutions, or of religious doctrines and traditions. Referring to the primary understandings and practices of a religious nature, each of these two characters informs us of a particular kind of religious perspective and reveals to us a typical Chinese understanding and interpretation of religious affairs and matters.

Zong as ancestral traditions

The understanding of *zongjiao* as an equivalent to superstition prevailing in the twentieth century confirms that the contemporary Chinese have diverted their views of religion from the traditional perspectives of *zong* and *jiao*. To rectify this diversion and to fully understand the similarities and differences between the English concept of religion and the Chinese term of *zongjiao*, we must examine the primary meanings of *zong* and *jiao* respectively.

The Chinese character *zong* was originally meant to denote various things, of which the most important are three: (1) the ancestral temple (*zu miao*), (2) the clan—a group of families with common ancestors (*zong zu*), (3) the chief spirit (*shen zhu*) or the ancestors worshipped in an ancestral temple. From the three meanings of *zong*, we can thus formulate a primary idea about what was taken as religion in classical China.

In the dictionaries of oracle bone inscriptions, different inscriptive forms for *zong* have been identified: The first one contains two parts: the outside part which is a pictographic radical for a roofed structure (house or shrine), and the inside part looks like the English character 'T' to be used to indicate a human made altar. In the second form, a horizontal short line (-) is added onto the top of the inside part, which has been interpreted as denoting sacrifice, that is, meat, wine, grains or fruits. In the third form, the inside part becomes more complex, containing not only the altar and the sacrifice, but also the action of offering sacrifice. The activity within the roofed house is further intensified in another form of this character, which contains the symbol of a cross inside. This, according to scholars, indicates four shamans practising some kind of rite which involved holding their arms crossed (Xu, 1990:811–812; Hongyuan Wang, 1993:188).

The basic part of the first three forms is *shi* which has become an important radical in the classical Chinese language which reveals to us vividly the sacred nature of early Chinese beliefs and practices. All characters that contain this radical are indicative of the ideas or actions involving a sense of awe, and are to do with sacrifice or sacrality. It has been speculated that the character *shi* might have been derived from the scene of holiness as perceived by the ancient Chinese, represented by a sacred stone, or a human-made altar. The pictographic presentation of the sacred stone that was believed to be the symbol representing supernatural powers indicates that animistic beliefs were characteristic of the ancient Chinese, while the human-made altar signifies an important step further in their consciousness of the relation between the human and the superhuman. The animistic beliefs reflect the religious beliefs and activities associated with 'natural worship' where all natural existences and phenomena such as the sky, earth, sun, moon, wind and so on were believed to have animistic spirits or souls and were thought to be able to bless and protect humans or inflict punishments on them. Archaeological discoveries have confirmed that natural worship activities were apparent throughout the lands of early Chinese civilization. This form of primitive religion not only yielded a complex system of beliefs that all natural phenomena had spiritual potency and power, but also led to a later monotheism, believing that all natural and human matters were controlled and commanded by a supreme power or being either called *Di* (Lord) or *Tian* (Heaven) (Li Xueqin, 2007:177–187).

However, 'natural religion' is only half of the story about early Chinese ideas and practices concerning important matters of life and death. The simple pictograph for a human-made altar that determines the meaning of *zong* tells us more about their further evolution, and about being increasingly integrated with daily life, revealing that the ancient Chinese not only made use of natural shapes to show their piety towards the beings or powers that were beyond their reach, but also consciously created their own sacred places for worship and sacrifice. The natural and the purpose-made are two of the most important criteria for us to appreciate the character of Chinese religion, and to assess the original religious beliefs and activities in early China.

The character *zong* informs us that religion was perceived as something that was related to sacrifice or worship that took place in a roofed building. However, to whom were the offerings made? Historical records such as the *Confucian Classics* tell us that in early China, two kinds of sacred place were consciously established and elegantly separated from each other. Each of them was dedicated to a particular category of deities and ritualistically prescribed sacrifices: sacrifices offered inside a building, at home or in a temple, were primarily to human deities, especially to great ancestors, while sacrifices made on open altars were mainly to cosmic or natural spirits such as Heaven, Earth, the Sun, moon, rivers and mountains. The two categories of deity might have been mixed together; for example, *Di* was both 'reserved for the supreme God (Shang-ti, Lord-on-High)' and 'used as a posthumous title to honour royal ancestors' (Julia Ching, 1997:60), but there was nevertheless a clear division between the two sacrificial sites on most occasions in early China.

From the analyses of the character and the reading of extant sources it has become clearer that whatever meanings the character *zong* might originally have, it was related to the veneration of ancestors, and was concerned with the family lineage. The association of *zong* with these activities has enabled us to conjecture that the initial appreciation of religion in early China probably originated from family rituals in the form of making sacrifices to ancestors, which in turn required piety, faith and devotion. When referring to the external features of religion, the structure and composition of this character gives us such an impression that Chinese religion grew up from sacrifices in family shrines or clan temples and from the faithful following and transmitting of the ancestral tradition. Further, Chinese religion not only originated from the family lineage but also took ancestor worship as its central canon. The newly excavated sacrificial sites such as ash pits, graves and primary temples of the Neolithic age are full of sacrifices, colourful potteries and jade items, and some of them contain drawings, clay phallus objects and female goddesses. Archaeologists confirmed that these were part of rituals for ancestor worship and were based on the belief that the spirit and soul of ancestors were still living (Li Xueqin, 2007:215–227). The central position of ancestor worship in early China was more obvious at a later age when (as the oracle bone inscriptions have shown) 'almost all the elaborate religious rituals of the Shang dynasty were meant for ancestors' (Tung, 1952:21). This practice was carried on and eventually became the central theme of Chinese culture and civilization, as many scholars have already observed: 'ancestor worship is not merely the ritual observances of the individual. It is rather the root from which grows the trunk of the lineage tree with its many family branches' (Thompson, 1996:32).

Lineage, transmission and devotion are thus three features which we have inferred from the character of *zong*. Since the ancestral tradition was transmitted from generation to generation, either by the genetic lineage of the clan and the family or by institutional groups and communities, *zong* gradually gained the meaning of a religious sect or school, in which the formation of a religious organization was understood as the result of the transmission of the original teachings from the founder or shapers in the same way as the transmission of the ancestral tradition. This understanding prevailed among the Buddhists, who, by tracing their separate routes of lineage to the Buddha or Buddhist masters, established various schools or sects (*zong*), such as the Pure Land School (*jingtu zong*) and Chan School (*chan zong*), of which there was a further division between the Southern transmission (*Nan zong*) and the Northern transmission (*Bei zong*).

Closely related to, and sometimes used in parallel with *zong* is the character of *jia*, which means 'the family' or 'home'. From the Former Han dynasty onwards, *jia* was also used to refer to groups or schools of religious and philosophical communities. The *locus classics* for the word *jia* is Sima Tan's *Essentials of the Six Orientations* (*lun Liu jia zhi yaozhi*, composed *c.*100 BCE), which describes six major orientations to political governance or philosophical ways of thinking, or more directly to the six groups of thinkers who shared keen devotion to particular texts (*yin/yang, ru, mo, ming, fa* and *daode*). These six 'families' were later adapted into a set of ten bibliographic subcategories by Liu Xiang (79–8 BCE) and Ban Gu (32–92 CE) in the *History of the Former Han Dynasty*.

As a pictograph, *jia* reveals to us vividly how a religious (and probably all other kinds of) institution was primarily established. The correspondence between a religious or philosophical organization and the family is so close that we may well say that the former is constructed exactly upon the structure of the latter, where the founder, equivalent to the ancestor, is called *shi zu* (teacher and ancestor), and the master acts as the father, *shi fu* (teacher and father) with his wife being called *shi niang* (teacher and mother), while disciplines correspond to the family code and tradition (*jia jiao*), rituals to family rites (*jia li*) and disciples to siblings (*shi xiong mei*), as shown in Figure 2.1:

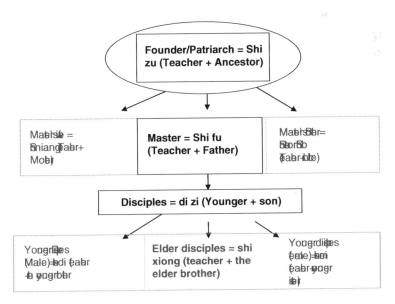

Figure 2.1 Family structure of religious and philosophical organization

In the characters of *zong* and *jia*, we have thus seen a number of the implications religion was conceived to have in classical China. First, Chinese religion is basically a backward-looking veneration. Religious ideas are believed to have all been embedded in the saying and conduct of the ancestors and founders, and religious ideals cannot be realized except by fulfilling ancestral expectations. In this sense, it would not be difficult for us to understand why the Chinese have bestowed so much on the sacred texts and on the images of classical exemplars; sages or immortals of the remote past would hence have had great effect on the people of today. Secondly, all religious activities are based on the central concept of order and harmony. Since religion is perceived as a structure of the family or clan, its internal relations are none other than those of the family. The family tradition cannot however be transmitted successfully unless its members of different generations are interlocked in a commonly venerated order. In the same way, central to religious teachings is the veneration of masters by disciples and veneration of founders and shapers by followers. Thirdly, based on the concept of order, religion is perceived as involving a search for conformity and is significantly enriched through complicated and complex rituals. Not only religion but also politics, education and community are all bound by various kinds of rituals (*li*) where the rites of passage and grand ceremonies on important occasions (such as the birthday and the day of passing away of the founder) are used to strengthen conformity. Through extending family rituals, this particular concept of religion has facilitated the acceptance of a socio-political unity in which the state is perceived of as an enlarged family and is therefore entrusted with the greatest responsibilities in religious life.

Jiao as the teaching transmitted from the past

In the oracle bone inscriptions there are several forms of the character *jiao*, composed of three basic parts: instructions, a son or junior and a hand holding a stick (Xu, 1990:347). Put them together, *jiao* can be interpreted as 'an authority' (father, teacher or ruler) who through instructions guides a child/student/follower to follow a good example.

Evolved from this form, the modern character for *jiao* is composed of two parts, *xiao* (filial piety) and *wen* (culture). Its intrinsic meaning points to the teachings transmitted from the past, or the instruction or education given by the authorities to bring about appropriate attitudes towards elder family members, or more directly indicates that a father, by instruction, brings his son into the conditions of filial piety. The combination of filial piety (love of children for ancestors or parents) and culture (civilized manners) speaks eloquently in itself for the fact that the Chinese understanding of religion is derived from teachings from the past which are concerned with the serving of the young to the old, the veneration of the past by the present and the cultivation of the self to cultural expectations. Because this teaching is transmitted from ancestors, what is taught becomes sacred, and requires faithful following, careful preservation and diligent carrying forward.

This indicates that the core of all teachings is not only related to the ancestral tradition, but is also regarded as the wisdom of the past, which has been and is being transmitted from the teacher or master down to younger generations. In a number of early texts, *jiao* is used in a general sense to refer to the wisdom of the sages. For example, in the *Book of Changes*, it is said that '[The sage] affords them a view of the divine way of heaven, and the four seasons do not deviate from their rule. Thus the sage uses the divine way [*shen dao*] to give instruction [*jiao*], and the whole world submits to him' (Wilhelm, 1989:486). In another Confucian text, the *Doctrine of the Mean*, *jiao* is associated with all kinds of cultivation of the Way: 'What Heaven imparts to man is called human nature. To follow our nature is called the Way (Tao). Cultivating the Way is called education [*jiao*]' (Chan, 1963:98).

Gradually *jiao* has specifically come to mean religious teachings; for example, in the section on the meaning of sacrifice in the *Book of Rites*, *jiao* is said to be concerned with the earthly and heavenly spirits of the ancestors: 'It is the union of *kwei* [the earthly soul] and *shan* [the heavenly spirit] that forms the highest exhibition of doctrine [*jiao*]' (Legge, 1885, Vol XXVIII:220). These moral and religious implications prepared the character to be used later specifically for 'religion'; for example, when referring to the religious movements in the second century CE, later Daoists used *jiao* to mean the sacred instructions imparted by Lord Lao the Most High (*Taishang Laojun*) to Zhang Daoling (a. 142), the so-called first Heavenly Master (*Tian Shi*) of a particular branch of Daoist religion. It is on this religious meaning of *jiao* that religious organisations, liturgies and practices were established. From then on, all the three teachings of Confucianism, Daoism and Buddhism have been known as the three '*jiao*'.

From the character *jiao*, we can read a number of principal ideas that characterize the Chinese perception of religion. First, religion as teaching carries with it a tone of conservatism and authoritarianism. Since teachings are transmitted from the elder to the young, the teaching must be treated with reverence and the old tradition must be preserved and followed. Although *jiao* is commonly used (often on polite occasions) to mean giving or receiving teachings or ideas useful or precious, its political and accompanying hierarchical connotation has often been so much manipulated that religious teachings are used to strengthen a particular political order, sometimes in the disguise of social etiquette and religious rites.

Secondly, religion as teaching lays an emphasis on its moral and educational function. Teaching of all kinds is associated with the education which the elders provide for the young. From this we can see clearly that religion is understood as growing up primarily from family ethical requirements (represented by *xiao*, filial piety), and is thus embedded in a strong moralistic tendency. This tendency was enforced as the core principle for all forms of traditional Chinese thought, religious, political, ethical or philosophical. Here terms such as philosophy, ethics, religion and politics and so on, are to be meaningful to the Chinese only if they are understood in an educational context. Failure to realize this, for example, has led a number of Western philosophers to the conclusion that Chinese thought consists of 'pronouncements' rather than 'philosophy' (Passmore, 1967:217–8). Robert Eno highlights this kind of misunderstanding as coming from the difference between Western and Chinese philosophy: 'the style of this [Chinese] philosophy is fundamentally different from that we have grown to expect from the analytical schools of Western tradition' (Eno, 1990:2).

Thirdly, religion as teaching naturally carries with it a transforming power. In the early textual uses, the character *jiao* denotes a set of moral teachings that the government used to instruct or guide its people: a nation is characterized by the way it *jiao* (teaches) its people; education is always part and parcel of a more comprehensive social programme to educate and transform (*jiao hua*). To be transformative, however, a teaching must be taught and studied. This transforming power is manifested through teachers or masters. Therefore, teachers or masters are religiously respected and politically praised, and are often endowed with a political role in Chinese societies.

Fourthly, religion as teaching opens the way both to religious pluralism and to religious orthodoxy. It is admitted that there are a variety of sources for teaching, and that a set of teachings can be transmitted through various master-disciple lines. Confucianism is thus *ru jiao*, the teachings of *ru*-scholars, of whom Confucius (later with the title of 'the Supreme Sage and Ancient

Teacher' and 'the Teacher and Model for Ten Thousand Generations') and other Confucian masters led the way; Daoism is *dao jiao*, the teachings of Laozi (the Supreme Lord) and other Daoist masters such as heavenly masters (*tian shi*), various categories of true men (*zhen ren*) and immortals (*xian*); Buddhism is *fo jiao*, the teachings of the Buddha or Buddhas; Christianity is *jidu jiao*, the teachings of the Christ (Protestantism) or *tianzhu jiao*, the teachings of the Lord of Heaven (Catholicism). However, as teaching *jiao* implies a set of religious beliefs or principles that the people accept as the sanctioned doctrine, and different teachings or transmission lines are subject to the needs of the state to 'teach' its people. The state is therefore entrusted with the responsibility to 'select' teachings of a good nature, and to reject those teachings that are perceived to be of a heterodox nature because of their tendency to affect people with a disruptive potential. As a result, the social *elite* represented by Confucian scholars tend to avoid designating their teachings as *jiao*. Instead they term their doctrine a kind of learning (*xue*) or the way (*dao*) and their school as a lineage (*jia*), while using *jiao* primarily to refer to popular Daoism, popular Buddhism or folklore, often in a deprecating tone.

The key teaching of Chinese religion is expressed by another character, *dao*, a term used by the ancient Chinese to denote an unfathomable, sometime mysterious, doctrine. The word '*dao*' has been translated variously as the Way, Nature, Reason, Logos, Law, Principle or the Word. Perhaps the most well-known usage of *dao* is in Daoism itself. However, any exclusive interpretation of this word for Daoism only runs contradictory to truth, because *dao* is in fact common to all schools of China, each of which is understood as part of the Way. Apart from Daoism (which has been plainly addressed as 'the family of *dao*'), the teachings of Confucius are termed as '*fuzi zhi dao*' (the Way of the Master), the orthodox Confucian lineage as *dao tong* (the transmission of the Way), while Neo-Confucianism is known as '*dao xue*', the learning of the Way. Buddhism is also taken as a form of *dao*, with the Eightfold Path to the Buddhahood being translated as the Eight Orthodox *Dao*. Many of the key terms of Christianity are also translated as *dao*; for example, the first sentence the gospel of John 'In the beginning was the Word' (Jn 1.1) has often been translated as '*Tai chu you dao*' – 'In the beginning was the *Dao*'.

Compared with the characters of *zong*, *jia* and *jiao* that reveal to us many external characteristics of a religious tradition such as the lineage, transmission, organizational structure and so on, the character of *dao* tells us more about the inner essence of Chinese religion. It is frequently used to refer to a deeper layer of human understanding or to point out to the highest level of cosmic existence or divinity. In this sense, it is even suggested that *dao* represents the ontological reality that is incomprehensible to an ordinary mind. The first sentence of the famous Daoist classic, *Daode Jing*, for example, reads that 'The Tao [Dao] (Way) that can be spoken of is not the eternal Tao [Dao]', while the author(s) of this text confessed that they called it *dao* only because they did not know its name (Chan, 1963:139,152). Confucius explained this difficulty from the viewpoint of the Middle Way: 'I know why the Way [Dao] is not understood. The Worthy go beyond it and the unworthy do not come up to it' (Chan, 1963:99).

The original form of this character tells us that when designating a religious tradition, *dao* is the way that has been opened up by the pathfinder and followed up by his disciples along the way, implying that a religion deals with the relations between the forerunners (the ancestor, the founders and shapers) and the followers (children, disciples and members), between what is taught and what is to be learnt, and between the universal Way and individual paths.

To the mind of a Chinese intellectual, the Way is universal because it is the source of all truths and is equivalent to the ultimate reality. The Way is also particular, because it provides individuals with the paths leading to the ultimate truth or enables them to have access to the reality. This indicates another characteristic understanding of religious tradition in China: religion as the Way-finding is syncretic and pluralistic. A religious doctrine is rarely taken as an exclusive system of beliefs and practices; more frequently it is considered to be one of many ways to the truth and one of many presentations of the same ultimate reality. In this regard most religious and philosophical traditions in China uphold a fundamentally pluralistic attitude and accept other teachings as different paths to the Way. Different presentations of the Way, the heavenly or the human, the spiritual or the secular, this way or that way, are believed to be the same in essence, coming from the same source and having the same or similar function.

Being the same, different forms of the Way reveal the same ideal for the world and reflect the same law of the universe; while being different, they each inform a distinctive path to the ideal and a unique approach to the supreme reality. It has become a widely accepted belief that not only is there an original harmony between the Way and the ways, but there are also harmonious relationships between this way and that way. This understanding developed to its full range in the argument for the harmony and co-existence of the so-called three religions or three doctrines (*san jiao*): these three doctrines might differ in form but in essence they were the same: 'A boat sailed over the water, while a carriage travelled on land, yet both were vehicles for moving from one place to another' (quoted in Shryock, 1966:118).

Zongjiao as religion

A particular concept of religion is always related to how the religious ultimate is perceived and understood. Thus, in the Abrahamic traditions, the concept of religion is primarily based on a belief in God who exists outside of the human race and has overall powers over them. God is portrayed first and foremost as an omnipotent Creator who creates the universe out of His own will. However, if we understand religion primarily as an ancestral tradition and its transmission, then religion would not necessarily relate to the supernatural and superhuman being. Using *zong* and *jiao* to refer to religion, the ancient Chinese made it possible for an understanding of the divine that is meaningful and functional socially, politically as well as spiritually, and for a closer relation between the divine and the human. This may well explain why in Chinese religion more attention is paid to the administration and regulation of the family, the state, and cosmic events than to creation, and why ancestors are believed to be spiritually caring for the well-being of their descendants, just as they had done so materially when alive.

The Chinese concept of *zongjiao* draws the divine nearer to the human world. In the state religion, this is a concept of a supreme being or power (*Di* or *Shang Di* or *Tian*), which functions as the final sanction of human behaviour, punishing the evil and rewarding the virtuous. Conceived of as an anthropomorphic being who is above humans, his origin is often said to have come from the great human or the great royal ancestor: 'In view of the close relationship between religious worship and family and clan, it is quite possible that Shang-ti was the chief god of the ruling family (perhaps even a deified ancestor)' (de Bary et al., 1960:5). Leslie Bilsky also supports this view of the supreme god as being originally from the family roots: *Shang Di* and *Tian* were

> celestial gods who had ultimate control over all human affairs and all natural events. Nevertheless, both gods, far removed from the normal sphere of human activities, undoubtedly had the more familiar ancestral spirits equated to them so that they could qualify for worship within the ancestral temple. (Bilsky, 1975:37)

Through *zongjiao* the concept of religion is essentially demystified and rooted in human experience and expectations. While having a profound meaning denoting superhuman existence, *dao* is fundamentally the Way of humans. In Daoist religion, *dao* can be personified; 'obtaining the way' (*de dao*) is an overall aim of all Daoist practices. In Confucianism, mysterious and profound as *Dao* may be, it is always considered to be encompassed in the human way of life, as declared in the *Doctrine of the Mean:* 'The Way (Dao) is not far from human beings. If a human being takes as the Way something that distances him from others, it cannot be the Way' (de Bary and Bloom, 1999:335).

Zongjiao also represents a different religious orientation. Because 'religion' refers to the bond between the human and the divine, there is always a danger that this bond will be broken, which for example, according to Christian theology is the wayward human betrayal of God's grace. Therefore a constant tension can be detected in early Christian texts between the divine and the human; the main theme of a religious tradition therefore had to be concerned with how humans were separated from, and how it is possible for them to become reconciled with, the Divine. Instead of separation, however, 'zongjiao' emphasizes communication, correspondence and mutuality, between the ancestor and the descendant, between the master and the disciple, and between the Way and the ways. If our understanding of *zong* is correct, then this understanding should mean that the religious ultimate derives from the transformed figure of the great ancestor or ancestors, who continue to support (but at the same time also rely on) their descendants, from which mutual benefits evolve. If we understand *jiao* rightly, a religious teaching must have some connection with filial piety (*xiao*), which implies that an old man needs support from his children, and that children must follow their parents. In this sense, we can say that in applying *jiao* to religious doctrines, the ancient Chinese actually illustrate that the mutual support of the elder and the young is needed for the continuity of ancestral tradition. In communication, *zongjiao* focuses on the ancestral teachings that are transmitted from generation to generation; in correspondence and mutuality, *zongjiao* points to the interaction between the human and the spiritual. If not provided with proper sacrifices, ancestors would be angered and would return to punish their unfilial descendants, bringing 'bad luck' to the family. If timely sacrifices had been properly made and residences chosen carefully, then the family would secure the blessing and protection of their ancestors.

With an emphasis on the divine creation, 'religion' tends to focus on delivery and salvation as the only path for humans to reach eternity. The separation of humans from God determines that humans must not be entrusted with the initial power or ability to be reunited with the divine; they must instead look to the divine for salvation, by which eternity becomes meaningful and realizable. With an understanding of religion as teaching and education, *zongjiao* thus makes it inevitable for the majority of Chinese intellectuals to have staunch confidence in the human capacity for transformation and perfection. In most Chinese religious and philosophical doctrines, humans are confirmed and reconfirmed with ability or potential to improve themselves; each individual is believed to possess the source and resource to reach perfection or enlightenment. The Chinese thus often take a positive attitude towards eternity and perfectibility. Believing that humans have the original capability of self-transformation or even immortality, many Chinese religious traditions find it unnecessary to adopt the concept of sins or sin, salvation and redemption as the centre of religious liturgy and rituals. Rather these traditions regard knowledge and wisdom as the focus of religious practices; this feature leads Hans Küng to define Chinese religions as 'religions of wisdom', thereby distinguishable from the prophetic religions (Judaism, Christianity and Islam) and from the mystic religions (Jainism, Buddhism and Hinduism) (Küng and Ching, 1990:xi–xix).

The concept of religion draws its elements from the relationship between the secular and the sacred, the temporary and the eternal, the mortal and the immortal, and the finite and the infinite. By the separation of the human from the Divine, the word 'religion' opens a door to the separation of religious life from social life, as witnessed in the New Testaments where people are called upon to abandon their secular life in order to follow Jesus the Christ. From this evolves – at least in theory and in early Christian Church history – the inevitable contrast and contradiction between the family and the church: the Church that controls the gate to the heavenly kingdom overrides the familial function and role in the spiritual life of the believer, while the priests who function as the link between humans and God overshadow the parents in guidance towards reunion with the Creator God. *Zongjiao* does not go as far as this. Rather it binds religion tightly with the family and, as the character of *jia* implies, claims that religion originates in the family, and that family is where transformation takes place. This is a view which led to enthusiastic engagement in debates between *zaijia* (staying home) and *chujia* (leaving behind the family) after Buddhism was introduced to China, which resulted in a major contest between Chinese understanding of Buddhism and its original tenets. This Chinese understanding eventually prevailed by which Buddhism was essentially reshaped to draw in the family as it became part of Chinese religion.

'Religion' and *zongjiao* uphold different concepts of holiness and sacredness. In the Abrahamic religions, holiness and sacredness are rooted in God and God's grace. The nearer to God and God's decree and the further away from the secular, the more likely recognition as holy is to be. In Hebrew *khadôsh* originally means 'to set apart' the Jews from other peoples: by extension the holy is thus differentiated from the profane, and the sacred is what is set apart, mysterious and inconceivable. The sacred and the profane are therefore contrasted in terms of space and time. The etymology of the sacred and the profane reveals to us the carefully defined spatial boundaries; *profanum* is indeed physically and materially outside a walled and separated *sacre*. Emile Durkheim has singled out this 'setting apart' as the property of the sacred, stating that: 'A religion is a unified system of beliefs and practices relative to sacred things, that is to say, things set apart and forbidden . . .' (Durkheim, 2008:47).

This kind of holiness is hardly seen in the concept of *zongjiao* where the emphasis is on a permanent presence; the Chinese term for holiness or sacredness is a combination of '*shen*' (the mysterious or spiritual) and '*sheng*' (sagacity), referring to the realm in which the supernatural and the human are integrated into a perfect unity by which humans have gained enlightenment or reached eternity. In addition, the characters of *jia* and *dao* refer to the reconciliation of the spiritual and the social, the absolute and the ordinary; they generate an understanding of the continuity from the secular to the spiritual, and from the mysterious to the conceivable. This coincides partially with R. Horton's view of religion, which 'can be looked upon as an extension of the field of people's social relationships beyond the confines of purely human society' (Horton, 1960:211). Since the transition from the secular to the sacred is a continual process, the sacred can therefore be practised, sought after and learned about: the Way exists everywhere, and whoever finds it or has grasped it would enter the realm of sacredness. It is in this sense that Confucius expressed his strong desire to fully understand the Way, and even stated that: 'In the morning, hear the Way; in the evening, die content' (Chan, 1963:26).

Since sacredness is what can be learnt, the sense of the holy concerning the classics is naturally cultivated. This reverence is similar to the Jewish attitude toward the *Torah*. However, what distinguishes the Chinese from the Jews is that for Jews the *Torah* is essentially the work of the omnipresent Yahweh or God, while for the Chinese the classics are regarded as the works of ancient sages who wrote down their discoveries by observing the patterns of Heaven and Earth in order to guide the people to a better life. This understanding is well illustrated in a passage from the *Book of Changes*, which describes how the ancient sage invented the holy book:

> The sage 'looked upward and contemplated the images in the heavens; he looked down and contemplated the patterns on earth. He contemplated the markings of birds and beasts and the adaptations to the regions. He proceeded directly from himself and indirectly from objects. Thus he invented the eight trigrams in order to enter into connection with the virtues of the light of the gods and to regulate the conditions of all beings'. (Wilhelm, 1989:328–9)

Religion and the Chinese way

At the beginning of this chapter, we raised questions about what religion is, and suggested that religion has been understood differently; no single criterion should therefore be adopted absolutely to judge what is religious and what is not. Subsequently we have argued that 'religion' binds humans to God who is beyond the human reach, and this bondage is fully manifested itself in human obedience to the divine decrees, while *zong* on the other hand, links ancestors to their descendants, and *jiao* points to the transmission of ancient teachings. This discussion has highlighted *zongjiao* as both different from and similar to 'religion', revealing a specific Chinese perspective of religion.

First, religion is primarily taken in China as a kind of 'teaching', and religious tradition is believed to possess a transforming power that can be used to change, strengthen or weaken a particular way of life. In the Chinese perspective, 'education' has thus become the central part of religious practice and wisdom the focus of religious ideals.

Secondly, religious ideas and ideals are considered primarily to be the embodiment of the ancient tradition, the transmission of which is the primary duty for the members of a community, in terms of a family or clan, or of a religious school or sect. Preserving and extending the chain from ancestors to descendents or from founders to followers is therefore recognized as the chief driving force for the Chinese to engage in religious activities.

Thirdly, the close relation between religion and the family on the one hand has enabled traditional Chinese intellectuals to be religious even though staying at home in order to focus on family relationships; on the other hand, this is a relationship which has cultivated a sense of the social-political-religious unity in which the state is legitimatized to intervene in religious matters. Raymond Dawson has observed in *The Chinese Experience*, 'Religion also did not attain that separate and independent status which a powerful church has sometimes achieved in European society' (Dawson, 1978:164).

Finally, seen as the Way, religious doctrines embrace both the ultimate reality and the ways to the ultimate truth, which, at least theoretically, opens up a door to religious pluralism and syncretism, allowing each individual or school or sect to explore his/her/its own path to that reality.

Questions for discussion

1. Why are there so many different definitions of religion?
2. In which sense has the character of *zong* defined Chinese religion in terms of ancestral tradition?
3. How can the Chinese concept of *jiao* be understood as the teachings from the past?
4. In which aspect can we say that each of the religious traditions in China establishes its organization upon the structure of the family?
5. Why is *dao* both universal and particular? How is the mysterious *dao* associated with personal life?
6. In the light of the typical meanings of religion in a Western context, what are the distinctive characteristics of *zongjiao*?

Religion in History

3

Chapter Outline

Another central theme in this book is the continuous interplay between current religious beliefs and practices in China and their historical context, against a background of thousands of years of cultural creation and re-creation, expansion and amalgamation. Indeed it is true to say that Chinese religion cannot be fully understood except in relation to its historical background, because it is this continuous interplay that has distinguished Chinese religion and history from those nourished in other cultures. It is a well-established tradition in China that history must be taken as the mirror for the present. Most contemporary issues or problems in relation to religion can be found in their sources or origin in history, and we may well gain insight by looking at their past.

Chinese religion demonstrates a strong character of accumulation and continuity, in which religion becomes part, or an extension, of history, while history is itself embodied, at least partially, in religious evolution and expansion. The close association of religion with history is primarily rooted in the universal perspective that the Chinese hold for the world in which religion, history, philosophy, politics, education and so on are all interrelated and inter-active. In particular, history is enriched through religious faith and practice while religion derives inspiration from historical images and reflection. For example, historical figures would receive the worship of the people if they actually, or were believed to have, contributed to the formation or expansion of civilization or to the well-being of the people; both the emergence of a religious tenet and the formation of a particular religious organization were always associated with particular historical dilemmas that called for spiritual solutions. Ideological, social and political events caused by religious faiths and movements formed the core elements of Chinese culture and history. Religion never failed to change in accordance with the change of time in the past, and there is every reason to believe that it will continue to renew itself in the future and to adapt itself to new circumstances.

Four seasons of religious history

How to write of religion in its historical context depends on what concept of time we follow. In the West, time appears to have a linear development; namely, from a beginning in the past to an end in the remote future. However, the Chinese concept of time differs radically; history is basically seen as circular movements that produce cycles which essentially repeat themselves. The contrast cannot be more clearly seen than in the difference between the Gregorian Calendar and the Chinese Lunar Calendar, where the end of one 60-year cycle only marks the beginning of another. Religion in Chinese history is often understood and interpreted as an organic developmental process, in the same way as that of a plant, or as the rotation of the sun and the moon. In this process there is a beginning, but this beginning is also the end of the previous cycle; there is an end, but this end is at the same time the beginning of the next cycle. Perceived in this way, Chinese religion in history 'evolves' in the same pattern as the four seasons run their course, following the order of spring, summer, autumn and winter, each of which is distinctively differentiated from others, but at the same time is closely related to those before and after it.

Spring is the season of rising up or the rebirth of new lives when religion was born to the Chinese world. This season covers a history from what has been revealed to us by archaeological remains and by mythological and legendary stories, to the time just before the formation of religious/intellectual schools that were to dominate the life in China for two-and-a-half thousand years. In this 'season' Chinese religion 'evolved' from separate faiths and occasional practices to a formidable force that commanded various aspects of individual and communal life and became the central part of a distinctive culture in terms of ideas, ideals, ways of life and systems of rituals and rites. In history, this season corresponds to the period from the time of the primitive religious practices that have been discovered, to the beginning of the disintegrating of China's unified world when the original and universal Way was to be replaced by various schools and their own transmission lines; namely, from the later Neolithic era to the end of the Western Zhou dynasty (?1045–771 BCE). This period can be further divided into several sub-eras: the primary religious beliefs and practices of the Neolithic age, the emergence of state religion, and religious faiths of the Shang (?1600–?1045 BCE) and Western Zhou dynasties.

Summer is the season of growing and unfolding, when all religious schools and sects achieved their specific forms, evolved, interacted and began to display distinctive features. All those distinctive features Chinese religion had demonstrated in earlier times expanded further in history, and this corresponds to a period from the intellectually 'axial age' of the Spring and Autumn (770–476 BCE) when tower-figured masters such as Confucius, Laozi, Mozi (?479–?381 BCE) and so on established their own doctrines to the beginning of the Tang dynasty (618–906 CE). Confucian transmission lineages were formed and expanded, but then encountered a huge set-back during the Qin dynasty (221–206 BCE). To revive, Confucian ideology was transformed and was eventually promoted to be part of the state religion or the official ideology sponsored by the state, and became the key player in education, government and religious life during the Han dynasty (206 BCE–220 CE). While Confucianism was from time to time overshadowed by other religious traditions during the following centuries, it also accumulated intellectual power and was prepared for its overwhelming prevalence in the future. Daoism gained popularity in two ways. First, Daoism evolved into neo-Daoist philosophy in the Wei-Jin dynasties (220–420) through intensive intellectual debates among the social *elites* that attempted to apply their mystic philosophy to ordinary life. Daoism also became a popular movement among the lower strata of the people, initially as revolutionary rebellions against political regimes but was later reformed as distinctively religious organizations. The amalgamation of Daoism-related religious faiths, naturalistic philosophy, medical practices and self-cultivation was overlaid by sophisticated rituals, moral teachings and doctrines of salvation, to meet the spiritual needs of the people. Buddhism was introduced to China, and quickly spread, initially as something akin to

Daoism, but soon established its own position as a 'new religion' that showed the people in desperation the road to a brighter next life.

Autumn is the season of harvest when all religious ideas and ideals began to ripen. In terms of dynastic eras, this corresponds to a period starting with the Tang, and ending with the replacement of the last dynasty (the Qing 1644–1911) by the Republic of China (1912–). In terms of religious institutions, this harvest is marked by four features: the maturity of Buddhist and Daoist schools, the synergy of the three major traditions (*san jiao*), the dominance of Neo-Confucianism in religious life, and the emergence of numerous new religious faiths and movements that were empowered by the syncretism of the three doctrines. On a popular level, people became more and more syncretic in their attitudes towards the teaching and deities of the three religions; religious masters deliberately moulded these three traditions into one, by which new schools or religious systems of a syncretic nature came onto the scene. While producing harvest and maturity, however, autumn also means a transition from summer to winter. It is no surprise therefore that in this period we can observe both the rapid growth of religious schools typical of the summer season and the withering to come of religious pursuits characteristic of the winter. Religion thus followed an uneasy path, punctuated by ups and downs, with both the joy of celebration and flourishing and the sadness and depression caused by political pressure and ideological narrow-mindedness.

Winter is the season of desolation but also of storage, when religions were suppressed, retreated or became inactive. Traditional religions were under mounting pressure and hostility from the beginning of the twentieth century. First, religious institutions in China were dismantled, damaged or left to dysfunction by the combining force of rationalism and republicanism, that discarded all traditional religious beliefs and practices as 'superstition' and as 'cheating non-senses'. The Republic of China discontinued the association of Confucianism with state education; radical intellectuals launched fierce attacks on Confucianism as the culprit for holding China back from advancement, and denounced Daoist and Buddhist beliefs and practices as superstitious, vulgar and counterproductive. Secondly, religious faiths and organizations were subject to the onslaught of extreme Marxism and Communism, which branded religion as nothing other than 'the opium of the people', and treated religion rather as a disease of the human race that must be cleared and cleansed. Not only the three major traditions of China and imported religions such as Catholic and Protestant Christianity, but also all other forms of religion among the common people were repressed, persecuted or forced into dissolution.

This was a severe time of testing for all religions. However, as hope for the beginning of spring is also embedded in winter, so Chinese religion retreated into itself and retained its essence, patiently waiting for the arrival of a new season.

The first light of rebirth and renewal was seen in the 1980s, when all traditional religions were reported as rising again throughout Mainland China; waves of antireligious feeling gradually subsided, and religious practices resurfaced (Pas, 1989:1). Many surveys report that religious beliefs and activities have become widespread and penetrative. Although bitterly cold winds still blow over religious sprouts and cool down religious enthusiasm from time to time, few would doubt that religion has since firmly moved into the season of spring when new ideas, ideals and practices are cultivated and begin to spring up.

The beginnings of religion

When and where did Chinese religion have its origins? This question is closely related to the view that one accepts concerning the origins of Chinese civilization itself. It is traditionally held among scholars that these beginnings go 5,000 years back in history, starting from Fu Xi (tr. around 2852 BCE) – a mythological founder of civilization, who was then followed by other legendary figures or cultural heroes such as the Yellow Emperor (tr. around 2697 BCE), the sage kings Yao (tr. around 2357 BCE), Shun, up until Yu the Great, the supposed founder of the Xia Dynasty (tr. 1818–1766 BCE) (de Bary and Bloom, 1999:xxvii). (All these legendary sage kings have been deified and become gods or deities in folk religion, as shown in Figure 3.1.). There are a number of problems with this claim, however. First, no evidence has ever been found concerning these legendary figures; their contribution should therefore perhaps be seen as more metaphoric than actual, marking the advancement of civilization. Secondly, newly excavated sites that date back to an earlier age than those established for these legends have revealed evidence of conscious religious activities by the people who inhabited the land. Therefore, a new perspective which encompasses this early history of Chinese civilization is needed to explain the origin of its religious activities and belief systems.

What can be said, however, is that conscious religious activities (and associated primitive systematic thinking) did not begin to develop themselves until humans became fully aware of suprahuman dimensions beyond them, and of their relationship to those dimensions. Evidence does point to Palaeolithic

Figure 3.1 Legendary Emperors Yao, Shun and Yu

beginnings, when the dead were buried according to certain rites and with burial materials such as powdered red iron ore, to prepare the soul for the hereafter. However, due to the scarcity of conclusive evidence, we are unable to form a definitive picture of religious thinking and practice at that time.

Primitive religious beliefs and practices

The most significant archaeological discoveries that shed light on primitive religion in China are associated with the sites of the Yangshao, Longshan, Dawenkou and Hongshan cultures, covering a period roughly from 5,000 BCE to 2,000 BCE. From those sites excavated were found such items as the 'pregnant woman' pottery, the 'Goddess Temple', the 'Coloured Goddess Head' and the stone-made tomb, as well as the jade dragon and other ritual or decorative items. These artefacts have provided new evidence for the origin of Chinese religion, which have not only 'expanded the history of Chinese civilization back for a further thousand years' (Su, 1999:108–110), but also 'made possible a scientific reconstruction of ancient civilization that had a profoundly religious orientation' (Küng and Ching, 1990:8). More than these, archaeological discoveries at the ancient Xishan City (about 6,000 years ago), at Zhengzhou City in Henan province, and the sacrificial pits (about 7000 years ago, discovered in 1991, 2004 and 2005) at Hongjiang Gaomiao in Hunan province, have provided convincing evidence of the religious practices that had existed considerably further back than traditional dating for the early stages of Chinese civilization (He, 2006).

Archaeological discoveries reveal a picture of a matriarchal society and a complex of religious rituals in the Neolithic age. For example, among more than 2,000 tombs of the Yangshao culture already excavated, such common features have been found as ritually built graveyards where tombs are uniformly aligned in the same direction, separate burial chambers for male and female, and special burial styles for the old and for the females, including small girls (Mou and Zhang, 2007:15). The discoveries of the Goddess Temple and the Goddess Head reflect the time when female ancestors were worshipped as the great mother womb from which all sprang, as in the legend of Nüwa the creator of humanity that became popular later (Lu, 1995:39). These feminist features of the early religious practices may have influenced the Daoist philosophy and religion that prevailed several thousand years later. Various pottery vessels discovered in the Dawenkou culture and other sites also display some aspects of nature worship, where the symbols of sun-moon-mountain are located at the centre of the pictures which they depict, showing a kind of nature worship that has since become deeply rooted in folk-religion in China. Ancestor worship, a central theme in late Chinese religion, was already rooted in the early practices of sexual organ worship, especially of the female.

The relationship between religion and myth is one which is constantly discussed among scholars on early China. A number of these scholars have suggested that in myth and legend is hidden the reason why Chinese religion has become as it is, substantially coherent in reformulating the Chinese way of life but significantly differing from other types of culture and religion (Patton and Doniger, 1996). It seems to be natural for some of these scholars to take it for granted that mythic stories reflect real history, and that the deities or heroes which the myths and legends describe represent the great ancestors of early tribal groups (Qi Liang, 2001:17–18). In fact, myth, history and religion were once inseparable in China; the figures of myths such as the Three Sovereigns (*san huang*) and the Five Emperors (*wu di*) are not only believed to be the true ancestors of the Chinese people, but are also taken as the initiators (or even founders) of various religious streams or traditions, representing both the divine order and the discoverers of this order for human beings. Either worshipped as supreme deities or as great ancestors, they mediated between the spiritual world beyond and the human world, the harmony between which is universally believed in early China to be crucial for religion, politics and education. This belief characterized the religious life of the so-called Three Dynasties (*san dai*), Xia, Shang and Zhou.

The spiritual and the human worlds

What was the nature of the spiritual world for early Chinese people? Various kinds of evidence have confirmed that their beliefs were of a polytheistic and animistic nature. For them there was a common order which the spiritual, the natural and the human must follow, the world of spirits (*shen*) and the world of humans (*ren*) were distinctive from each other and yet closely associated.

In the *Book of History* (*Shang shu*) and the *Sayings of the States* (*Guoyü*), a collection of historical conversations from major states of the Spring and Autumn period, we have found a classical narrative about the relationship between the spiritual and the human worlds. It is said that originally human and divine beings did not intermingle, and the communication between them could be enabled only by sorcerers and sorceresses whose wisdom and righteousness enabled them to receive the illustrious spirits on one hand, and to effect the order both for spirits and for humans and to assign each of them with different positions and responsibilities on the other. Guided by the order, the spirits conferred prosperous harvest upon humans, and humans offered sacrifices up out of gratitude.

However, this order was broken due to the rebellion of the Li tribal people in the south who threw the world into disorder and discarded all cherished virtues. As a consequence, humans and spirits became confusedly mingled, and they were no longer properly distinguished from one another. Both the spiritual and the human worlds were in utter chaos, and natural calamities occurred repeatedly. When the Sage King Zhuan Xü (tr. the third millennia BCE) took over the throne, he ordered a return to the old standards, and cut off the direct communication between Heaven (the spiritual world) and Earth (the human world), so that spirits and humans were held in their own places, and there were no longer mutual encroachments or over familiarity between them (Fung, 1952:22–23).

This narrative reveals to us much more than a legendary story about sage kings and their sovereignty. A number of characteristic features of Chinese religion can be drawn from it. First, central to the concern of the Chinese is the relationship between Heaven as the spiritual world and the earth as the human world, and an order must be present to regulate this relationship. Secondly, what sustains this order is virtue (*de*), and it is moral virtues that enable certain people to contact spirits, and to mediate between the spiritual and the human. Without or losing moral virtues the order would be disrupted or broken, which would in turn lead to natural disasters and spiritual corruption. Thirdly, the spiritual and the human are two separate worlds, each having its own duties and positions, and must not be intermingled. Here comes the importance of ritual and ceremony in Chinese religion. Ritual is the way by which the spiritual and the human are properly distinguished, associated and regulated, and is the method through which humans are trained, educated and cultivated.

This narrative also implies that there were two stages in the early religious history of China; namely, the religion without regulation by the state, and the religion under the control of the state. In the first stage, sorcerers and sorceresses regulated the relation between humans and spirits through their own virtue and intelligence. It was believed that if virtues were abandoned or abused and the order was broken, spirits would move out of their own positions and intrude into the human sphere. All these represent a state of primitive religion when people naturally communicated with, and worshipped the spiritual world without much mediation or interference. In the second stage, a conscious effort was made to create various offices in charge of ordering things, matters, events and duties, and of assembling heavenly spirits, earthly spirits and humans each in their own place. In place of the original direct contact between humans and spirits was a new order through which ordinary people could communicate with spirits only indirectly; namely through government-appointed officials with a complex system of rituals and ceremonies. From that time onwards, religious initiatives were taken over by the state, sacrifices regulated by official priests, and beliefs and practices controlled through regulations and executive orders. Overall rule was exercised not only by the patriarchy of the people, but also by the high priest who communicated with the spiritual world on behalf of his subjects; the two positions were often combined into one single person, the king. It was out of these political activities that the ancient state religion emerged.

Scholars claim that the ancient state religion in China started to function in the first of the three dynasties, the Xia dynasty (an era traditionally believed to have preceded the Shang), developed in the Shang and fully matured during the Zhou dynasty. Most of the Xia as the first of the three dynasties is still of an uncertain status because of insufficient archaeological evidence; some scholars are therefore sceptical about its existence, suggesting that 'the existence of the Hsia is not yet verified' (Keightley, 1984:488). Archaeological discoveries of the past 50 years or so, such as cities, tombs, ritual items and ceramic vessels dating to the 2000–1000 BCE, however, have shown that diverse Neolithic societies had occupied the landmass of present-day China before they were gradually brought together to become a culture that we recognize as Chinese (Rawson, 1996:11). More and more scholars are convinced that the sites of the Erlitou culture found in Henan and Shanxi provinces of Central and North China coincide in time and in space with the Xia dynasty as described in ancient texts (Loewe and Shaughnessy, 1999:72). What, then does the Erlitou culture reveal to us in terms of the state religion? According to Sarah Allan, the Erlitou represented an *elite* culture, associated with a set of religious practices centred on ancestral offerings, and revealed through primary markers of a common set of motifs and ritual forms, dictated by the state. This type of religious culture anticipated the themes of the later ages such as the so-called 'society of great harmony' (*da tong*) and the 'Golden Age' that were venerated by Confucians (Sarah Allan, 2007:461–496).

Monotheism and pantheism

The second of the three dynasties, the Shang, shows a clearly defined and fully developed form of the state religion. From the oracle bone inscriptions we can see that the spiritual convictions of the Shang royal house were centred on the belief in *Di* or *Shang Di*, the Lord or the Lord on High, who presided over the world and was the source of the human ruler's power and authority. *Di* was regarded as the ultimate power over all natural and human affairs, from which issued commandments for human behaviour concerning right and wrong. *Di* determined human affairs in at least the following five ways: he sent the rain down to the earth; he might hold the rain in check and send down famine instead; he brought victory to the army; and he brought fortune as well as misfortune to the world (Tung, 1952:12–13). Evidence shows that the Shang people believed that all matters concerning natural events and changes, such as wind, rain, calamities, disasters, and all human affairs, such as good and bad fortune, happiness and sorrow, harvest and famine, victory and defeat in war, unfolded according to the will of *Di*. It was *Di* who presided over the divine order through his agents or messengers, the lesser spiritual powers or beings, such as gods of wind, rain, thunder, mountains, rivers and the four directions (Directions of South, North, East and West). The association of *Di* with many other deities is believed to have taken place at an early stage of the Shang dynasty when the consolidation of the empire incorporated the religious beliefs of conquered neighbouring tribes into its royal sacrificial system, and assimilated various gods of theirs into the pantheon of *Di*. The new gods were then either worshipped sacrificially at the altar for *Di* himself, or at their own, separate shrines.

Belief in the supreme high authority above, who was infinite, all-encompassing, all-knowing, and universal, became the centre of religious life in early China. This was manifested not only in belief in the Lord on High of the Shang dynasty, but also in the worship of *Tian* or Heaven by the Zhou and subsequent dynasties right up to the early twentieth century. *Tian*, originally simply meaning 'sky', had become equivalent to the Lord on High by the beginning of the Zhou dynasty and, as the highest authority, was the focus of religious belief and closely linked with human authority on earth. The people of the Zhou believed that *Tian* determined their fate, that the Mandate of Heaven (*Tian ming*) provided justification for their dynasty, and that *Tian* would bless the good and punish the evil. These ideas are found in bronze inscriptions on various ritual vessels dating from the early years of the Zhou dynasty, and retained in the early classics such as the *Book of History* and the *Book of Poetry* (*Shi jing*), a collection of 305 poems of the Shang and early Zhou dynasties, both books being traditionally believed to have been edited by Confucius.

As well as the lesser spiritual beings, the Supreme Power or Lord, either in the name of *Di* or *Tian*, was also assisted in the execution of his will by royal ancestors who were particularly concerned with the performance of their descendants on earth. Therefore, worship of ancestors (including making sacrifices to them and invoking their names in divination) was essential for the continuity of the royal house. Equally, it was believed that the support and blessing of ancestors would not be bestowed unless descendants offered up to their dead proper sacrifice in exchange for a spiritual assurance from above that the royal linage would be strengthened and continued. The mutuality between the commemorated dead and the conscientious living remains the central thread of religious belief in China.

This close relationship perceived to exist between the Supreme Lord on High and human authority on earth would become distorted and darkened if worldly political struggles weakened rather than strengthened human faith in the power of the Lord. This was precisely the situation towards the end of the Western Zhou Dynasty, when communities were devastated by natural disasters and state cruelty, and prayers and pleas met with silence. Where was the Mandate of Heaven? Why would the supposedly kind and benevolent Heaven allow such pain and suffering to afflict the people? A group of new thinkers then emerged who began to search for alternative interpretations of the deeper meaning of life. It was they who marked the beginning of the axial age in China, taking Chinese religion into a new phase, the summer season.

Growth of religious schools

In this new period of growth, Chinese religion achieved its full and comprehensive development, including the formation of such schools as Confucianism and Daoism; the dissemination of key religious ideas such as *dao*, *yin-yang*, and the five elements into political, social and religious life; the establishment of Confucianism as the state ideology; the transformation of Daoist philosophy into specific religious movements; the introduction of Buddhism and the formation, transformation and adaptation of major Daoist and Buddhist schools.

The period of Spring and Autumn is crucial not only to the political and cultural history of China, but also to its religion and religious evolution. It was in this period that earlier comprehensive religious beliefs and practices were transformed and crystallized into different schools or traditions, such as Confucianism, Daoism, Legalism, Moism and so on. These schools were further developed and expanded (particularly in conjunction with new ideas and practices such as *yin-yang* and the five elements) during the Warring States (475–221 BCE) period. The unfolding of religious traditions continued throughout the two Han dynasties (206 BCE–220 CE) when a transformed form of Confucianism was established as the ideological authority of the empire, Daoism was equipped with religious rituals, tenets and monasteries, and Buddhism was introduced to and accepted in China. In the following 400 years, however, Buddhism became a sweeping power over the spiritual belief and practice of the Chinese people, which inevitably affected and changed the forms and content of Confucianism and Daoism, and intensified the interaction between the so-called three religions (*san jiao*).

Confucianism

Confucianism is a Western term for a Chinese tradition called '*ru*', referring to the group of people who were proficient in ritual and education in early China, while Confucius is the Latin transliteration of *Kong Fuzi* or Master Kong (551–479 BCE). According to his biography in the *Records of the Historian* by Sima Qian (?145–?86 BCE), Confucius' ancestors came from a branch of the royal Shang house; he became one of the well-known teachers in his 30s and many people, poor or rich alike, came to him to study ritual, poetry, history, music and so on. In the same way as his contemporaries, Confucius pursued a public career in his home state (*Lu*). Disappointed with the ruler of the state, however, Confucius gave up his government position and left together with a group of his disciples to wander among neighbouring states for 13 years in search of an 'enlightened' ruler who would put his ideas into practice. Failing to find such a one, Confucius returned home, devoting the rest of his life to editing the classics and to educating students (Lin Yutang, 1994:29–160).

The most reliable source on Confucius and his teaching is a short collection of his sayings or dialogues (probably compiled by the second generation of his disciples) which later became known as *Lunyu*, the *Analects*. These records indicate that Confucius retained traditional beliefs in the power and Mandate of Heaven, believing that his mission to transmit ancient culture was from Heaven, and arguing that if a person offended against Heaven, there would be nowhere he could turn to in prayer. When asked why few people understood him, Confucius replied, 'I do not complain against Heaven, nor do I blame Man. In my studies, I start from below and get through to what is up above. If I am understood at all, it is, perhaps, by Heaven' (Lau, 1979:129). With his concern for human problems and desire to find solutions for them, Confucius turned much of his attention from the cults of spirits and ghosts to the exploration of the Universal Way (*dao*) that he believed could guide and prescribe human activities. He injected humanistic elements into a deeply superstitious culture and channelled spiritual power into serving a human purpose. When one of his disciples asked him what wisdom was, for example, Confucius declared that wisdom was to 'devote yourself earnestly to what must be rightly done to the people; respect spiritual beings, while keeping a distance from them' (de Bary and Bloom, 1999:50). When asked about how to understand death and how to serve the spirits of the dead, Confucius admonished that if not yet able to understand life and to serve humans, we would not be possibly able to understand death and serve spirits (Lau, 1979:107). Concerning sacrifice to gods, Confucius emphasized the importance of sincerity and reverence of heart when conducting such rituals, because the word 'sacrifice' encompassed the word 'presence': 'sacrifice to the gods as if the gods were present' (Lau, 1979:69). For him, humans should gain experience in their believing and in carrying out what they believe, and his requirement that serving the dead as if they were alive was both religious and educational; this we can see from what was said by Zengzi (born ?506 BCE), a disciple of Confucius: 'When proper respect towards the dead is shown at the end of their life and continued after they are far away, the virtues of the people will have reached their highest point' (Lau, 1979:60).

Focusing on improving the quality of human life, Confucius emphasized the importance of family, community and government, laying responsibilities on the ruling class and believing that the influence of moral virtue far outweighed the effect of penal law. Central to his moral curriculum for teaching was a set of traditional ritual formulae known as *li*, which includes rites, ceremonies, moral codes and rules of propriety. Teaching on the subject of rituals, Confucius did not intend to train his students simply to follow rules but inspired them to become virtuous people, the most important virtue being *ren* (humaneness, benevolence or humanity). A person of *ren* was called by Confucius a *junzi*, translated as 'gentleman' or 'superior person'. For Confucius and his followers the people of *ren* were the only legitimate persons to rule and govern, since they had a heart of love and they would act always in accordance with the rules of propriety. By instilling such teachings Confucius hoped that the world would return to the harmony which reigned when it was ruled by sage-kings in ancient times.

After the death of Confucius, his disciples and students spread to various states, finding employment in government, education or editing ancient texts. Different approaches to, and diverse understandings of, Confucius' teaching led to different interpretations of the Confucian Way. By the time of the Warring States, eight distinctive schools had emerged claiming to be truly Confucian. Among them, Mengzi (?372–?289 BCE) and Xunzi (?313–?238 BCE) pioneered two different approaches to the world view of Confucius. The Mengzi school on the one hand championed an idealistic way in which all humans are said to have been born with a good nature; by cultivating one's nature and nourishing one's heart, anyone can thus become 'a sage', the paragon of virtue. Mengzi regarded himself as defender of the Confucian way, and therefore took it as his mission to fight against the advocates of heretic doctrines such as Yang Zhu who advocated that individuals should preserve their own life first, and Modi who proclaimed that universal love rather than family affection was the foundation of world peace. The Xunzi school on the other hand, presented an argument opposite to the position of Mengzi, arguing that humans are born with an evil nature, and must therefore be trained and disciplined through the teachings of the sages, educated under the guidance of teachers, and restricted by *li*. In so doing, people would be able to overcome their selfish desires and eventually reach the highest ideal. During the Qin and Han dynasties (221 BCE–220 CE), Xunzi's interpretation of Confucianism was in the ascendant, but his position in the Confucian tradition then declined rapidly; by the time of the Song Dynasty (960–1279) Mengzi had emerged as the most orthodox transmitter of the Confucian way, and was regarded as the 'Second Sage' after Confucius.

Confucians were, however, persecuted and Confucian classics burnt during the short-lived Qin dynasty (221–206 BCE). After the replacement of the Qin by the Han, Confucians gradually recovered from this reversal, but formed a somewhat different doctrine: 'Having clearly realised that they were in an eclectic culture, Han Confucians started a long process of adapting their doctrine to the need of the empire' (Yao, 2000:8), the movement then strove to establish a new type of state religio-political theory by adding a moral dimension to religious and political practices. For them, the government must employ sets of *li* (the codes of conduct and rites) to regulate its affairs, to appreciate civil as well as military merit, and to accept a system of social distinctions which determined an individual's relationship to his kin, neighbours, superiors and inferiors. Dong Zhongshu (?179–?104 BCE), the greatest Confucian scholar of the Han era, was instrumental in setting up Confucianism as a pattern for orthodox state conduct during the reign of Emperor Wu (r. 141–87 BCE). This revived Confucianism was characterized by synthesizing different traditions (including Daoism, Legalism and the school of yin-yang and five elements) and by a theologically or teleologically interpreted view of Heaven and its linkages with humans.

Gradually the worship of Confucius achieved the same rank as the worship of Heaven and the worship of royal ancestors, and became one of the 'three pillars' sustaining the imperial religion (Shryock, 1966). Veneration of the life of Confucius as among the highest of human achievements was revitalized by the followers of the New Text School (*jin wen*) who took Confucius as the Saviour of humankind, treating the Confucian classics as vehicles for the revelation of sacred messages. Confucius was considered the 'Uncrowned King' (*su wang*) whose mission was to bring order and peace to a chaotic world. By the beginning of the Common Era, worship of Confucius had become compulsory for all schools and government institutions and branches. Offering sacrifices to the 'Supreme Sage and Ancient Teacher' (*zhisheng xianshi*) remained part of official ceremonies at all levels of society for more than 2,000 years, until 1912.

Daoism

Daoism takes many (often interacting) forms, the two main principal modes of these being philosophical (*dao jia*) and religious (*dao jiao*) Daoism. As the term derives from a work attributed to a possibly mythical figurehead, however, it is debatable whether Daoism is an appropriate generic term to denote the beliefs of the group of people who claimed during the Spring and Autumn period to have found the Right Way. At this time, Laozi was the most renowned Daoist sage. According to Sima Qian, Laozi was an elder contemporary of Confucius and the author of a book of 5,000 characters either called after him the *Laozi*, or entitled *Daode Jing*, the *Classics of the Way and its Power*. Laozi is said to have composed this book at the request of a pass-keeper named Yin Xi before retiring from the secular world (Pas, 1998:195). However, since there is no concrete evidence to date to confirm the existence of Laozi or his composition of the book, modern scholars tend to think that the book (which collects sayings and aphorisms of individuals who proclaimed the value of living in harmony with nature) was compiled by unknown scholars over a considerably long period during the time of the Warring States.

Central to the *Daode jing* is the concept of Dao. This is a concept which is metaphorically said to be the beginning of the universe, the law of the world and the source of life (Lau, 1963:30), the unfathomable power sustaining all things and every living being. Dao is illustrated through metaphoric names in the book, such as 'the ancestor' (*zong*), the 'mystical female' (*xuan pin*), the 'spirit of the valley' (*gu shen*) and the 'One' (*yi*). It is claimed that to gain eternity, humans must return to the Dao or become one with the Dao, by following a philosophy of 'non-action' or 'no striving' (*wu wei*), as one of its ultimate principles.

It was this philosophy which was further expanded in the *Book of Zhuangzi*, named after the advocator of the Daoist way who was traditionally believed to have lived in ?399–?295 BCE. As in the book of *Daode jing*, Zhuangzi also believed that civilization and culture corrupted human hearts and destroyed the harmonious relationship between human beings and nature. Like many other early Daoists, such as Guan Yin (?–?) and Yang Zhu (fourth century BCE), most of whose works were unfortunately lost, Zhuangzi preferred to lead a life in harmony with nature rather than a life that was glorious for a moment but was soon destroyed. He proclaimed that the ideal life was the one of union with Dao; this was a union, which could not be achieved except in the emptiness of the heart, which he called the 'the fasting of the heart' (*xin zhai*). Concerning life and death, Zhuangzi strongly believed that these were nothing but different stages of cosmic transformation; there was no justification for us to be joyful over the coming of life, or fearful towards the coming of death; they were but two forms of the great Dao. For him, 'life and death, existence and annihilation, are all a single body' (de Bary and Bloom, 1999:109).

Ironically this kind of philosophy was later adapted to provide theoretical justification for the pursuit of immortality through medical and meditational practices. Practitioners of such were called *fangshi* (the prescription-masters) who achieved fame during the Qin and Han period for medical and spiritual treatment of illnesses, but claiming that they had found effective ways to longevity or immortality. These people travelled around to cure and heal the sick, not only using herbs and medical skills but also formulae, charms and rituals. Their skills and knowledge encompassed astrology, geomancy and alchemy, and they were renowned for their grasp of the meaning and implications of life and death; some of them even claimed to be able to communicate with immortals (*xian*) or to become immortals themselves through their encounters with immortals.

The search for longevity, if not immortality, was of primary significance to early Daoist religion, in search of which numerous practices were explored and followed: alchemic, dietary, gymnastic, respiratory and sexual exercises, plus 'magical herbs' or 'immortality elixirs', as well as praying to immortals or gods or spirits. All these were melded to give a religious form to Daoism and to construct various kinds of 'theocratic regimes' (Thompson, 1996:88) during the Later Han dynasty (25–220 CE), when leaders of a number of messianic movements (often with a political agenda) claimed to have had the Supreme Way revealed to them either by Laozi, or some other mighty powers or beings, who had commissioned them to lead the people to the realization of great and eternal peace on earth. The leaders of the Yellow Turbans (Zhang Jue (died 184 CE) and his brothers), for example, organized a military movement based on religious Daoism in eastern and central parts of China, calling for the confession of sins and the practice of meditation; this was the way, they believed, to achieve the Great Peace (*tai ping*), a Daoist utopia of harmony, wisdom and social equality. Slightly earlier than the Yellow Turbans, a politically ambitious medical practitioner named Zhang Ling or Zhang Daoling (dates unknown) claimed that Laozi appeared to him in a dream, telling him that the Mandate of Heaven had been removed from the Han house, and this mandate had now been entrusted to him by the Heavenly Master who was responsible for the chosen people. It is said that acting on the divine command, Zhang went to West China to preach Daoist teachings and establish Daoist communities. From this ministry grew a movement called the Way of Five Bushels of Rice, a name it gained from the fact that each member of the sect was obliged to give five bushels of grain to provide for the community and for the relief of the poor. Zhang Daoling's mission was inherited by his son, Zhang Heng (dates unknown) and grandson, Zhang Lu (active 155–220), who further developed his teaching and organized communities into religio-military units, and headed a small kingdom for a short while. The lineage developed into what was later known as the 'Way of Heavenly Masters' (*tian shi dao*), a religious community centred on the Heavenly Master who acted as mediator between the unfathomable Dao and believers. It was clear to the dynastic rulers and generals of that time that these so-called Daoiost movements were threatening the established order. The imperial government and warlords thus joined forces against them, suppressing them with violence. Rapidly or gradually these pioneers of Daoist religion died out, but their ideas and practices had nevertheless paved the way for a yet more powerful and fully equipped religion that bears the name of Daoism.

In due course Confucian virtues such as humaneness, righteousness, loyalty and filial piety were all adopted as part of the Daoist practices, although the highest virtues were said to be those as called for by Laozi: flexibility, femininity, humility, non-action and tranquillity. Unlike earlier Daoist philosophers who disregarded spirits other than the profound Way as irrelevant, however, the new Daoist religion claimed that gods, goddesses, spirits and deities dominated the world and human life and that all misdeeds and wrongdoings individuals committed were watched and recorded and could be expiated only through reciting sacred texts (notably the *Daode jing*), confession and penance consisting of community service such as repairing bridges and paving roads. These religious Daoists also developed sets of practices typical of all later sects, such as 'nourishing one's vital power (*yang qi*)', 'avoiding cereals (*pi gu*)', 'preserving the One (*shou yi*)', and carrying out breathing, meditational and physical exercises.

A number of early texts played an important role in arming the religious movements with religious views of the world. The most influential of these were *Tai ping jing* (a book illustrating how great peace could be achieved internally and externally), *Zhouyi Cantong qi* (a collection of Daoist commentaries on the *Book of Changes* which is generally considered to be the earliest work on alchemical techniques) and *Yellow Court Scripture* (*Huang ting jing*, which is dealing with issues of visualizing the inner gods dwelling in the body and the circulating of *qi*, the vital power). The doctrines and speculations in these texts were further developed by a number of significant Daoist theorists and practitioners. Ge Hong (283–343), for example, formulated his understanding of Daoist immortality and its related practices in a book entitled *Baopuzi* (*The Master who has Embraced Simplicity*, probably completed in 320), in which how to become an immortal is discussed and elaborated in detail. In the same way, Kou Qianzhi (365–448) claimed to be entrusted by Laozi, the Supreme Lord, with the mission of reforming Daoism and institutional disciplines and rituals. Kou was responsible for the revival of the Heavenly Master tradition in the north. In the south, Lu Xiujing (406–477) brought classification to Daoist texts and gave a theoretical illustration of the established *Lingbao* tradition that had developed under the influence of Buddhist devotion to bodhisattvas, emphasizing the ritual and worship of heavenly deities. Tao Hongjing (456–536) then consolidated the newly developed *Shangqing* tradition, the scriptures of which concentrate on meditative and visionary techniques. These sects and their further development constituted different dimensions of religious Daoism, enabling Daoist religion to play a key role in the intensive interaction with Confucianism and Buddhism.

Buddhism

Buddhism was formally introduced from the Indian subcontinent via Central Asia around the beginning of the Common Era. The Chinese came to know of Buddhist teaching initially through the translated texts (or sutras) of Theravada and Mahayana traditions, which revealed to them a new and 'alien' doctrine.

'Buddhism' is derived from the 'Buddha' that refers to 'the One who knows', or 'the Enlightened One'. The person behind this title is believed to be a prince born in or about the year 543 BCE, to the family of *Sakya*, from which he derives his name, Sakyamuni (the Sage or Saint of the *Sakyas*). While his personal name was *Siddartha*, he is also addressed as *Gautama*, believed to come from the name of the clan (*Gotra*) to which his family belonged. *Gautama* is used widely among Southern (*Theravada*) Buddhists, while *Sakyamuni* is more prevalent in Northern (Mahayana) Buddhism.

Central to the Buddhist tradition are the 'three jewels': the Buddha, the *dharma* (law) and the *sangha* (order). The conception of impermanence is the key to the Buddha's teaching. By impermanence is meant that all beings, whether in the forms of gods, humans or of other creatures, are transient, fleeting and impermanent; their present life is only one of endless reincarnations. While the Buddha did not deny the existence of gods, he nonetheless subjected them to the same law of cause and effect. The change of all beings is explained by the word *karma*. *Karma* does not simply mean 'fate', but refers to the sum total of the deeds performed in previous existences, resulting from the forces brought into action; just like a seed that naturally develops into a fruit, so an action naturally leads to a certain kind of result (Peter Harvey, 2001:67). Whatsoever gods, humans and creatures are now reaping is a result of what they have sown in previous existences, of which they may be utterly ignorant.

According to Buddhism impermanence underlies the conception of suffering. There are four fundamental Truths in Buddhism concerning suffering. The first is that as all things existent are but passing, all that is born is surely to die, and all that is created to dissolve; hence life itself a 'suffering' or pain. The second truth explains the cause of suffering: suffering comes from desire or craving, which produces re-existence and re-becoming and which is bound up with passionate greed. The third truth is the way to end suffering. Suffering is the result of desire or thirst; if desire or thirst can be extinguished, then suffering will be brought to an end. One will be thus liberated from the ties of rebirth and reach nirvana, a state of non-attachment to conditioned experience. However, to reach this state, the noble eightfold path must be followed: right understanding, right thought, right speech, right action, right livelihood, right effort, right mindfulness and right concentration. This is the fourth truth of Buddhism.

Such a doctrine brought a 'new' religion and subsequent 'alien' practices to the Chinese, and yet was not totally different from those of native Chinese traditions. In the first period of Buddhist presence in China, the major target of the immigrant or native masters was to familiarize the Chinese with the religious concepts and ideas of the Indian subcontinent; in this they employed their parallels with Daoism and were naturally tempted to express their beliefs in Daoist terms and to demonstrate Buddhist tenets as being closely linked with Daoist doctrines. The idea that a soul lives forever in accordance with *karma* was likened to that of Daoist immortality, the Buddha was equated with the Daoist supreme deity or Laozi the founder of Daoism, while the Buddhist vegetarian diet and meditative practices were allied with the Daoist control of respiration and abstinence from certain kinds of food. The substantially theistic culture of Daoist and the State religions made it easier for *Mahayana* Buddhism to be embraced by the Chinese rather than the *Theravada*; the *Mahayana* belief that the existence of all phenomena is empty and illusory, and that only the Absolute remains, undefinable and eternal (Ch'en, 1973:10) was particularly welcome among ordinary people.

The initial 'honeymoon' gradually gave way to mutual suspicion and reproach, however. Buddhists in China (foreign as well as native) soon realized that this yoking of two originally different systems would inevitably produce fault ideas that were misleading and ambiguous; great efforts were then made to interpret Buddhism from their own religious perspectives, and new approaches to religious doctrines and practices were pioneered through digesting and re-absorbing essentially Chinese elements into a reconstructed version of Buddhism. This movement led to the emergence and growth of Buddhist lineages and schools, with some retaining the substantial form and content of the original Indian subcontinent philosophies, and others being new developments and with distinctively Chinese characteristics. Among the early shapers of new forms of Chinese Buddhism were Dao An (312–385) and Hui Yuan (334–416) whose doctrinal views represent an amalgamation of devotional practices, trance and thaumaturgy, as well as a more intellectualized mixture of Dark Learning (*xuan xue*) and *Mahayana* notions. By the end of this period, Buddhist schools had come to fruition, and then grew rapidly, targeting different layers of population, some appealing to intellectual and social *elites* and others aiming at the common people. Buddhism had thus evolved into a formidable social power, accommodating not only homeless vagrants but also 'retired gentlemen', the *literati* who tried to avoid an official career (E. Zürcher, 1972:74).

Maturity of religions

After about 1,000 years' growth, all the branches of Chinese religion discussed reached maturity as witnessed by the flourishing of major Buddhist and Daoist schools, the full integration of the three doctrines, the dominance of Neo-Confucianism (itself a syncretic religio-politico-ethical system) and the springing up of new religious movements.

Integration of three doctrines

Religious harvest first came in the form of Buddhist and Daoist schools. During the Sui-Tang period (589–906), all major Buddhist schools such as *Tiantai, Huayan, Chan* (Meditation) and *Jingtu* (Pure Land) reached mature forms, which prevailed throughout the country and beyond. Daoist schools such as Heavenly Masters (*Tian shi*) or Orthodox One (*Zheng yi*) claimed to have continued the line of transmission since Zhang Daoling and the masters frequently received the honorary titles from the imperial court, while Perfect Truth (*Quan zhen*) aimed at becoming true persons (*zhen ren*) by following ritual, inner cultivation and an ascetic way of life in the Song era (960–1279). Characteristic of these Buddhist and Daoist schools is a syncretism that was itself rooted in Chinese culture and social conditions, which functioned as a melting pot for religions, and in which all doctrines and practices, indigenous or imported, melded in mutual adaptation, mutual adoption and mutual transformation.

From the very beginning Confucianism and Daoist doctrine were both opposite and overlapping. This remained true in the following centuries, with each developing its own doctrines while adopting useful elements from the other. Each claimed to cherish similar concepts such as *yin-yang* and the five elements, as well as sacred texts such as the *Book of Changes*. Archaeological discoveries recognize a close relationship between early Confucianism and Daoism; for example, although the bamboo version of the article entitled '*Taiyi shengshui*' discovered at Guodian Tomb no.1 in 1993 is a Daoist paper, yet it has a close relationship with Confucian beliefs as confirmed by the researches of a number of scholars (e.g., Chen Guying, 1999). Through a long term of mixture and interaction, Confucianism and Daoism eventually became two sides of the same coin, opposite but interdependent. On a social level, Confucianism presents itself as more positive, active and engaging, while Daoism appears as more detached and passive, and reticent in committing to social and political matters. In terms of ethical principles, Confucianism places stress on family and communal collaboration and its collective benefits, while Daoism focuses on personal freedom and individual choice. In the religious sphere, Confucianism emphasized the educational importance and effect of ritual and faith, while Daoist principles centred on relief from suffering and on spiritual well-being.

It seems that both Confucians and Daoists were aware of their differences, but at the same time of the need to collaborate. While Confucius rebuked the followers of Laozi as 'consorting with birds and beasts' (Lau, 1979:150), it is also said that he praised Laozi as the spiritual dragon, learned rites from him (Sima Qian, 1959:2140) and adopted from him an ideal similar to Daoist 'non-action' as being the highest achievement in politics (Lau, 1979:132). In the so-called Neo-Daoism of the Wei (220–265) and Jin (266–420) periods, Confucian classical learning and the mystical teaching of Laozi and Zhuangzi were twisted together to form 'mystical learning' (*xuan xue*), representing the 'first serious attempt to synthesise Confucianism and Daoist philosophy' (Yao, 2000:90). Religious Daoists incorporated Confucian virtues into their own system, considering moral cultivation and ethical action as necessary for anyone to achieve immortality, as represented by Ge Hong, who 'saw himself as a Taoist [Daoist] in his inner being, while acting as a Confucian in his social life' (Pas, 1998:188).

During the Tang era, Confucian scholars strove to reconstruct its doctrines and to strengthen its influence over government, education, community and the personal life of the individual, which paved the way for the full revival of Confucianism in the Song dynasty. Daoist priests built upon achievements in earlier ages, namely, editing and publishing the Daoist canon; improving Daoist rituals; developing technologies for making immortality elixirs (*wai dan*, external alchemy) from cinnabar and other elements; and producing inner power (*nei dan*, internal alchemy) by circulating and nourishing *qi*, the vital energy of life. The interaction between Confucianism and Daoism was in this way intensified, and further deepened by contact with Buddhist precepts. Confucianism and Daoism benefited in terms of metaphysical deliberations and meditational practices from Buddhism, while Buddhism gained itself a full ethical and political acculturation through its contact with Confucianism and Daoism. As a result metaphysics and reasoning deliberations were enhanced in Confucian and Daoist schools, while Buddhist schools took on the distinctively Chinese features as discussed above. This is an 'intertwining' recognized by Hans Küng: 'not only did the two main wisdom religions of Confucianism and Taoism become intertwined, they also absorbed a large number of Mahayana Buddhist influences – not, however, without giving them a deep Chinese colouring' (Küng and Ching, 1989, p.xvi).

The syncretic progress between the three doctrines was thus achieved in tolerance and mutual benefit. The reconciliation between them resulted in the common sense view that each of the three doctrines had its merits, and could exist and function alongside with the others. It then became accepted among the majority of the *elite* and the ordinary people that the three doctrines should be taught in parallel and as mutually complementary, because they were different only in terms of form and method, not in essence. They were hence seen as different vehicles to the same destination, or different approaches to the same goal, no matter what it was termed, sagehood (Confucianism), immortality (Daoism) or enlightenment (Buddhism). This all embracing perception led to the apparent co-existence of the three doctrines/religions, and the subsequent emergence of the three-in-one religious beliefs and practices which characterized the Sui and Tang dynasties onwards.

The three doctrines did not of course operate in vacuum. They were subject to the economic and political conditions of the times; cooperation and tolerance between them were thus frequently disrupted, or damaged by confrontation and attempts at mutual containment. Believers competed fiercely with each other for prestige, social recognition and above all, imperial patronage; this competitive behaviour brought about alternating social or political favour or disfavour of one over the others, and caused, directly or indirectly, the persecutions of the government towards one or more of the religious movements. The most noteworthy of these events were the suppression of Daoism in 555, when Daoists were ordered to become Buddhist monks (Pas, 1998:xxviii), and the persecution of Buddhism in 842–5 when Buddhist monks were forced to return to secular life, their properties confiscated and monasteries destroyed (Kenneth Ch'en, 1964, 232). In the latter case, devastation was also inflicted on other religious traditions of a foreign origin such as Manicheism, Nestorianism and Zoroastrinism, which had enjoyed a comfortable co-existence with Buddhism but which were now totally disbanded and stamped out.

Less violent methods were also employed to establish a working order or an order of preference among the three doctrines. A frequently adopted form was the 'three-doctrine-debate' sponsored by the imperial court, through which the emperor judged each on its merits and decreed a preferential treatment to them. One of these early attempts was made in 569, when Buddhists and Daoists were assembled in court to discuss the relative merits of the three doctrines with 100 (Confucian) officials; the outcome of these deliberations was the emperor's decree in 573 that Confucianism ranked the first, Daoism the second and Buddhism the third (Ren and Liang, 2006:113). Although at the beginning of the Song dynasty this kind of debates were formally prohibited, their different forms and scales still took place between Daoists and Buddhists; for example, those held at the court of the Mongol Yuan dynasty in 1255, 1258 and 1281 after which Buddhism was claimed to be the winner and Daoists the loser (Pas, 1998:32). However, with changes in the degree of enforcement over the next 1,000 years, the decreed order that Confucianism came first and was then followed by Buddhism and Daoism remained an effective point of reference around which the government and intellectuals could structure and construct religious devotions important to the people of China.

Dominance of Neo-Confucianism

Confucian revival had its beginnings in the Tang Dynasty, when a number of intellectuals and officials launched a movement calling for a return to ancient sources of Chinese tradition to rid China of foreign influences. This movement explored the central themes of early Confucian texts such as *xin* (heart/ mind), *xing* (nature, specifically human nature) and *sheng* (sagehood). These themes were extensively developed by Confucian scholars of the Song and Ming eras, leading to a renaissance of humanistic and rationalistic Confucianism, which have been termed as 'Neo-Confucianism' in the West. This was a new approach to cosmological, ethical and personal issues, which challenged Buddhist and Daoist spirituality. Leading Confucian scholars such as Zhu Xi (1130–1200) and Wang Yangming (1472–1529) were stimulated by Buddhist and Daoist teachings and by the ongoing debate among different approaches within Confucianism. Neo-Confucians sought to systematically answer the questions raised by Buddhism and Daoism, believing that they found their answers in 'The Four Books' – the *Analects of Confucius, The Book of Mengzi,* the *Great Learning* and the *Doctrine of the Mean* – and in the metaphysical views explored in *The Book of Changes.* The real value of Neo-Confucianism was thus not only in its 'return' to classical Confucianism but also in a fundamental transformation of Confucian doctrines, which enabled leading scholars to construct a comprehensive and complex doctrinal system that satisfied the spiritual and social needs of the age.

Neo-Confucians were not simply scholars who indulged themselves in theoretical deliberation and philosophical debate. They were also very practical, applying their understanding to society at large and attempting to solve serious problems which they believed prevented communities and individuals from developing in the right way. Some Neo-Confucians emphasized that family rituals were of great importance in cultivating a good character, while others gave more weight to an individual's spiritual cultivation, such as practising 'quiet sitting' (*jing zuo*) and ridding oneself of selfish desires. For example, Zhu Xi wrote on the codes of family conduct and rituals (*zhuzi jiali*) for the members of his clan; he also believed that learning could help overcome obstacles such as personal desires and feelings caused by the faulty functioning of vital energy (*qi*) in the mind and body. As a further example, Wang Yangming propagated the idea of the unity between knowledge and action, insisting that as soon as an evil idea appeared, a person had already committed a wrongdoing. These ideas and practices became the foundation of spiritual and moral training in later ages.

New religious movements

The thrust of Neo-Confucianism was thus to distil new and applicable moral principles from various religious and philosophical doctrines, and to put them in place as social and political criteria, by which everybody and every institute is judged and evaluated. It was thus only too natural for Neo-Confucians to encourage the interference of the state in religious matters in line with their moral principles in order to maintain the status quo. Under a powerful government, new religious ideas and practices could not help but to begin life as secret societies; new religious ideals in this way became intermixed with political ambitions aiming at changing the established order. Towards the end of the Yuan dynasty (1279–1368), for example, revolutionary movements made use of millenarian beliefs in *Maitreya* or *Mile* in Chinese. These beliefs were based on the expectation that *Maitreya* the Buddha of the Future would come at the end of the age. Followers of the White Lotus Religion (*bailian jiao*) thus developed into the army of the Red Turbans, whose leader was regarded as a reincarnation of the *Maitreya* Buddha. Rebellion became religiously motivated with the message that the reincarnation of *Maitreya* signalled a change of dynasty. Further, the founder of the succeeding dynasty, Zhu Yuanzhang (r. 1368–1398), who rose from the Red Turban movement, named his dynasty the Ming (Light) to align himself with the widespread beliefs of the significantly sinicized Manicheism ('Religion of Light').

Established after the anti-Yuan religious rebellions, rulers of the Ming dynasty (1368–1644) were clearly aware that secret religions represented a double-edged sword and so decreed the disbandment of all societies which bore the names 'White Lotus' or *Maitreya* as soon as they had consolidated their ruling position. However, secret societies continued to demonstrate their power and threatened the order of the state throughout the Ming era. Examples of these rebel movements were the insurrection led by Tang Saier (date unknown) in 1420, who claimed to be the 'Mother of the Buddha' (*fo mu*); the revolutionary movement of 1489 which asserted that '*Maitreya* descending from Heaven will rule the world'; and the *Wu-Wei* (Non-Action) Religion founded by Luo Qing (1424–1527), all of which began as secret societies, bearing the hallmarks of millenarian movements. When the Manchus became the new rulers of China, secret societies and religions combined their forces and instigated rebellions against the 'barbarian rule', aiming to restore the Ming – as many as 72 such revolts occurring during this period. After the first Opium War (1840–42), most secret societies and religions additionally directed their attacks against foreign invaders and missionaries, culminating in the massive movement known in the West as the Boxer Rising (1898–1900), *yi he tuan* in Chinese, the Righteous Harmonious Fists secret society.

Besides their rebellious and millenarian nature, new religious movements were distinguished by the following common features. First, most of them worshipped a supreme god or goddess who was named after Buddhist or Daoist deities, such as *Maitreya* or the Eternal Mother (*wusheng laomu*). Secondly, the majority of the new religions transformed Buddhist *kalpas* (immense tracts of time) into various doctrines enshrining the cycle of cosmic birth and death. Some of them, for example, propagated the idea that there was a *kalpa* of the past in which the Buddha *Dipamkara* resided, the *kalpa* of the present at which *Sakyamuni* presides and the *kalpa* of the future when Buddha *Maitreya* would be supreme. Others of a more Daoist nature would term these three *kalpas* as the three periods of Green Yang, Red Yang and White Yang, with the colours signifying the different stages of the cosmic power's evolution. Thirdly, they declared that, by converting to their religion, a person could seek sanctuary during the chaos of the *kalpa* end-times and then rise to the Heavenly Paradise. Fourthly, their founders often claimed to be the reincarnation of *Maitreya* or the Eternal Mother, who had descended to save the good and punish the evil. Lastly, their doctrines and practices were of a strongly syncretic nature, intertwining the worship of *Sakyamuni* the Buddha, Laozi the founder of Daoism, and Confucius as major deities, the pursuit of Buddhist and Daoist spiritual practices such as calming the heart, reducing desires, contemplating on/visualizing of gods or goddesses, and the use of Confucian moral codes as religious disciplines, the three religious traditions were accepted as complementing popular beliefs supporting each other (Bowker, 1997:94).

Religious decline and rebirth

In 1911, the last imperial dynasty was overthrown, and the new Republic of China established in 1912. Revolutions and wars had devastated the economy and torn apart traditional society. Fundamental questions urgently needed to be answered: why did China fail to protect itself from the onslaught of foreign powers? How could China be revived in order to stand as an equal with other countries? Liberal intellectuals and republican politicians ascribed the weakness and failure of China to the traditional structure of the state and to traditional ideology and religion. Thus, in place of the dynastic infrastructure modern political structure, social reform and secular education were installed, introduced from the West, but not without a significant transformation. The search for a new China led to the May Fourth Movement (1919), in which science and democracy were seen as two powerful weapons in the fight against 'the old culture' in the form of codes of conduct (li), loyalty, filial piety, chastity and righteousness. There were two criteria for judging what should or should not be retained as part of the Chinese new culture: whether or not a cultural element was attached to the old systems of past dynasties (anti-democracy) or whether or not it was 'superstitious' (anti-science). As traditional ideologies, religions were believed to have failed in both tests, and not to bring any benefit to society; they must therefore be jettisoned or replaced by new ideas and ideals.

Decline of the three religions

Of the three established religions, Confucianism was the first target of revolutionary forces. Having just established itself in Nanjing in 1912, the republican government issued decrees to separate the learning of Confucian classics from moral education and abolish the cult of Confucius in public schools. Radical intellectuals and students alike shouted loudly 'Destroy the old curiosity shop of Confucius'; the majority of the Confucius temples were no longer used to honour the sage (Chan, 1978:18-19). Efforts were made to revitalize Confucian learning and Confucian religion by political conservatives, Confucian values were used to launch the New Life Movement promoted by the Nationalist Party in the 1930s, and Confucian learning was advanced by a number of prominent Modern New Confucians. Despite this, Confucianism was more and more confined to the sphere of pure philosophical study and historical research.

Buddhism had a comparatively brighter but brief glory in the 1920s and 1930s, when a number of distinguished philosopher-monks explored the modern values of Buddhist doctrines, and led Buddhism in the direction of a universal faith that would bring material benefits to the people and society. Daoism followed a slightly different route. Facing a rapidly changing society, Daoists became aware of their weaknesses in protecting themselves and preaching their message. The Central Association of Daoism was set up in the White Clouds Temple in Beijing as the national organization for Perfect Truth Daoism in 1912, while the sixty-second Heavenly Master attempted to found the national organization for Orthodox One Daoism in Shanghai.

However, these measures did not save Buddhism and Daoism from further decline, and in 1928 the nationalist government issued decrees to seize or dismantle a large number of temples and shrines dedicated to Daoist deities such as Guandi (Lord Guan, a deified general of the Three Kingdoms period,

220–265), God of Soil or Earth (*tu di*), God of Hearth (*zao jun*), Dragon Kings (*long wang*), goddesses and other spiritual beings. Most of the temples were in fact confiscated to be used as schools, government offices and military camps. Although these measures were not carried out thoroughly and the extreme elements of the policy were soon moderated, they added further pressure on Buddhist and Daoist organizations that had already been struggling to survive.

Resilient religions

Comparatively speaking, the religions of the common people were less affected in the first half of the twentieth century by the rationalism and atheism that dominated social *elites*. With the weakening of the governmental control, organized religions in the form of secret societies, professional guilds and communal groups even flourished in the countryside and cities alike. However, to survive, they also attempted to attach themselves to different political forces and military powers. For example, the Way of True Emptiness (*zhen kong dao*) aligned itself with the nationalist government, the Pervading Way (*yi guan dao*) made an alliance with the Japanese invaders, and the Society of Red Spears (*hong qiang hui*) eventually joined the communists. For the majority of people, who were neither members of secret societies nor dedicated followers of the institutionalized religions, communal rituals and practices were part of their daily lives which remained largely unchanged for centuries, regardless of the government or religious jockeying for power. This situation dramatically changed in the 1950s, however, when the communists took power and abolished all superstitions and religious societies that had a connection with the nationalist government or were formed under the influence of foreign forces, in order to foster a new and patriotic emotion among religious and non-religious people.

Religious suppression

Nationalists appeared to be relatively tolerant of religious organizations and in some sense even supported religions, largely because a number of the leaders of the Nationalist Government were themselves Buddhists or Christians, but communists on the other hand regarded most religions as superstitious and (potentially) anti-revolutionary. Communist policymakers in the 1950s adopted a system of watching, restraining and controlling religious activities.

They held that, as the 'opiate of the people', religion weakened an individual's will to fight against abuse and repression; further, they believed traditional religions were closely related to feudalism and the nationalist government, and were used to suppress people and exploit the working classes; that Buddhists and Daoists were parasites because they relied on the working people for food and clothing while they did no useful work themselves and that Christianity was a tool in the hands of imperialist countries that intended to invade China and exploit Chinese people. These attitudes and political doctrines resulted in a series of policies that aimed to bring all religious organizations and activities under supervision and control. Under such directives, a religion or religious organization was allowed to exist only if it accepted and acknowledged the leadership of the Communist Party and only if its adherents were patriotic in the face of foreign interference and willing to serve the people and the socialist cause. As an indigenous religion explicitly or implicitly sponsoring individual freedom in religious matters, Daoism suffered more than other institutional religions: it 'was forced to abandon its apolitical and detached position and was obliged to adapt to the new political conditions' (Dillon, 2009:105).

Anti-religious feeling culminated in the events of the so-called Cultural Revolution starting from 1966 when thousands of high-school and university students reacted fervently to the appeal of Mao (1893–1976) and turned themselves into Red Guards who, in their eagerness for emancipation from the trammels of 'old ideas, old culture, old customs, and old habits', smashed cultural heritages including Confucian, Buddhist and Daoist temples, Christian churches and ancestral graveyards; 'Priests, monks, and nuns have been driven out of temples' (Chan, 1978:145). They attacked any institution or orgnization that had connection with, or content of, old cultures, such as education, drama, literature and local customs. Extreme measures were adopted to eradicate religions, and to eliminate the influence and effect of old traditions. Religious believers were subject to physical and psychological abuses and were forced to give up their faith and change their thought and behaviour. For a time, China became a country virtually without any active religion.

Renewing religion

The end of the Cultural Revolution signalled the moderating of extreme policies towards religion. A new official policy regarding the freedom of religious belief was declared in 1982 by the Chinese government (Pas, 1989:6). After this, various religious institutions were gradually restored, and most religious buildings and properties such as temples and churches that had been confiscated or occupied before were now returned to their dispossessed owners. There has been a remarkable increase in overt religious activity since the 1980s; attendance at traditional Daoist and Buddhist temples and the presentation of votive offerings have increased over the past 20 years ((Dillon, 2009:103–104). Thus, religion started to recover its traditional ground in the 1980s and has since entered a 'new season' where religious activity is growing and expanding so rapidly that some scholars even declare that the new acceptance of religious faiths is tending to an 'excessive' level that has not been reached since the late Qing times, and this manifests a degree of individual freedom never experienced before in China (Thomas H. Hahn, 1989:81).

There is no doubt that religion is still under the strict guidance and direction of the government and the communist party. But in general, religious tolerance has increased, and religious observances and beliefs have become increasingly important to ordinary people. Not only are political recognition and legal protection extended to major institutional religions such as Buddhism, Daoism, Christianity and Islam, but freedom and tolerance are also granted to individuals and local communities to engage in traditional religious activities. Ancestor worship is practised widely, and families offer lavish sacrifices to the dead during festivals or on birthdays. The settings of family graves in rural areas are again chosen according to the advice of masters of yin-yang and *fengshui* (geomancy). Local shrines and temples, where gods or goddesses are regularly offered food and incense, have become re-established once more. Buddhist monasteries and Daoist temples are attracting growing numbers of people, and alms-giving is common among pilgrims. Implicit religions – activities or organizations with a secular shell but a religious content – aimed at improving health and lengthening life span are developing their doctrines by means of synthesizing certain aspects of Confucian virtues, Buddhist tenets, Daoist views and Christian ideas, especially in the name of practising *qi* (*qi gong*, an exercise of strengthening one's vital energy by breath control and meditation).

Either in the name of restoring traditional culture or in the interests of maintaining spiritual well-being, religious beliefs and practices are in general diversified, empowered and animated by deep embedding in day-to-day life. Although religious movements have been revitalized or redirected in a modern context, we have reason to suggest that the Chinese are continuing their religious way of life in new situations and with fresh inspiration.

Questions for discussion

1. The cyclical change of the four seasons is often used to explain the nature of religious life in China. What justification is there for such an interpretation?
2. 'Chinese Religion is deeply rooted in myth and legend.' Discuss.
3. How much can we gather about the main features of religious tradition in China from archaeological discoveries?
4. How did Confucianism, Daoism and Buddhism gain full maturity in their parallel, confrontation and coexistence?
5. Why was Neo-Confucianism so important for religious life in the later part of imperial China?
6. Why is it said that the most part of the twentieth century was comparable with the season of winter for Chinese religion?
7. Do religious activities in mainland China today justify the statement that its religious spirit has entered the spring season?

Religion as Culture

Culture and religion are interrelated facets of civilization, essentially of the same nature but with different characteristics and functions. Neither operated in isolation in China till the modern age, when both political ideology and social structure were substantially transformed under the influence of the West. Religion in traditional China was an intrinsic part of the culture which in turn provided social relations and structured orders in which religion operated. In this sense 'Chinese religion can be defined as a cultural system that governs the rites of passage and the annual festivals celebrated by the people of China'; in contemporary times, Chinese religion 'has survived all attempts to usurp its pre-eminent, fundamental position at the roots of Chinese cultural and social life' (Saso, 1990:1). The typical features of Chinese religion are in this respect 'related intimately to Chinese culture and history' (Bush, 1977:xiii).

Religion and culture

Religion and culture in China are characterized by their interpenetration and interdependence. Religion fosters a sense of cultural identity in individuals, families and communities, and thus manifests an inclusive culture that nurtures the religious orientations typical of the Chinese. Religion in this context not only strengthens the core values and meanings of Chinese culture, but also functions through such cultural symbols as rites, customs and communal activities. Religious identity is therefore crucial to the coherence and continuity of Chinese traditions, and religious teachings and practices have become the most celebrated part of its culture. In a sense, the relationship between religion and culture can be likened to that of the body and the mind/soul, where culture is the 'body' of religion while religion is its 'mind/soul'. Central to the Chinese understanding of human life is a conviction that body and mind/soul are inseparable from each other; and this conviction lays the ground for all religious practices ranging from ancestor worship to rites of passage. In the same way, religion cannot be separated from culture, and traditional culture would have become a meaningless form without religion. Religion must be understood in its cultural context and culture cannot be fully appreciated except through a religious lens.

Zongjiao and *wenhua*

The Chinese terms for culture (*wenhua*) and for religion (*zongjiao*) reveal to us a great deal of specific meaning and value, important for our understanding of Chinese religion. *Wenhua* is a combination of two originally separated characters, *wen* and *hua*. In classical Chinese, *wen* stands for the results of human activities and the achievements of intellectual expansion and social evolution; while *hua* refers to the transformation and education of individuals and society. The pictographic form of *wen* in oracle bone and bronze inscriptions portrays a frontal view of a man with tattoo on his chest. Since tattoo symbols in ancient China were related to natural or ancestor worship, it has been conjectured that the origin of *wen* was rooted in reverence towards the past and the worship of animated natural entities such as the sun, moon, stars, fire, rivers, mountains and animals. Although no evidence has so far yet been found concerning tattoos on the human body, there are discoveries of red body paintings and tattoo drawings on pottery, bone and jade items (Mou and Zhang, 2007:24–25). From the original meaning of 'a man with tattoos', *wen* gradually derived the connotation of 'a decorative pattern' or 'fine lines', and has finally come to embody a variety of meanings such as writing, characters, scripts, language, literature, composition, culture, the civilized, the gentle and so on.

The character of *wen* speaks volumes for the primary position of religion in Chinese culture and civilization. Many scholars have indeed concluded that there was no distinction in origins between religion and culture, and ascribed the source of art and social customs, philosophy, politics and even nationality to religious beliefs and practices. According to Tang Junyi (1909–1978), a leading New Confucian scholar of the modern era, for example, the spirit of Chinese philosophy, morality and politics are all directly derived from the original idea of reverence to Heaven; this reverential spirit is the root of social, political, moral and cultural life (Tang, 2005:41, 328). Heaven in ancient China is believed to be the place where ancestors would continue their spiritual existence; thus, revering Heaven always simultaneously carries the meaning of revering ancestors. In this sense, it seems reasonable to suggest that culture (*wen*) and religion (*zong*, revering the ancestral tradition) share the same root meaning in terms of piety and sincerity towards spiritual authorities.

Not only do religion and culture have a common source and root meaning, but they are also invested with the same social function and spiritual value. This can be seen from the connotations of '*hua*', the second character of the Chinese phrase for culture. Its pictographic form in oracle bone inscriptions, for example, shows the people's comings and goings. The pictogram is then expanded to indicate 'changing' or 'transforming', a process by which natural phenomena and human beings would turn 'anew' to the influence of good teaching and guidance. On the part of humans, this renewing process is itself one of modelling as well as being taught and guided, in which education and ritual performance play a key role. At this point culture and religion join together again. As discussed in Chapter 2, religion (*jiao*) is primarily understood as a process of teaching and education, and is intended to transform people from an unenlightened state to an enlightened state, by externally following ritual and rites, and by internally cultivating sincerity and reverence. This is a dimension of meaning which equally loads the Chinese character of *hua*.

Cultural religion

No religion can be totally separated from its cultural roots and contexts. Religion in China thus reflects what is spiritually aspired to and inspired by its culture; its beliefs, rituals and practices are often shaped or moulded into particular forms of cultural systems or sub-systems with expectations and orientations which are uniquely Chinese. Religion is in this sense deeply woven into the broad fabric of individual, family and social life, and is an integral part of Chinese culture.

This culture is essentially human-focused, synthetic and practical. These features have worked together to demonstrate a distinctive Chinese character in terms of divine-human relationships, cultural transformation of different faiths, and programmatic arrangement of religious activities. This character differs from the three Abrahamic religions, for example, where God, the supra-human and supernatural being, has set prerequisite rules for humans, and then only by following these rules can humans be awarded with His grace and bless-ing. In Chinese religion, however, divine beings or powers are often moved by human requests, and their response changes along with human behaviour. In religious Confucianism, for example, Heaven (*Tian*) measures human situa-tions by moral criteria, awarding the good and punishing the bad, and is itself a projected moral force that both represents and enforces the five virtues of benevolence, righteousness, propriety, wisdom and trustfulness. Because of this, the primary concern of Confucians is not only about reverence towards Heaven and the Mandate of Heaven, but also about how to cultivate human virtue, as the *Book of History* states: 'The king should have reverent care for his virtue' (de Bary and Bloom, 1999:36). For Confucians, virtue itself is a demonstration of reverence for Heaven. In Daoism, divine beings and immortals are all embodiments of Dao, which is both transcendent and imminent. In this sense, only those who help ordinary people and relieve their pain and suffering would rank among divine beings. Hence, the most popular figures of spiritual power in Daoist religion are the so-called Eight Immortals who are believed to help the righteous and honest and to punish the selfish and arrogant. Indian Buddhism, as another instance, was gradually transformed or reshaped by Chinese culture after its introduction. This cultural reshaping process is vividly evidenced in two examples: one is the cultural transforma-tion of *Avalokiteśvara*, the *bodhisattva*, from a male form to a delicate, beautiful and slender female, who becomes fused into the popular figure of the Giver of Children or the Goddess of Mercy (see Figure 4.1). The other example is the change of *Maitreya* from an unimportant role in the Indian tradition to a popular and important figure in the form of a fat, laughing image as the 'Pot-Bellied Mi Le' or the 'Laughing Buddha' (Ch'en, 1973: 7–8).

The humanistic face of the divine and its relation to the human world are nurtured in Chinese culture. With all its aspects mutually related and affecting one another, Chinese culture upholds a belief in the interrelatedness of this life and the life beyond. Whatever we do in this life will inevitably affect what we become in the next; and the well-being of the spiritual realm would change along with what is carried out in the human world. This belief is the

Figure 4.1 Guanyin, the Goddess of Compassion

prerequisite for ancestor worship and much of the continual family and clan ritual and sacrifice. In the *Book of Rites* and other classics where materials recording earlier religious beliefs and practices are contained, we find more or less consistent narratives about how the ancient Chinese viewed this and next life, which has become the backbone of religious beliefs in China. The Chinese believe that two kinds of essence must be present to create and maintain life in a human body: one is *hun*, meaning the spirit, the other is *po*, the soul; when *hun* coming from heaven and *po* from earth dwell in the human body and combine together, a new human individual is born; by the time of death, the soul returns to the Yellow Spring of the earth, and the spirit goes up to heaven: 'The intelligent spirit returns to Heaven; the body and the animal soul return to the earth' (Legge, 1885, xxvii:444). The spirit and soul are to be recalled by their descendants through ritual and sacrifices, to come home and to dwell in the spirit tablet erected in the main hall of the house. The spirit and the soul that have returned are called *gui*, literally meaning 'returning':

> When a man is born, [we see] in his first movements what is called the animal soul. After this has been produced, it is developed into what is called the spirit. By the use of things the subtle elements are multiplied, and the soul and spirit become strong. They go on in this way, growing in etherealness and brightness,

till they become [thoroughly] spiritual and intelligent. When ordinary men or women dies a violent death, the soul and spirit are still able to keep hanging about men in the shape of an evil apparition. (Legge, 1991, Vol. V:618)

If these spirits and souls are not properly treated, such as provision of proper funeral rituals and sacrifices, they will become haunting or hungry ghosts, causing disease and harm to animals and human beings in the household or community. To avert this harm, the family or local people must carry out special religious services to console these unquiet spirits through proper sacrifice and ritual.

The cultural features of Chinese religion gained momentum from the fact that religious teachings and tenets were centred on the family and on family virtues (see Chapter 5), since the traditional social system was based on the family, not on the individual. To preserve the family, practical Confucianism, religious Daoism and popular Buddhism all insisted that filial piety be the foundation of social and spiritual life. Buddhism is a showcase of how religion became culturally inhabited and reshaped in this context. Original Buddhist teaching before its introduction to China was primarily concerned with the individual liberation that is achieved by gaining enlightenment and escaping from the world of bondage including family life. Such a starkly dualistic vision of the world as two separate secular and sacred realms naturally met strong resistance in Chinese culture; more appealing to China in the Mahāyāna Buddhist teaching was that individual liberation was to be attained not so much by escaping from the world of bondage, but by achieving it within the world of suffering, as proclaimed in the *Fanwang sutra*: 'A bodhisattva should give rise to the heart of filiality of the Buddha-nature, a heart of compassion, always helping all people to achieve felicity and happiness' (de Bary and Bloom,1999:429). This kind of liberation in the world is compared to the lotus flower that 'can only blossom when rooted in the muddy bottom of pond' (Gregory and Ebrey, 1993:19). More than that, to demonstrate that this liberated spirit was not a tradition against Chinese values, Buddhist masters drew attention to the fact that numerous Buddhist sutras called for love of parents; they forged a body of apocryphal literature, and added to the translated sutras lengthy commentaries that placed filial piety and loyalty at their centre. In due course, Buddhism was successfully absorbed by forming its own doctrine of filial piety and loyalty, as claimed by Huiyuan (334–417): 'they who rejoice in the way of *Sakya* inevitably first serve their parents and respect their lords', ... 'though inwardly they may run counter to the gravity of natural relationships, yet they do not violate filial piety; though outwardly they lack respect in serving the sovereign, yet they do not lose hold of reverence' (de Bary and Bloom, 427).

Religious culture

A powerful culture in China has thus reshaped religious forces into acceptable forms. However, religious forces are not inactive, or passively receptive to cultural reshaping and transforming. By its very nature religion actively influences culture and enables culture to be spiritually oriented and manifested through its tenets and practices. Therefore the relationship between religion and culture is not only concerned with absorbing religion into Chinese culture, but also with how the culture itself is immersed in and shaped by religion.

Behind many seemingly secular cultural events and ceremonies are hidden deeply religious purposes or convictions; all dimensions of Chinese culture are, in this sense, heavily coloured by religious themes or beliefs. C. K. Yang has provided a comprehensive survey of religious culture in traditional China by examining the important places of religion in Chinese society: temples and shrines dotted the entire landscape, while different places of worship stood as symbols of social reality; the Chinese world was intimately related to the spiritual worlds of gods, spirits and spectres. Religion has influenced all aspects of daily life such as food, clothing, shelter, travel, marriage, birth, death and life crises. Historiography and philosophy are under the influence of religious interpretation, while 'among the untutored populace – children and adults alike – a day scarcely ever passed without some thought being devoted to the supernatural meaning of one's daily activities' (Yang, 1961:17).

In terms of literature, the four famous traditional fictions depict or imply a particular type of interaction between the human and the spiritual world. The *Journey to the West* (*xi you ji*) is a fictionalized account of the legends around the Buddhist monk Xuanzang's (?602–664) pilgrimage to India during the Tang dynasty (618–906) to fetch the *Tripitaka* Sutras. In his journey he was effectively supported and assisted by his three disciple-protectors (Monkey, Pig and Sandy). There was many a demon power in the disguise of human, animal and plant forms who attempted to catch or kill the Monk but were all defeated by his disciples with the help from *Guanyin* the Bodhisattva and many other Buddhist and Daoist deities. The Buddhist and Daoist character of the *Dream of the Red Chamber* (*hong lou meng*) is clearly seen in its artistic design, thematic ideal and scenic unfolding, and the intercommunication between gods/goddesses and the heroes/heroines overarches its themes and plots. The central theme of the *Water Margin* (*shui hu*) is to enhance the Confucian virtues of loyalty and righteousness which is supported and illustrated by magical powers or immortals of Daoist religion, while the *Romance of the Three Kingdoms* (*san guo yanyi*) carries a meaningful twist to Confucian and Daoist ideas and ideals. Apart from them, other popular novels are also of a religious theme. For example, 'The Investiture of the Gods' (*Fengshen yanyi*) tells the stories about how the Zhou conquered the Shang with the help of gods and spirits; hence the battle for a new dynasty evolved into battles between two opposing camps of deities or immortals, most of whom were killed in battle but after the Zhou triumphed, were canonized as gods and became part of the Chinese pantheon (http://en.wikibooks.org/wiki/Category:Chapters_of_Fengshen_Yanyi).

In China, religion cannot be totally separated from politics. It is a normal practice both in the past and present times that spiritual powers are invoked to ensure cultural and social solidarity or to create stability or change in a political regime or society. All dynasties in the past would justify their rule by referring to the mandate of Heaven and by sacrificing to Heaven as a way of laying claim to its legitimacy, while all rebellions in turn would justify their actions through associating themselves with a sort of the ultimate spiritual power. Thus, by conscious alignment with political forces, religion could either thrive or wither depending on the favour or disfavour of government authorities (see Chapter 6).

Daoism and Buddhism were instrumental in the formation and evolution of Chinese medicine and health practices such as *qigong* and martial arts. Many Daoist masters were themselves medical doctors or practitioners, composing famous medical treatises which are still relevant to today's medical practices. The Daoist diagnostic treatment of an illness is based on the spiritual understanding of the human body in which a heavenly component and an earthly component are crucial for health and life; 'If they are partially gone, man becomes sick. If they are completely gone, man dies. If they are partially separated from the body, the occult expert has means to retain and restrict them' (de Bary et al., 1960:260). *Qigong* itself is a unique physical and mental practice that is aimed at corporeal and spiritual well-being and harmony, the initiation and development of which was inseparable from Daoist and Buddhist understanding of the cosmos, human body and mind, as well as the interaction between the human and the spiritual world.

Religion has contributed much to the basic motifs in Chinese arts, particularly architecture, painting, music and calligraphy. Few pieces of elaborate traditional decoration omitted the religiously inspired patterns of the cloud, the dragon, the phoenix or fairies (Yang, 1961:18). Indeed, the masterpieces of Chinese painting and architecture are all related to religious inspiration and aspiration. For instance, water-mountain paintings reflect the spirit of Daoism, and, later, Chan Buddhism; distinguished buildings are often places of religious worship, or are designed to strengthen the mutually beneficial relationship between the spiritual and the human world, or are intended to ward off evil influence or intrusion. Sculptures, frescos and other artistic forms are often of a Buddhist, Daoist or Confucian nature where religion and culture are fused together perfectly.

The impact of religion on culture leads to particular customs and preferences that constitute an important part of the Chinese way of life. This includes the almanac which the people follow, the festivals they celebrate, and the food they consume. Food for the Chinese is not merely something for survival or to fill the stomach, but is also taken as an important path to the harmony of the twin powers of *yin* and *yang*, to balance the five elements, and to well-being in spiritual growth. There are numerous taboos or prescriptions on what to eat and what not to eat at a specific time, for medical as well as religious reasons. Festivals in the Chinese calendar are all essentially religious or carry with them strong religious convictions. For example, the Chinese New Year marks the replacement of the old by the new, and it is important that all behaviour and action during the festival are focused on ridding the community or the family of the demons and misfortunes of the past year while celebrating the arrival of the New Year and good fortune. The *Qingming* festival in the spring and the *Hanshi* festival in the autumn, on the other hand, are occasions for making good shelter for ancestors and providing food for the spirits of the dead.

Religious culture in China is fully manifested in the home, which is not only the convergent point for personal and familial life but also a shrine for religious activities. In a traditional Chinese home, ancestral spirit tablets, statues of Buddhist and Daoist deities or Confucian sages, and pictures and symbols of communal or family gods are displayed and offered sacrifices on a regular basis. Home is also the primary place where an individual goes through various stages of life such as birth, adulthood, marriage and death. In the same way as for the tombs of the dead, a house compound is built on the principles of geomancy or *fengshui* (wind and water) which are intended to ensure maximum good fortune and offset evil influences by harmonizing *yin* and *yang* powers.

The humanistic character of Chinese religion further integrates the religious and the cultural, making it possible for spiritual cultivation to be gained through a familial, social and political living and by various secular activities and pursuits. For example, it is believed that human spirit can be cultivated and nurtured in the practice of calligraphy, painting and music, and that spiritual well-being can be strengthened or improved through morning or evening exercises such as *taiji* and *qigong*. It is also believed that spiritual cultivation can be achieved through a particular method that is fitting to a particular place and a particular time, and can be enriched by fulfilling moral responsibilities to other people, the family, community and the state.

Moralizing religion

Since Aristotle, ethics has been a separate discipline in the West and the modern era is marked by that of an essentially law-centred culture. Differing from it, traditional Chinese culture took morality into the heart of its social and spiritual systems. This has brought about two consequences. First, Chinese religion is substantially humanistic, underpinned by human-centred concerns and practice-led principles. Secondly, moral norms and virtues penetrate all social and cultural aspects of human existence, with which religious teachings and practices are imbued. Religion and morality are thus interlocked in a very special relationship: moral virtues are at the centre of religious faith and practice while religion strengthens the binding force of moral norms and rules.

Morality and *daode*

The Chinese term for morality, *daode*, has much wider references than its English counterpart implies. As we have already examined in Chapter 2, *dao* (the Way) refers to the essence of religious and philosophical doctrine; when used in a religious sense, the term implies that religion is itself 'a way' opened up by a 'pathfinder' who is followed by his disciples along a spiritual path. *Dao* is also infused with a metaphysical or ontological meaning to represent the origin of the universe or the principle of universal change. In this sense, *dao* is often seen as the source of eternity, by which the world came into being and in which all beings acquire life. *Dao* is therefore both transcendental and immanent, as the Way that dominates the natural, human and spiritual worlds, and as concrete ways or paths that can be followed by individuals. From the universal Way to manifested paths, *dao* penetrates all things through its suffusing power of *de* that allows each individual being or thing to be distinctive and unique.

Although often translated as 'virtue', *de* in Chinese originally signifies a personal quality or ability, as a kind of 'power' or 'charisma' by which a king is able to rule the state without resorting to force or violence. In this sense, *de* is defined as 'to obtain'; a virtuous king is thus said to be the one who has obtained 'the Way', namely, received the endorsement of Heaven and ancestors, had capable ministers to support him and acquired gifted people to work for the good of the state. Gradually, *de* becomes 'a moral-making property' that is able to confer a kind of 'psychic power' to influence others, or even to control one's nonhuman surroundings. This kind of power is naturally manifested as a personal 'virtue', a virtue accumulated through personal cultivation or endorsed by spiritual powers. When obtained, 'virtue' enables one to be transformed from a crude and uncivilized being to a cultivated and refined person; or from a body of senses and instinct to a spiritual being.

Since *dao* is universal to all beings and things, and since all humans are able to attain *dao* through individual moral effort and cultivation, then it is only natural for the Chinese to believe that the nature of each individual is linked with the nature of the universe, the particular with the universal, and the finite with the infinite. In their moral world, the universe and the human body has become one, and the secular (familial, social and political) has acquired a transcendental meaning. Since spiritual goals can be achieved through daily life, and since religious beliefs can be outwardly demonstrated by moral effort, religion in China is thus essentially moralized.

Moralized traditions

It is evident that Confucianism, Daoism and Buddhism all take morality as a doctrinal foundation, where transmission and cultivation of moral virtues are undertaken as necessary paths to religious and spiritual attainment. Nevertheless, the roles which each of these traditions actually play in ensuring moral uprightness in personal, familial, social, political and spiritual life are different: Confucianism, from this perspective, provides moral principles while Daoism and Buddhism apply and sanction them.

Morality as described is characteristic of Confucian theories and practices. The spiritual aspirations and moral concerns of Confucians imbued all traditional codes of life, rules of propriety, patterns of behaviour and guidelines for social and personal life. In this sense we may well say that Confucianism is an ethical religion. Central to Confucian morality are the five relationships that are guided by the following moral virtues: loyalty of the subject to the ruler or state, benevolence or righteousness of the ruler towards the subjects and people; filial piety of children towards their parents and love and kindness of parents towards their children; submission of the wife to her husband, and respect and love from the husband to his wife; respect of a younger brother for his elder brother and the care of an elder brother to the younger and finally, trustfulness and sincerity between friends. These five relationships and ten virtues are not only central to dealing with political, social and familial matters, but also to ruling over all religious organizations and their activities; they are set up as the sole standards for distinguishing the good from the bad, the right from the wrong, for promoting or downgrading the ranks and positions of particular spirits or gods, and for judging the merits or demerits of a person in the afterlife to determine the destinations when reincarnated.

Morality is also at the centre of Daoist religion. Clearly contrasting with Confucianism, early Daoist masterpieces such as *Daode jing* and the *Book of Zhuangzi* advocate an amoral approach to social and personal problems. However, these early Daoist texts also advocate various kinds of ethical standard to judge right and wrong. Gradually, differences in moral attitudes and standards between Daoism and Confucianism were reduced, minimized or simply disregarded. Indeed, when religious Daoism came onto the stage, deliberate efforts were made to blend its naturalism with Confucian moralism. The founder of the first religious movement in the name of Daoism (Zhang Daoling) was himself originally a Confucian scholar, who injected Confucian values into reinterpreted Daoist teachings. This process was furthered by his grandson Zhang Lu, who is alleged to have produced a pamphlet entitled *Laozi xianger zhu*, a first religious commentary on *Daode jing*. In this commentary, Laozi is transformed from a philosopher who addresses rulers of the states to a deity, the Supreme Old Lord (*taishang laojun*). The commentary also changes the import of the original text from attacking Confucian virtues to praising and adopting its moral virtues as important steps in personal and social salvation (Pas, 1998:197).

Attempts to incorporate moral values into religious ideals and beliefs in early Daoist scriptures were significantly amplified by later Daoist masters, particularly Ge Hong, who manipulated Confucian moral virtues into necessary conditions and means for attaining the religious ideal of longevity and immortality. Ge Hong in particular emphasized Daoist aspects of moral virtues such as calmness of mind and freedom from anxiety, simplicity in life, sympathy with all creatures, happiness over others' happiness, sadness over others' suffering, helping others in need, harming nobody and nothing and speaking no evil words. However, at the same time, he also consciously aligned himself with Confucian virtues, claiming that those who aspired to immortality must be rooted in loyalty, filial piety, harmony, obedience, benevolence and trustfulness. According to him, all Daoist books are 'unanimous in saying that those who seek immortality must set their minds to the accumulation of merits and the accomplishment of good work. Their hearts must be kind to all things. They must treat others as they treat themselves, and extend their humaneness (*jen*) even to insects'; he warned that 'If they do not cultivate moral conduct but merely devote themselves to occult science, they will never attain everlasting life (de Bary et al., 1960:262, 264).

On its arrival in China, Buddhism seemed at odds with the tension between its religious ideals and the moral virtues which the Chinese cherished at that time. It seemed outrageous for some Chinese that Buddhists were unable to attain enlightenment unless they had renounced all secular emotions, responsibilities and moral virtues. On the part of Buddhist scholars this was a problem they must solve quickly. Solutions were explored during an initial process of Buddhist sinicization, when scholars not only selected and translated Buddhist sutras in the light of Confucian moral standards, but also attempted to inject its morality into Buddhist doctrine. For example, Sun Chuo (314–371) declared in *Yü Dao Lun* or *A Discourse on Illustrating the Way* that among the twelve classical Buddhist sutras, four have taken filial piety as an important theme, while Yan Zhitui (531–?) assimilated the Buddhist five precepts (*wu jie*) into the Confucian five principles (*wu chang*). In practice, Buddhists even claimed that 'if a son of the family becomes a Buddha, all his ancestors of the seven generations will gain buddhahood,' and that 'cultivation not inside but outside of one's family is not to give up filial piety but to carry it out in a broader sense' (Mou and Zhang, 2007:352).

Further, through reinterpreting the Buddhist doctrine of causation, Buddhism strengthened its claim on moral superiority over other traditions. Although one of the Buddha's primary teachings is transcendence of the self, in popular *Mahayana* interpretations, Buddhist causation has become a sort of merit and demerit system, according to which the form of reincarnation is determined by current actions. The form into which one incarnates comes from what has been done in a past life or lives, and what can be reaped in the next will be determined by what is sown in this life. This ethically interpreted cause-effect chain is thus used to explain why many must go through repeated incarnations in the cycle of life-death-rebirth. In this way, popular Buddhism in China not only gives morality a religious sanction, but also provides a religious answer to the question of why the virtuous are often unrewarded, while the vicious so frequently profit.

To further their moral appeal, Buddhists introduced to China a totally new concept of hell, as an additional assurance for the moral to be rewarded and the immoral to be punished. The Buddhist hell is based on a well-organized underground god system which is entrusted with the task of the final cleansing and judgement, using various tortures to punish the sinful souls in accord with their wrongdoing, while rewarding the righteous with a new birth in favourable circumstances, without undergoing further torments, again in accordance with their good deeds. For those who have led a wholly sage life, rebirth in the Western paradise will be attained, so as to escape finally from the repeated suffering of reincarnation.

Moral karma

Thus, one of the fundamental ethical tenets in China is the heavily moralized karma belief that the good will be rewarded while the bad punished, either in this world or in the next. The idea of, and belief in, a kind of moral retribution were already influential in China before the arrival of Buddhism. The *Book of History* (*Shang shu*) states, for example, that the fall of a dynasty was caused by the loss of the Mandate of Heaven which is in turn caused by the failure of the ruling House's virtue. Thus, the toppling of the Yin or Shang dynasty was equated with the fall of their Mandate because: 'they did not reverently care for their virtue' (de Bary and Bloom, 1999:37). For Confucius, human error will cause displeasure to Heaven; if this error is too grave an offence, then there will be nowhere to turn in prayer (Lau, 1979:69). More evidential statements are found in the writings of the Han Confucian scholar Dong Zhongshu (?195–?105 BCE) in his discoursing on the human cause of natural disasters. According to him, all natural and social calamities were rooted in the faults of the state:

> When faults have just begun to germinate, Heaven sends forth fearful portents to warn and inform the ruler of these faults. If after being warned and informed, the ruler fails to recognize the cause of these portents, then strange anomalies appear to frighten him. If after being frightened he still fails to recognize the cause of his fear, only then do misfortunes and calamities overtake him. (de Bary and Bloom, 1999:305–306)

However, this kind of moral retribution is usually confined to the ruling class; it is more political than religious. It was the Buddhist belief that became popularized in visual and religious terms, a perception of hell where the evil were punished, and a paradise where the virtuous triumphed. In judging by whether or not one followed the Way, early Chinese Buddhists drew attention to the consequences of one's behaviour: 'If one has the Way, even if one dies, one's soul goes to an abode of happiness. If one does not have the Way, when one is dead one's soul suffers misfortune' (Ibid, 424).

Gradually the primary target of the morally interpreted karmic belief shifted from focusing on life after death to encouraging people to do good and to deterring them from doing evil. Daoists were equally anxious to adopt this doctrine, by designing different ways to fulfil it in personal, familial, communal and social life. They made it the centre of their beliefs and practices that rewards for good deeds and penalty for evil doings were controlled by spirits who resided in the human body and in the home. No evil thought or action would escape the watchful eye of these gods; spirits on the other hand were responsible for prolonging or shortening people's life span according to the number and nature of their good and evil acts. Those who have committed evil will have their lifespan significantly decreased, or undergo repeated sufferings in a life that is surely stricken with illnesses, calamities and disasters.

Not only humans but also all gods and goddess are subject to moral retribution. Spirits, immortals or gods are regarded merely as different embodiments of moral virtues, attained through previous virtuous living; and their divinity is believed to be vulnerable to undermining by moral degeneration. Thus, as a human being can accumulate virtuous merit and thereby enter the spiritual world, so a god or goddess can either rise in the hierarchy of deities through cultivating virtues or righteous actions, or be forced downward because of immoral or reckless action. Transfiguration between humans and gods is thus fundamental to Chinese religion whereby no status is permanent, except for moral virtues. Under this system of moral retribution, it is widely held that any god or goddess can incarnate to human form if he or she has committed a moral wrong; in the same way, a human being is able to become a god or goddess if he or she has done sufficient good works. Moral virtue is therefore laid down as an important path for human beings to attain the status of a god or an immortal or a Buddha or bodhisattva.

Since both divine and human beings are equally susceptible to the influence of moral or immoral behaviour, moral virtue becomes the sole criterion to judge one's worth, to measure the quality and quantity of one's life and to determine whether one would be mortal or immortal. As a result of this doctrine, a variety of instruments were designed to measure the goodness of a person or god, and to induce people to do good by promising them an eternal and happy life. In the Daoist tradition, a number of ledgers exist to count one's merits or demerits in daily activities, using mixed moral codes from all three teachings. These have a religious dimension since they urge not only the leading of a morally justifiable life, but also the cultivation of the belief that to accumulate a certain number of merits will guarantee the status of an earthly or heavenly immortal. As an example, the below chart is constructed from the earliest ledger of merits and demerits that served as a model for later morality books, 'attributed to a Daoist named Youxuan zi who stated in the preface, dated 1171, that the ledger was a divine revelation made through him by the Taiwei Immortal' (de Bary and Bloom, 905) (see Figure 4.2).

Conduct that results in merit	Merits	Conduct that results in demerit	Demerits
Saving someone from death penalty	100 per person		
Exempting someone from imprisonment	40 per person		
Saving the life of a domestic animal	10 per animal	Killing an animal for food	6 per animal
Saving the life of a nondomestic animal	8 per animal	Buying meat and eating it	3
Saving the life of an insect or watery creature	1 per creature		
Giving assistance to the widowed, the orphaned or the poor	1 per 100 coins spent	Not providing assistance to the poor	1
Printing scriptures	10 per 100 coins spent	Humiliating the poor	50
Remonstrating with people not to fight	1 per person	Provoking someone into a fight	3 per person
Recommending intelligent, capable and virtuous people to office	10 per person	Not recommending a capable person to office	1
Praising someone's good deed	1 per instance	Not seeking teaching from worthy people	1
Not telling about someone's bad deed	1 per instance		

Figure 4.2 A Ledger of Merits and Demerits (de Bary and Bloom, 905–906)

Religious means

This kind of ledger was also adopted by Buddhists and Confucians who encouraged their followers towards moral conduct in order to realize their goals. Equally true is that religion is taken as a means to a moral end; that is, moral virtues draw on religion to strengthen their function and acquire spiritual sanction. Thus religion and morality are mutually supportive: a strict moral code is often the essence of religion, while religion ensures that the human and spiritual world observe that moral code. Religious beliefs strengthen and magnify moral value, while religious ritual and practice enhance moral consciousness and habit.

A number of religious instruments have been used to encourage followers to observe the designed moral code. One of these is an association of human life with a predetermined concept of destiny or fate (*ming*). Believing in such a predetermined fate is rooted in the Chinese world view, which affirms that for all human beings the destiny assigned by Heaven governs how long they may live and what they can achieve. This destiny involves happiness and enjoyment, or suffering and pain, depending on what kind of fate one has. Whatever an individual human can achieve in life depends on one's destiny too. In Confucius' *Analects*, for example, a conversation is recorded between two of his disciples; one of them complains that all others have brothers, but he alone has none. The other replies that as long as one demonstrates virtues within and without, why should he be worried about not having any brothers? This naturally leads to a conclusion that since life and death are a matter of Destiny, we must accept what we can have in life (Lau, 1979:113).

Apart from the concept of destiny, other religious means to encourage people to perform their moral duties include setting up religious models for people to follow, propagating the idea that a morally perfect person can become an immortal or a sage or a *bodhisattva*. For those who have no wish to become either, two additional ways are in place to encourage them to do good: the moral being will lead a happy and trouble-free life because of their virtuous character, and a virtuous person will be incarnated to the heavenly or Western paradise after death.

A more effective means for religion to enforce its moral codes is to deter its followers from doing evil. In all Buddhist and Daoist temples, there are statues of spiritual beings whose supernatural powers will terrify the guilty and remind wrongdoers that punishment awaits them. Through the popularized pictures of hell and its Ten Courts, people come to believe that when dead all will go before the judgment seats: Those who are virtuous in life will suffer little and will be reincarnated to the Western paradise or to birth as noble and rich; those who commit moral wrongs will be tortured, judged and reincarnated as miserable and poor beings or will even be born in the form of animals or insects.

Harmony

Religion as culture also has at its heart the core concept of harmony, as Julia Ching suggests 'We may call these [Confucianism, Daoism and Buddhism] the "religions of harmony" because of the known Chinese effort in directing effort to harmony between the human and the cosmic, as well as harmony within society and with the self' (Ching,1993:4). In religious terms, harmony is not just a state of peaceful living or a stable social structure, but also of harmonious relation or unity between spirits and common people, between ancestors and descendents, and between Heaven and humans (Yao, 1996:31–32).

Harmony and *he*

Harmony in Chinese is termed 'he', an earlier written form of which has been found in bronze inscriptions as picturing a music instrument (panpipe). This means that for the ancient Chinese, harmony is primarily associated with music, derived from the 'harmony of sounds and tones'. Music is not merely an object of aesthetic appreciation but more importantly, it is a moral and religious indicator or criterion for the world order and human flourishing. In the section on music in the *Book of Rites*, for example, music (*yue*) is said to be composed of tones (*yin*), and demonstrates the highest achievement of human comprehension and appreciation:

> Tones rise from the human heart and music is related to the principles of human conduct. Therefore the animals know sounds but do not know tones, and the common people know tones but do not know music. Only the superior man is able to understand music. (Lin, 1994:559)

In this sense music reflects as well as creates harmony through touching the human heart and tuning human conduct. The association of harmony with music is also recognized by other schools; for example, the Daoist work, the *Book of Zhuangzi* points out that 'The *Book of Music* speaks of harmony' (Watson, 1968:363).

Harmony is believed to be the original state of Heaven and Earth which can be expressed through music. Music and rituals are central to the Confucian perception of the world, as stated in the *Book of Rites*: 'Music is the harmony of Heaven and earth, rites are their order. Through harmony all things are transformed; through order all are distinguished' (de Bary et al., 1960:168). However, harmony is not only a natural state, but also includes human effort, involving creatively mixing and combining different elements to form a new unit. In this sense, it is said that 'Harmony results in the production of things'; this process can be illustrated by the formation of a kind of soup when the cook 'mixes the ingredients, harmoniously equalizing the several flavours, so as to supply whatever is deficient and carry off whatever is in excess' (Fung, 1953:35, 36). Through the metaphor of soup, the early Chinese thinkers reveal that harmony does not simply identify one element with another, replicating what we already have, or merely putting different things together. Harmony is itself a process of creation; in the process of producing something new, it is itself a process of transformation and reproduction.

From this root meeting, the notion of harmony is gradually expanded to become a grand philosophical and religious scheme that underlies what the Chinese regard as their universe. This view is composed of the following elements:

(1) The cosmos is a harmonious unity where Heaven and earth, stars and mountains, creatures and things, all exist in harmony and each, great or small, has its or his/ her own proper position and value;

(2) All things or beings flow from the same source, either called *dao* (the Way) or termed as *taiji* (the Supreme Ultimate), and are driven by the same forces (yin-yang) and ruled by the same laws (*li*). The harmonious world is not created by a creator or God, but is formed through self-transformation.

(3) Cosmic harmony evolves in constant self-transformation, driven by changes, a process full of movements, exchanges and interactions.

(4) Harmonious changes are not of a linear but a cyclical movement, in which the end is linked with the beginning, in the same way as the rotation of the four seasons, or as the night following the day that is followed by the night. Therefore, returning to the beginning is characteristic of harmony.

(5) Cyclical changes that are central to harmony have made the Chinese universe an organic process of growing and declining: the peak is followed by the decline, while the ebb always indicates the return to the beginning of new growth.

This view is cultural as well as religious. Apart from a limited number of cases where millenarian ideals are claimed, all religious schools, movements and scriptures are deeply rooted in the belief in harmony, encourage self-cultivation and self-transformation, and are aimed at returning to the original state that is described either as the golden age, the ultimate harmony or simply the paradise.

Harmony as religious ideal

From this perspective, harmony can be said to be the supreme ideal and the essence of Chinese religion. In popular religion harmony is identified as two gods or two immortals, each holding a lotus flower (*he*, which has the same pronunciation as the character for harmony). According to one version of folklore, the gods of harmony are said to be two Buddhist poets of the Tang Dynasty (618–906): Hanshan (691–793) and Shide (?–?). Buddhism is thus believed to be the guardian of harmony. For Daoists, attaining to *dao* or returning to the origin is what matters. *Dao* itself is perfect harmony, from which all things flow. The evolution from *dao* is itself a process of organic harmony, in which the chain of organic production leads from *dao* to the myriad creatures, while these myriad creatures all 'carry the *yin* and embrace the *yang* and through blending of the material force [*qi*] they reach harmony' (Chan, 1963:160). The beginning is marked as the 'height of harmony' and 'to know harmony is called the constant' (Lau, 1963:62).

Harmony underlies all Confucian doctrines, where harmony is taken both as the means to the ideal and as the goal of self-cultivation. It is said in the *Doctrine of the Mean* that when all feelings and emotions 'are aroused and each and all attain due measure and degree, it is called harmony' (Chan, 1963:98). Harmony is also a social, political and religious ideal that is often identified with the Grand Unity (*da tong*). This Grand Unity is believed to have existed in the ancient golden age under the rule of the sage-kings, to be reclaimed or recovered through ethical and political programmes. What Confucians have in mind is a harmonious world in which all human beings are brothers and sisters, and all things are companions (Chan, 1963:497). Ritual is important, but without harmony it would be useless. Indeed, among the functions of ritual, 'the most valuable is that it establishes harmony. The excellence of the ways of ancient kings consists of this. It is the guiding principle of all things great and small' (Chan, 1963:21).

Harmony is not confined to religious and philosophical doctrines, but has also penetrated all aspects of Chinese culture. For example, in medicine, health is regarded as a harmonious condition where *yin-yang* forces and the five elements are in balanced and mutually supportive relations, while illness results from their disruption or in a situation where the harmony between these forces and elements is disturbed. In traditional medical vocabulary, sickness is often called 'disharmony' (*bu he*) or 'contrary to harmony' (*wei he*). The same applies also to the mind or soul. If *yin-yang* forces and the five elements are in proper order, then spiritual well-being is maintained, and we will have psychological and spiritual peace and harmony; on the contrary, if their harmony is disturbed, we will suffer from mental diseases. Herbs or acupuncture would need to be allied to balance the disrupted order and to regain health by restoring the original harmony.

Yin and *yang*

Central to the understanding of harmony is the unity between *yin* and *yang*, the two forces behind all existences, lives, movements and changes. *Yin* and *yang* are considered to be the origin of the cosmos, and the source of vitality. In philosophical terms they are the powers or principles by which the world comes into being and through which all gain energy and vitality, but in folklore they are embodied as two gods or the two forces that enable beings to gain divine power.

Yin and *yang* are opposite to each other, but their relation is far more complicated than opposition; they together form an organic polaristic unity. In contrast to a dualistic world that is characterized by opposition, separation, finality, closeness and independence, the polaristic world of *yin* and *yang* is characterized by interconnectedness, interdependence, openness, mutuality, indeterminateness, complementarities and correlativity. *Yin* and *yang* are related to each other intrinsically, both self-determinate yet determined by the other. The changes between them are therefore not 'substantial', but transformational; and accordingly, all changes in the universe are not revolutionary but evolutionary; not destructive but constructive.

Yin and *yang* are popularly symbolized in nature and personified in human representations, where *yang* is associated with heaven, day, the sun, fire, heat, outer, male, light, warm, masculine and aggressiveness; while *yin* symbolizes earth, night, the moon, water, dampness, inner, female, dark, coldness, femininity and passivity. These two sets of phenomena or qualities do not parallel each other; rather they are interrelated to form harmonious pairs: heaven and earth, father and mother, male and female, the sun and the moon, fire and water, light and dark, and so on.

More than mutually complementary, *yin* and *yang* contain each other. All natural, social and human entities have both *yin* and *yang*, containing in their nature yin and yang qualities: yang qualities include generative power, aggressiveness, forcefulness, harshness and masculinity, while yin qualities manifest in procreation, yielding, weakness, softness, kindness and femininity. All phenomena and realities possess both kinds of qualities, albeit in different degrees – here it is degree or quantity that decides. This can be seen clearly from one of the most popular Chinese symbols, ☯ where *yin* and *yang* are divided by a curve, not a direct, line and there is a small circle of the opposite colour in both yin and yang dominant areas. The curved line between *yin* and *yang* means that the relationship between them is subtle, while the small circle of the opposite colour in each area means that they are included in each other. The balance of yin and yang is thus the basis of the cosmic harmony, and to sustain their balance is the only way to keep well-being and prosperity in nature, in the state, in the family and in the human body.

The five elements

Harmony is not only presented as the mutual complementation of *yin* and *yang* forces, but it also manifests as the mutual production or negation of the five elements. While using the 'elements' as a convenient translation, we must point out that this does not accurately reflect what the Chinese term *wu xing* implies (Fung, 1953:21). The meaning of *wu xing* is much wider and more active than the five elements in English, ranging from five principles, five agents, five powers, five movers and five phases to five activities. These are applied to all aspects of the natural and human world, manifested as five seasons, five directions, five colours, five virtues, five inner organs and so on and so forth.

The five elements represent what the Chinese believe are the five most important forces of the universe: water, fire, wood, metal and earth, corresponding to its five factors or activities or aspects. The order starting from water is first used in one of the oldest books of China, the *Book of History*, where water is listed in the first place because, as it is later explained, water is produced by Heaven (in the form of rain), fire is listed as the second because it is produced by earth (dryness); wood is generated in water and is therefore listed as the third; metal is obtained in fire so that it is ranked as the fourth, while earth (soil) in the form of dust is the destiny of all things.

Crucial to the harmonious world are the two orders of the five elements, one being that they mutually produce each other and the other being that they mutually overcome or negate each other. By production (*sheng*) the Chinese mean to give birth to, to give way to, to generate, to lead to, or to beget, and the one who produces and the one who is produced are therefore likened to the relation between father and son (Chan, 1963:279). Wood produces fire as fuel, fire produces earth since in fire all turns into ashes, earth produces metal in the way that metal ores grow in earth, metal produces water either because it attracts dew in the night or because metal has the property of liquefying in fire, and water produces wood as water nourishes plants.

The harmony of the five elements lies not only in their mutual production, but also in their mutual conquest, in which the circular order overcomes any excesses to enable the world to sustain balance. The order of mutual conquest is not simply a counter-order of mutual production. Conquest (*ke*) here means that the nature of the first is contrary to that of the second, and the first is stronger than the second; therefore, it can control the second. Wood conquers earth either in the sense that wooden spades dig the earth up and make shapes of it or that the roots of plants penetrate the earth; metal conquers wood in that it cuts or carves wood; fire conquers metal because fire can melt metal; water conquers fire as it extinguishes fire; earth conquers water in the way of damming water and constraining it. In the same way as the mutual production order, the mutual conquest order is also applied to all aspects of life. For example, it has been used to construct the five main departments of the state. The minister of each department represents a special element, holds the particular quality of that element and carries corresponding responsibilities, but is controlled and supervised by the minister of another. Thus, the minister of the Department of Agriculture represents the nature of wood. He controls the Department of Works whose nature is of Earth, but is supervised by the minister of the interior department who is representative of metal. In turn the Interior Minister is supervised by the Minister of War who is representative of fire, while the Minister of War is supervised by the minister of Justice representing the nature of water. The minister of Justice is supervised by the minister of Works as the representative of Earth. At the end of this circle, the Minister of Works is controlled by the Minister of Agriculture in the same way as earth is conquered by wood. Through mutual controlling and mutual producing, it is believed that the state would be efficient and balanced, and the social and political order achieved (de Bary et al., 1960:202–204).

Heaven and humans

What *yin-yang* and the five elements represent is a harmonious world in which all things and beings are driven by the same forces and follow the same laws. Harmony is therefore not only seen in the balance of natural forces, in harmonious social relationships, in inner equilibrium and in balanced personal temperance, but primarily in the interrelationship between Heaven and humans.

'Heaven' here is a translation of *tian*, the earlier written forms of which represent either the Being which is greater than humans, the sky above us, or the destiny where we all end. Invested with such complex connotations, the meaning of Heaven is both cultural and religious, and its relationship to humans has many facets. As Nature, Heaven refers to what is meant in English the cosmos, the universe, the natural environment, natural laws, material entities, ontological reality and so on. Its relation to humans is therefore both metaphysical and ontological. As the spiritual power, Heaven is identified with the Lord on High (*shang di*), embodied as the High God, or popularly as the Jade Emperor (*Yu huang*, see Figure 4.3); it is also substantialized as the province of spiritual beings which ancestors, spirits and immortals inhabit. Its relationship to humans is therefore both religious and spiritual. As the source of moral virtues, Heaven is identified with the principles of all existences, and is venerated as the model of moral conduct which humans must follow; and its

Figure 4.3 Jade Emperor and his entourage God of Venus, Lord Laozi, God of Fortune and God of Longevity in his shrine at the top of White Clouds Mountain, Biyang County

relationship to humans is therefore ethical. While separated into these three areas, the Heaven-human relationship must not be defined by any of them; its different aspects cannot be totally independent from each other. Metaphysical, spiritual and ethical dimensions are meaningful only in their interrelationship and interdependence.

The relation between Heaven and humans in Chinese culture and religion is far more intimate than that in other cultures. Heaven and humans are by no means two separated realms; rather they are mutually dependent or mutually included. The practicality of Chinese culture does not allow humans to be independent of their natural and spiritual environment; in this culture humans are affected, or at least influenced by what happens in Heaven. One of the visible examples for this is that humans would feel sad in bad weather, but would be highly spirited on a sunny day. Although very superficial, this example illustrates well the Chinese belief that Heaven and humans share common forces and 'emotions', so much so that one would be consonant with the other in all aspects of changes.

Heaven and humans not only share fundamental powers, but are also said to be within each other. The oneness of Heaven and humans is initially a Daoist understanding, by which Daoists argue for epistemological agnosticism; for example, Zhuangzi declares that 'Heaven and Earth came into being with me together, and with me, all things are one' (Fung, 1952:235). A similar view, albeit from a different ethical perspective, is also expressed by Mengzi, who claims that: 'All the ten thousand things are there in me' (Lau, 1970:146). These views were then accepted and expanded by idealist Confucians, meditational Daoists and Chan Buddhists who transformed the oneness of Heaven and humans into a spiritual starting point for humans to embark on the journey to return to the beginning, or to be one with the origin. Heaven and humans are therefore no longer two separate existences but a holistic unit. Because of the oneness, Heaven and humans are naturally in harmony; even though at times temporarily in contradiction, it is believed that they can easily and will surely return to perfect balance and harmony.

The oneness is also expanded from material and substance to apply to principles and relations, as claimed by Dong Zhongshu: 'The norms of the people's ruler are derived from and modelled on Heaven' . . . 'Since human beings receive their lives from Heaven, accordingly they appropriate Heaven's humaneness and are thereby humane'; this relationship explains the need for all human virtues such as 'reverence toward Heaven', and 'affection for parents, brothers and children; it also underlies all cultural refinements and inner principles such as being loyal, trustworthy and caring, acting according to what is right, and being wise as to distinguishing right from wrong (de Bary and Bloom, 1999:295, 301). The imperative that humans must model themselves on the pattern of Heaven is the ontological and ethical foundation of harmony, by which parallel relationships in the family, society and the state have developed. Husband and wife, father and son, brothers and brothers, the ruler of the state and his subjects, friend and friend are none other than reflections of the principles of Heaven and Earth, and are guided by their laws.

In the Chinese context religion and culture are thus closely knit together, demonstrating distinct culturo-religious characteristics through morality and harmony. Religious beliefs are rooted in ethical concerns, while religious practices are aimed at regaining the original harmony. These features are fully revealed in the family and political contexts which will be dealt with in the following two chapters.

Questions for discussion

1. What is 'culture' in a Chinese context? In which sense can it be said that culture has functioned as religion in China?
2. 'Chinese religion is a moralized faith system'. Discuss.
3. What does the Daoist ledger of merit and demerit reveal to us about the characteristics of Chinese religion?
4. How can you understand that harmony is the central theme of both Chinese religion and culture?
5. What are *yin-yang* and the five elements? Why should we say that the five elements are not an accurate translation of the Chinese term '*wu xing*'?
6. What is 'Heaven' in Chinese culture and religion? Why is it said that the Heaven-human relationship is the foundation of Chinese religion?

Religion in Family Contexts

5

Chapter Outline

The family is at the centre of religious life in China, and to a great extent, determines and shapes the form and content of the spiritual practices of the Chinese people. First, the family is in one sense where religion originated; Chinese religion had much to do with ancestor worship, from which various systems of beliefs and practices evolved and expanded. Secondly, the family is the prime place for religious activities which facilitate individuals' spiritual maturity, primarily through rites of passage and other ritual-related activities. Thirdly, the household is where a huge number of deities and spirits are believed to be located, watching closely over each member of the family. These deities are believed to be instrumental in bringing benefit or damage to family well-being and good fortune. Fourthly, the family is viewed metaphorically as a microcosm of the world, the peace and harmony of which is believed to depend, essentially, on the peace and harmony of the family. In a word, religion in China is woven into the broad fabric of family and social life; a proper understanding of the family is therefore crucial for a full view of Chinese religion.

Family and religion

In anthropological and genetic terms, the primary purpose of the family is for marriage and offspring reproduction, but it nevertheless bears culturally and religiously much more than this biological interpretation. The traditional Chinese family is a culturally complex integration of all biological, personal, social, political and religious elements. It is the place where the family tradition is transmitted: parents exercising an influence over children while children receiving moral and religious education from the elders. The family is often seen as a miniature of the state; its affairs and businesses are thus imbued with layers of social and political meanings and values. More importantly, the family has provided an intimate context in which family members cultivate moral virtues or go through cultural transformations, often in a strong religious context. Thus, every traditional Chinese home is virtually a religious shrine, containing spirit tablets of ancestors, and pictures and idols of many household deities (Yang, 1961:16). It is in the family where sacrifice to religious objects is made, rituals for important festivals are performed, the rites of passage are undertaken, and religious commitment and pious emotion are cultivated and nurtured. The family is therefore the prime place not only for the enrichment of the individual's secular life, but also provides a necessary context for his or her spiritual growth.

The impact of the family on religion can also be seen from the fact that, as discussed in Chapter 2, all religious organizations in China are established with the same structure as that of the family, where the founder is equated with the ancestor, the master with the father, discipline with the family code, and relations between disciples and believers are formed in the same way as those between brothers and sisters. With substantial interpenetration of the family and religious life, it is no surprise that a significant part of religious doctrines and practices is designed to ensure family prosperity or intended to solve family problems.

While the integration between the family and religion is rooted in Chinese culture, Confucianism is nevertheless credited with preserving, clarifying and promoting this family-focused framework. It can in fact be said to be a family-centred religion of which the most sacred five objects for religious worship are Heaven, Earth, the Sovereign, Parents and Teachers. Under the influence of Confucianism, sacrifices to ancestors in the state religion are paralleled to those to Heaven and Earth – the most sacred beings or forces in the Chinese universe. The Confucian world is sustained by five constant relationships (*wu chang*), namely, ruler-subject, father-son, husband-wife, elder-younger brothers and friend-friend. Of these five relations, the centre is obviously kinship, while others are its extension or application. For instance, in the ruler-subject relationship, the ruler is analogous to the father, and the subject to the son; the state is seen as the enlarged family; the relationship between friends is actually the extended relationship between elder and younger brothers. Thus, in a typical Chinese society, the family is a miniature of the state, while the state is an enlarged family. All social, political and religious relationships evolve around familial relationships, and principles or norms that are used to guide family relationship, are also applied to social, political and religious contexts or situations.

Concern for the human predicament prompted early Confucians to give acute attention to political disorder and social instability, of which they deduced the primary cause to be the lack of family virtues. It is for this reason that Confucius taught his students to cultivate a good character in a family context, because for him family virtues are the roots of the Way; only when these roots are established can the Way flourish, as explained by one of his disciples: 'It is rare for a man whose character is such that he is good as a son and obedient as a young man to have the inclination to transgress against superiors; it is unheard of for one who has no such inclination to be inclined to start a rebellion' (Lau, 1970:59).

Mengzi saw the ultimate importance of extending family virtue to all families in a country, arguing that he who loves his parents and cherishes his own family would then naturally feel affection for all parents and families, and when this love and respect is extended to all things in the universe, world peace and universal harmony will then naturally follow:

> Treat the aged of your own family in a manner befitting their venerable age and extend this treatment to the aged of other families; treat your own young in a manner befitting their tender age and extend this to, the young of other families, and you can roll the Empire in your palm. (Lau, 1970:56)

It is in this context that Confucians cultivated the strong conviction that social, political and religious life starts with the family, and that family virtue itself starts with self-cultivation. This self-cultivation plays an important role in Confucian spirituality; it is taken as the pivotal point of reconstructing world peace. The *Great Learning*, one of the four sacred books for later Confucians, explicitly says that cultivation of the personal life is the foundation or root of the human world (Chan, 1963:87).

On the surface, it may seem that family virtues such as parental affection, brotherly love, and filial piety are mostly secular and therefore more of a social tool than a religious aspiration. However, in a Confucian context, the familial, the political and the religious are all bound together; family virtues are essential for all these areas of human existences, and are therefore viewed as intrinsically spiritual. Of the virtues that govern family relations, the most important for Confucians is that used for regulating children to honour their parents – filial piety (*xiao*). In its original form, *xiao* is a pictograph representing an old person supported by a young one, and was therefore concerned with honouring ancestors. Gradually, it evolved into the virtue of the son or grandson in his attitude and conduct towards his parents and grandparents. In the *Classic of Filial Piety* (*xiao jing*), it is said that 'filiality begins with service to parents, continues in service to the ruler, and ends with establishing oneself in the world [and becoming an exemplary person]' (de Bary and Bloom, 1999:326). While this remains confined to human flourishing and moral goodness, the following phrase however, effectively elevates filial piety above the secular to the religious realm, in which Heaven, earth and humans are united into a harmonious entity: 'Filiality is the ordering principle of Heaven, the rightness of the Earth and the norm of human conduct' (Ibid, 327).

Binding all family relations, including that between husband and wife, to cosmic forces and spiritual powers was particularly popular in all ages of Chinese history. For example, Ban Zhao (?48–?112), a female *literata* of the Later Han dynasty, published an extremely influential pamphlet entitled *Lessons for Women* (*nü jie*), in which it is claimed that 'The Way of husband and wife is intimately connected with *Yin* and *Yang*, and relates the individual to gods and ancestors' (Deborah Sommer, 1995:109). Based on the harmony between the cosmic and the spiritual, it seems therefore that Confucians do not treat family virtues as purely secular norms; rather they have injected into them a spiritual value. This had been illustrated as long ago as the eleventh century by Zhang Zai (1020–1077), a prominent Confucian scholar who declared that 'When the time comes, to keep himself from harm – this is the care of a son. To rejoice in Heaven and to have no anxiety – this is filial piety at its purest' (Sommer, 1995:188).

In such a cultural and social context, it is natural for all ideological and religious systems or schools to place Confucian family virtues at their own centre. The gravity centre of the family in traditional China determines that it was a politically sanctioned common sense that without filial piety and brotherly love, and without a virtuous husband-wife relationship, the state would surely collapse, and the world be reduced to chaos. Encouraged by this kind of Confucian doctrine, the imperial government adopted various ways of enforcing family virtues; among these, many were unambiguously religious. For example, the exemplars of filial sons, chaste wives, obedient brothers and honourable mothers were praised by imperial decrees; their memorial archways or buildings became sacred places for pilgrims and continue to be admired in the contemporary time; extraordinary stories created about them in the past have passed indelibly into memorable traditions. Some of these exemplars were even deified based on a belief that extraordinary virtue was of a divine nature, enabling one to be spiritually transcendent or religiously awarded; it was also strongly believed that violation of family ethics would surely lead to severe punishment by spiritual powers.

The family-religion alliance is not confined to Confucianism; it is also applicable to other religious doctrines. Religious Daoists and Buddhists operating in such a family oriented culture thus tend to make every effort to align their spiritual pursuits with family virtues. The status of a complete person (*zhen ren*) in Daoism and the Buddha (*fo*) in Buddhism is equivalent to that of a Confucian sage. To reach this state, family virtues are said to be one of the most effective pathways. For example, many immortals in popularized Daoist religion are said to have been filial sons and daughters, who, by taking care of their parents with extraordinary devotion, have achieved eternal life. A considerable number of Buddhist monks and nuns entered into cloistered life out of commitment to Buddhism in order to fulfil the vows of their parents, or to atone for the sins of their parents or to save their parents from suffering punishment.

Although focusing on individual cultivation of Dao as the way to immortality, the majority of religious Daoists would never discard family virtues in their own spiritual pursuits. Instead they view the fulfilment of responsibility to the family as necessary for religious goals. A not insignificant part of the Daoist rituals is intended to meet the need to cleanse the household of spiritual contamination, of expelling evil forces (*gui*) from the house or out of individual family members, or of bringing in good fortune to the family. The association of Daoists with *fengshui* or geomancy is particularly strong; *fengshui* masters tend to make great use of Daoist doctrines and rituals to predict or determine good or bad fortune for a grave or a dwelling place.

The initial conflict between Buddhism and the family-focused religion of China soon gave way to mutual complementarities; Buddhist missionaries and masters absorbed a great many familial elements into their new interpretation of Buddhist doctrines. For example, the Buddhist apocrypha which were created in the early stages of Buddhism in China include the texts 'extol filial piety, ancestor worship, and funerary rites' (Twitchett and Loewe, 1986:850). The family thus gradually became the point of convergence for Buddhist practice; its prime contribution to the integration of the family and religion was in the area of mourning and funeral rituals. As an example, the Buddhist ritual of chanting sutras (*nian jing*) as the way to deliver suffering souls unto heavenly paradise (*chao du*) occupies an important position in family religious practice; few well-to-do families would not invite Buddhist monks to provide a seven or forty-nine day service for the deceased. Buddhist monasteries that bear the name of 'promoting filial piety' (*Guang xiao si*, the Temple of Glorifying Filial Piety) are not unusual throughout China. Buddhism has bent itself to the family demands and provided the rituals not only for the dead, for exorcism, but also for other family matters. As Tsui observes, for example, although for 2,500 years Buddhism had distanced itself from anything to do with marriage, nowadays, monks have seen fit to invent a Buddhist marriage ritual as an evidence for Buddhism supporting the established order of human life in *samsara* (Tsui, 1989:307).

In a traditional family, the individual is viewed as one section of a long chain, connecting ancestors of the past and descendents of the future. As members of the family, individuals are not only responsible for themselves, but also, often more importantly, for the family. Fei Xiaotong (1910–2005), one of the prominent anthropologists and sociologists in modern China, has provided unambiguous evidence that 'to honour their family and to bring glory to their ancestors' continues to be the most consistent meaning of life among traditionally educated men and women (Fei, 2006:5). Evidence also shows that in contemporary China ordinary people are still enormously influenced by traditional family values, and a large portion of religious activities either take place in a family context, or are driven by concerns for family fortunes, especially among peasants in rural areas. It was found in a 2005 survey, for example, that the primary motives for rural women to visit temples and to provide offerings to gods were out of concern for their family: female members of the family would often 'pray for the safety, health and prosperity of their family', and would seek spiritual help to 'bring good luck to the family' (Yao and Badham, 2007:146).

Life and family lineage

This family-focused culture naturally nurtured a pro-life and pro-family lineage attitude, which led to the emergence of two orientations in Chinese religion. These two orientations characterize the Chinese view of life and death and underlie the motivation to engage in spiritual activities, which have in turn strengthened the association between religion and the family.

The first characteristic aspiration is a strong belief that life itself is the centre of religious practices, and that the blessing of a long life is an important part of the religious ideal. Unlike religions in other cultures where transcendence is the focus of religious faith and practice, in China it is the cult of a long, healthy and happy life that underlies cultural attitudes and views. In the *Book of History*, a long life is already viewed as a priority for personal happiness: 'of the five happiness, the first is long life; the second is riches; the third is soundness of body and serenity of mind; the fourth is the love of virtue; the fifth is an end crowning one's life' (de Bary and Bloom, 1999:32). All five aspects of happiness converge on the benefits of a good and healthy life, and this convergence later exerts a huge impact on all religious doctrines and practices.

Although Confucianism often opts for the moral quality of life over the preservation of physical life itself when there was a conflict between the two, Confucian masters nevertheless cherish the ability to live peacefully and happily, and relate longevity to moral virtues. For example, Confucius considered only those who were virtuous and kind as capable of leading a long life. It is for this reason that Mengzi was against those who put their lives in danger without a good reason: 'one who knows destiny does not stand under a wall in danger of collapsing. To die in the course of fulfilling the Way is a proper destiny, while dying in manacles and fetters is not a proper destiny' (de Bary and Bloom, 155).

It is well known that unlike later religionists, Daoist philosophers reject any unnatural means to prolonging one's life. However, it would be misleading if by this we say that they did not value life at all. In fact, preserving natural life is characteristic of Daoist attitudes. Words like '*jiu*' (eternal), '*chang*' (long), for example, play an important role in the *Daode jing*'s deliberation on the new world view. The concept of 'eternity' undoubtedly influenced the later Daoist cult of immortality and the folk-religion where the 'Goddess of Eternal Life' (*chang sheng niangniang*) was the focus of worship among local communities. While claiming that life and death are none other than two parts of the great transformation and that a 'true person' (*zhen ren*) would neither fear death nor be over joyful in life, Zhuangzi nevertheless taught his disciples that 'Follow the middle, go by what is constant, and you can stay in one piece, keep yourself alive, look after your parents, and live out your years' (de Bary and Bloom, 1999:103).

Thus, for religious Daoists, it is not only a moral duty to self and family but also one of the strongest religious aspirations to live a long life. For this reason, they have adopted a variety of natural ways to cultivate health and immortality; these include herb medicine, meditation, *qigong*, dietetic or sexual practices, apart from producing the so-called immortal elixir. Immortality in Daoism and folk-religion is hence not to exist as an eternal soul without a physical body, but a perfect combination of eternal soul and eternal body. In some Daoist beliefs, immortals are able to enjoy, and actually do enjoy, all the kinds of pleasure and happiness that humans would wish for: youthfulness, healthiness, soundness and tranquillity.

In contrast, Buddhists in general believe that all living beings are of no value in the eternal cycle of incarnation and call upon their followers to take a self-abnegating attitude towards the human body (*chou pi nang* or revolting skin bag). However, this does not prevent them from appreciating life itself, and many Buddhist masters do accept some of the Daoist and Confucian views that it is morally and religiously desirable to live a good and healthy life. The importance which is bestowed on long life (*chang sheng*) is the central theme of many early texts, although gradually Buddhists transformed this yearning for longevity into the aspiration to attain the paradise of *Maitreya* or *Amitayu*, the Buddha of infinite life (Twitchett and Loewe, 1986:850).

The second orientation characteristic of Chinese religion is motivated by the ultimate importance of sustaining the family lineage and of ensuring the purity of the biological blood line. In a historical context, after patriarchy replaced matriarchy, the family lineage could be sustained only by the continued succession of male descendents, since it was believed that only male members were able to carry out sacrifices which were acceptable to ancestors. The duty to provide male offspring was therefore the single most important responsibility to the family, because without a son and grandson, the family bloodline would cease to exist.

This view was further strengthened by the Confucian filial piety. Mengzi, the second sage (*ya sheng*) of the Confucian tradition, for example, said unambiguously that 'There are three things that are unfilial, and the greatest of them is to have no posterity' (de Bary and Bloom, 1999:140). Thus, many of the Confucian family codes, rites of passage and other household rituals were built around the need to fulfil this responsibility. Male successors were consequently allowed, and even encouraged, to have more than one wife or concubine to increase the chance to continue the ancestral bloodline. The position of a wife or concubine in the family would be enormously enhanced if she had a son. This also led to the popular cult of a particular *bodhisattva* (*songzi Guanyin*), a Daoist immortal or goddess (*songzi niangniang*) who was believed to bless the women and the family with the birth of a son.

Concern for the ancestral lineage also necessitated extra measures to ensure its biological purity. For this purpose, a sophisticated family code of conduct was put in place in order to reduce or even prevent direct contact between female and male members within the household and between young girls and the outside world. In the *Book of Mengzi*, for example, there are already very strict rules forbidding a sister-in-law to touch her brothers-in-law; indeed, Mengzi had to argue in favour of loosening these restrictions in a particular situation when a sister by marriage was in danger of drowning (David Hinton, 1998:133–134). Practices forbidden in these codes became virtually 'taboos' in traditional families in later imperial China, and were also enforced by a variety of literature, stories and myths, involving spirits and ghosts. It became commonly accepted that violation of these rules was not only subject to punishment under family codes, but also to spiritual condemnation. While chaste wives were established as community and religious models of decorum or were deified, adulterous women were believed to be subject to the most horrific tortures and punishments in hell.

Ancestor worship

Ancestor worship is the underlying foundation of Chinese religion and is also the key reason for the close association of religion with the family. What then does the term 'ancestor' (*zu*) signify in Chinese? Different views or theories have been put forward to explain its root meaning. For some, 'ancestor' originated in the fertility or the reproductive power of the male. According to Guo Moruo (1892–1978), a distinguished scholar on Chinese history and culture, the pictographic part of the character *zu* is a symbol of the penis (Guo, 1931:1–10). For others, however, this character represents the female sexual organ (Qi Liang, 2001:168–178).

Ancestor worship is far more complex, significant and fundamental to Chinese religion than a mere fertility cult. It is a bedrock belief running through all stages of Chinese civilization and playing a crucial part in the state as well as folk-religion. Early records show that ancestor worship was primarily initiated for a religio-political purpose; the patrilineal system revered the patriarchs when alive, who then became objects of worship after death. From the oracle bone inscriptions we can see, for example, that ancestors in the Shang dynasty were of two kinds: those of the 'lineal' and those of the 'collateral'. The lineal ancestor was called '*da zong*', and the collateral '*xiao zong*'. The eldest brother who had inherited the throne, or had been made heir apparent, later became the lineal ancestor; but if he had no son, then his brother would be next in line to ensure that a son of the bloodline would become '*da zong*', while he himself would become *xiao zong*. For each generation, only one ancestor was worshipped as *da zong*, together with his spouse (Tung, 1952:12–21).

It has been found through the oracle bone inscriptions that the spirits and ghosts of ancestors were treated with great awe in the Shang era, and that the king revered his ancestors and their great governmental ministers as still living. The royal ancestors were believed to reside in Heaven, to retain the same rank and authority as when they were living, to possess the same emotions and enjoy the same pleasures and possessions as in their time on earth. Ancestors were also believed to have spiritual power, assisting the Lord on High, or Heaven, in the execution of various orders; they thus became the focus of divination and religious rituals, as Tung has observed: 'The one hundred thousand pieces of oracle bones and shells contain little but the questions the reverential Yin kings [the kings of the Shang dynasty] put to their ancestors and the answers in the forms of cracks . . . almost all the elaborate religious rituals of the Yin dynasty were meant for the ancestors' (Ibid., 19, 21).

Ancestor worship thus came to dominate religious, political and communal life in early China, where the royal ancestral temple held the most important place in the state as the political symbol of sovereignty. The temple was more than simply the location for sacrifice to ancestors, however; it was the place where divination was carried out, where a new king was enthroned or an imperial marriage was announced. It was also the storehouse for things of value and military weapons. It was the place where kings held audiences with officials and feudal lords, where orders concerning both civil and military matters were issued, where the ruler and ministers heard news of victory in battle and where they dispensed rewards and awards to meritorious officials (Bilsky, 1975:66). With various modifications, this tradition continued until modern times, a tradition gradually extended from the state religion to ordinary families or clans. The ancestral temple (*zong ci*) for each clan, as seen from our introduction to the Chen clan temple at the beginning of Chapter 2, carried great weight as the civil centre for the whole clan where important decisions were made, education was maintained and disputes were resolved.

Along with the replacement of the Shang by the Zhou, views concerning ancestors and their worship underwent a profound change: new elements such as virtue and ritual were then added. A new belief in the 'Mandate of Heaven' was introduced with the political intent of justifying a change in dynastic governance, or to pass judgment on unworthy rulers. It was claimed, for example, that the Shang lost its rule, because the last Shang king had forfeited the mandate from Heaven by reason of his immoral behaviour and unethical conduct. This led the Duke of Zhou to devise a religiously strengthened mechanism by which kings and nobles were placed under the dual, but interrelated, supervision of Heaven and the might of the ancestor. At the centre of this mechanism was the warning that the ancestral powers to protect and bless their descendents functioned only if a new ruler was virtuous and diligent.

A cautionary event is recorded in the *Book of History* which sets out clearly the 'conditions' for a continual dynastic rule. Two years after the conquest of the Shang dynasty, King Wu caught a fever and was very ill. His brother, the Duke of Zhou, erected three altars to the three past kings and offered up as sacrifice precious jade items. The Duke then prayed earnestly that the three kings should punish him rather than his brother, the king. This prayer represents an important pointer in the history of Chinese religion because it illustrates all the central tenets of ancestor worship in the religion of the state: first, an illness can be caused by ancestral displeasure; secondly, the king rules the country by his own virtue, not merely by the virtue of the ancestors; thirdly, ancestors have measures available to ensure a king to fulfil the mandate of Heaven; fourthly ancestors need the services and sacrifices of their descendants to continue their existence in the spirit world. This is shown in the last sentence of the Duke's plea to the former kings: 'Do not let that precious Heaven-conferred Mandate fall to the ground; then [all] our former kings will also ever have security and resort' (de Bary and Bloom, 1999:34).

Ancestor worship then spread to ordinary people of all social ranks and sustained Chinese families. As the epicenter of Chinese religion, ancestors function as more than the biological source of the descendants, however; they are venerated because of the complex threads by which they are linked to their descendants in a variety of ways: cultural, religious, moral and communal. First, ancestors are held in awe as they are seen as family or clan heroes who created the past and who laid down the foundation for the way of life by which all its members, present and future, are able to lead a human life. Secondly, ancestors hold the key to questions concerning the source from which we come and to which we will return. Unlike the Judeo-Christian tradition where living beings are created by God out of nothing, it is strongly believed in China that the existing things must come from something that already existed and beings from the former beings. Since ancestors are former beings, they are therefore viewed as the root of current and future beings. Thirdly, ancestors are taken as exemplars for the present and for the future, and ancestor worship contains both commemorative and educational elements.

This culturally enriched ancestor worship requires sophisticated ritual, a ritual that is effectively employed to create a religious and communal environment, in which living people are firmly linked with a glorified past. An early example of such ancestor worship, as recorded in the *Book of Poetry*, illustrates its august ceremonial gravity as follows:

> The fruit is sliced and pickled. To be presented to our great ancestors, That their distant descendant may have long life, And receive the blessing of Heaven . . . Then we present, then we offer; All round the fragrance is diffused. Complete and brilliant [sic] is the sacrificial service; Grandly come our ancestors. They will reward (their descendants) with great blessing, Long life, years without end. (Legge, 1899:370)

This was a ritual intended not only to seek blessing from the ancestors but also for its interrelated educational purpose. For thousands of years this ritual was followed and observed, to augment the belief that ancestors were not only living but also powerful in influencing the present and future. With each ritual performance, participants and audience would recognize and acknowledge anew that the great achievements of the ancestors must be praised and remembered and that their great virtues must be re-acted in today's life. It has become a deep-rooted psychological heritage in the minds and hearts of the Chinese that when ancestors were properly worshipped, the past will be glorified, tradition renewed, family or clan members educated and good future assured.

The educational function here is clear, as is the moral and communal purpose. Ultimately, however, all relevant beliefs and rituals surrounding ancestor worship already point to its religious substance; ancestors are ritually deified as gods and are believed, although 'living' only in ritual and through sacrifices, also to possess supra-human power, an ability to protect the descendants from the invasion of vicious forces, or to ward off undesirable influence that might damage the familial fortunes. In this sense ancestors are equivalent to family deities, the blessing of whom is believed to be necessary for a good life. The power of ancestors is thus viewed as an ability to determine the quality and extent of the family life. From various extant texts and the ritual processions that are still practised today we can see that the spirits of ancestors are believed to be able to 'return', and if appeased with regular sacrifice by their descendants in accordance with proper rituals, these returning spirits would be beneficent. But they could also be maleficent if appropriate sacrificial rites were not performed, or if they were totally ignored. In the latter case, these ancestral spirits would instead become 'hunting ghosts', causing disease or death to the household.

It follows therefore that ancestors exhibit at one and the same time both power and vulnerability. Their vulnerability means that the power or existence of ancestors depends upon the sacrifices provided by their descendants, and their returning to the family is possible only if their spirit tablets are displayed in the house or clan temple, as shown in Figure 5.1. Their power is demonstrated by the fact that through ancestor worship the family is placed under the safekeeping of spiritual beings, acting as a spiritual mechanism to prohibit people from doing something against the family interests. More importantly, ancestor worship cements the living and the dead into a relationship of interrelation and interdependence. Ancestors are not in nothingness and forgotten, because they are continually held in awe and are entrusted with the

Figure 5.1 Ancestral Temple of the Mao Clan

responsibility of protecting their descendents. Living generations are neither totally separated from their past from two perspectives. First, their forebears continue to 'live' through their remembrance and ritual sacrifices; secondly, striving for the blessing and protection of their forefathers ensures the existence and continual flourishing of the family and its enterprise.

The spiritual value of ancestors is further magnified through a conscious association with the supreme power of Heaven. It is believed that the spirits of ancestors function as mediators between Heaven (the Supreme Lord) and humans. Indeed, even in a less religious context, it is a commonly accepted view that 'the root of life is in Heaven and Earth, while the root of humans is in former ancestors' (Sima,1959:1167). From this perspective, to worship ancestors, is to show gratitude towards family founders, and is also an indirect expression of gratitude towards the supremacy of Heaven and Earth. Human moral value is therefore judged by sincerity and dutifulness towards Heaven, ancestors and the family, as Dong Zhongshu confirms: a ruler is good if he 'reverently enacts the suburban sacrifice [for Heaven], dutifully serves his ancestors, manifests filial and brotherly love, encourages filial conduct, and serves the foundation of Heaven in this way' (de Bary and Bloom, 1999:300).

It is also widely believed that through religious and secular acts in relation to Heaven and ancestors, human virtues can be promoted and glorified. In this sense, ancestor worship carries with it a strong spirituality: the respect given to ancestors is seen as the way to reach the ultimate realm of human values. The *Book of Rites* has put it this way: 'In the sacrifice to God in the suburb, we have the utmost expression of reverence. In the sacrifice of the ancestral temple, we have the utmost expression of humanity. In the rites of mourning, we have the utmost expression of leal-heartedness' (Legge, 1885, vol. xxvii:413).

Under the influence of Confucianism, Chinese religion has in essence become focused on this world; ancestor worship is thus intended to not only highlight the importance of harmonious family relationships, but also to promote moral virtues for communal stability. While sacrificing to ancestors is to 'bring about a return to the beginning' (de Bary and Bloom 1999:342), reverence towards ancestors is taken as a way to strengthen filial piety towards parents, and to follow faithfully the family tradition; the *Book of Rites* confirm this view: 'The noble person, while [his parents] are still alive, reverently nourishes them, and when they are dead, he reverently sacrifices to them; his thought is how to the end of life not to disgrace them' (de Bary and Bloom 1999:340). Either as religious or as familial ritual, sacrifice to ancestors requires sincerity and reverence. Here, Confucius places an emphasis on individual participation in religious and communal ritual. When commenting on the saying that 'sacrifice to the gods as if the gods were present', he further stated that 'Unless I take part in a sacrifice, it is as if I did not sacrifice' (Lau, 1970:69). The implication is thus that by personally participating, one experiences the spirits of ancestors, experiences the highly spiritual process of rituals and experiences an inward refinement of one's character.

Although the political and social infrastructure of ancestor worship has been partially dismantled in a series of political revolutions throughout the twentieth century China, the majority of ordinary people nevertheless preserve some of its elements and remain emotionally attached to their forebears.

In some cases, however, rationalist and Marxist indoctrination has led contemporary Chinese attitude on the mainland to polarize. The mainstream ideology and the majority of intellectuals exhibit a rational and often agnostic attitude towards ancestors; rural communities on the other hand tend to stick more closely to traditional values and continue, at least partially, with what has been inherited from their ancestors. It thus seems that ancestor worship, if still followed, has become more a question of custom and culture than religion and morality, particularly in the city and among educated people. However, research does show that reverence towards ancestors and the familial tradition may not totally be a thing of the past; it is still a living tradition for a good portion of the mainland Chinese population, as demonstrated in a 2005 questionnaire survey where 21.2 per cent of the people reported that they had experienced the influence or control by their ancestors in the previous year, while 27.6 per cent agreed with the statement that providing timely offerings to ancestors would gain their blessing and protection (Yao and Badham, 2007:34).

Household deities

It follows therefore that there is seemingly no lack of the divine dimension in the Chinese way of life; this dimension can be termed variously as the supernatural, the invisible, the holy, the numinous, the sacred, the spiritual or the transcendental. All these meanings and references crystallized as a variety of deities in the Chinese pantheon, which can be classified into different categories according to their functions, and each of which is supposed to be responsible for a defined area or aspect of material and spiritual life. In a sense, ancestral spirits function as a special category of deities in terms of their huge importance for the continuation of the family lineage and for the quality of family life, as we have already examined in the above section, although whether or not ancestors should be treated as gods is still an open question among scholars; for example, Shryock already contended that 'That the sacrifices to ancestors are similar to the sacrifices to Heaven is not in itself proof that the ancestors are gods' (Shryock, 1966:79).

Apart from the spirits of ancestors there are also heavenly and earthly gods who control and administer all natural phenomena and human affairs, and are ultimately responsible for the correlation between these two realms. There are communal gods who are responsible for the well-being of the people in a specific location or are in charge of a particular aspect of local life. There are 'trade gods' who protect the artisan, agricultural and commercial professions, and ensure that proper orders are followed in particular fields. Finally there are household gods, who reside in the house and take care of family business, affairs and household well-being.

The household is not only the place where ancestors are revered and worshipped, but also the site where numerous household deities reside and function. The importance of these deities for the spiritual and material well-being of family and its members is next only to the ancestors themselves. Embedded in the depths of the Chinese mind and heart is a hunger for the blessing, protection and help of spiritual forces and supernatural powers, of whom the closest are those deities residing in their own homes. It is strongly believed among the ordinary Chinese that even with the utmost exertion, human abilities and efforts alone are neither sufficient to guarantee physical and mental health, nor enough to ensure economic success or family harmony. The property and health of the family and the prosperity and harmony in the home need the blessing and protection of spiritual beings. This belief is the underlying reason why people are utterly convinced that only through properly conducted rites of ancestor worship can integration and perpetuation of the family be viable, and is also the key reason why household deities have such an important position in Chinese religion.

Ancestors and household deities are thus two special categories of deity in the spiritual world of the Chinese, both protecting the well-being of the family. It seems that the spirits of ancestors and household deities are parallel in their importance for the spiritual and material well-being of the family. The function of ancestors lies in the close relationship between them and descendents and this makes ancestors not simply spiritual beings, but also the intermediaries between the human and the spiritual world. On the one hand they are thought to hold supra-human powers to bless or condemn the family as a whole, or to reward or punish its individual members, but on the other, the function of rewarding or punishing requires the assistance from gods in order to be carried out. In this respect, household deities are frequently put on the spot, functioning as the agents of the ancestral spirits or the supreme authorities of the spiritual world.

In other words, the complex ancestral role is supplemented and strengthened by household deities who share the same concern for the well-being of the family, and whose functions and responsibilities often intermingle with, and complement those of ancestors. Early records in China testify to this complementarity: 'Ancestor worship was supplemented by that of household and agricultural deities, the former including the gods of the gate, doors, stove, and well' (Twitchett and Loewe, 1986:567). The parallel and mutual complementation between ancestors and household deities continues in contemporary China, where 'most household altars are quite similar. The tablets for ancestors, Master of the Site (*di zhu*), Heaven God (*dang tian*), Kitchen God (*zao jun*) and Door God (*men guan*) are commonly found in families practising local religion' (Overmyer (ed.), 2003:74).

A wide range of such household gods are worshipped in the family altar, shrine or temple, with considerable divergence in practice between different regions or areas. The most popular of the deities given a prime place in the house or family altar throughout China include: the Jade Emperor (*Yu huang*); the Buddha (*fo zu*); The Supreme Old Master (*taishang laojun*, the deified Laozi); the Sage (Confucius); the god of earth (*tu di*); the kitchen god (*zao shen*); Guanyin (the *bodhisattva*); the god of fortune (*cai shen*); the principal god of the household (*hu zhu* or *jia zhu*); the god of the well (*jing shen*); the bed god (*chuang shen*), and gods of the gate (*men shen*). Of these gods, some are of a more general or universal application, such as the Jade Emperor, the god of earth, the god of fortune and Guanyin, since they look after not simply the family but also all the people in the world. They do not therefore belong to the household category. Thus, the gods normally catalogued as household deities are in general those who primarily reside in the house or the compound, and who take responsibility either for the whole family, or for part of the family property and business.

Of the household deities the most popular and colourful is the 'kitchen god' or 'stove god', who 'goes back to time immemorial, perhaps the eighth century B.C' (Ching, 1993:210). Like the god of earth who is usually depicted as a divine pair (lord and lady) in folk-religion, the 'kitchen god' is also represented by a pair (lord and lady) in some regions: lord of kitchen (*zao wang ye*) and his female companion, lady of kitchen (*zao wang nai*) are often depicted as

Figure 5.2 God and Goddess of Kitchen

a smiling and affectionate old couple, looking after the stove and taking care of family matters as shown in Figure 5.2. The kitchen god is believed to have a special mission in the family, as a kind of registrar, watching over all its members. According to folklore, the god(s) watch the behaviour of the family members and listen to their conversations carefully in a year and then they will ascend to Heaven (where the Jade Emperor resides) to report what has been seen and heard of the family on the 23rd day of the 12th month; the Jade Emperor will then determine, based on the report of this kitchen god, whether to reward or to punish particular members of the family, or the family as a whole. With such an import role at stake, a variety of ritual acts are designed to find favour with this god before his ascent to Heaven. In line with the pragmatic nature of Chinese religion, some of the rituals designed to honour this god are intended to 'bribe' him so that he will report to the Jade Emperor only those good things of the family but omit the bad; others are intended to celebrate the replacement of the old time cycle by the new, so that the family will go smoothly into the next period of life. The valediction ceremony when the kitchen god ascends to Heaven is therefore one of the most joyful religious events in the family. It is a ritual which comprises the following aspects: burning incense, offering sweets/food, putting into the fire the old picture of the god together with other symbolic items, such as a paper horse that is supposed to be necessary on his journey up to Heaven. It is believed that the god ascends to the sky on the rising flame and smoke. In order for the return of the god, a new picture is put on the wall above the stove or in the kitchen before the arrival of the new year; in this way, the god can reside in the picture once again when he returns home from the court of the Jade Emperor.

Within the house compound every item or area is believed to have a god or goddess to oversee activities. For example, the well, which was and is, in many private households in rural areas, located within the courtyard, has a god who will go to the east sea to report to the dragon king on the last day of the year. It is customary that the well then will be covered on that day and will not be reopened until the second day of the New Year, when the god is believed to return home. Before the act of reopening, a ritual of burning paper money or incense is enacted to offer sacrifices; sweets are also customarily offered with the prayers in order to make sure that the well will continue to provide sweet and pure water. Another important pair among household gods is the lord and lady of bed. Prayer and sacrifice to them includes, for example, offering tea for the lord, and wine for the lady. The purposes of the offerings are threefold: to draw down blessings for future babies especially to protect against the dangers of birth or sickness; to have deep and healing sleep and to pray for harmony of husband and wife.

It is an ancient belief that all household deities are ruled by a supreme god who takes overall control of the spiritual life of the family, as well as co-ordinating various spiritual activities within the house. This is a tradition which is carried on in many local communities. Like the head of the family (usually the father or grandfather), the supreme god of the household is in charge of general business, spiritual well-being and material matters. For the house, this god functions in parallel to the god of city (*cheng huang*) for the town, or the god of earth (*tu di*) for the village or local area. Different names have been found in different areas for this god; he is sometimes addressed as '*jia zhu*' the ruler of the family, or '*hu zhu*' the ruler of the household, or '*di zhu*' the ruler of the site, or '*jia tang*', the patriarchal god. His picture or name (written on a red paper) is usually placed alongside those of Guanyin (the Goddess of Compassion) and the god of fortune on the central wall of the main-room, below which, incense and other offerings, such as fruit and food, are displayed.

One of the most important duties of household deities is to protect the family; this explains the special status which the Chinese have bestowed on the gods of the gate. The gate guardian gods go back to ancient times in China and have since undergone change and evolution. Originally, gate gods were two figures carved of peach wood representing two brothers, Shen Shu and Yu Lu, who were believed to protect the household from demons. In legend, they were the gods assigned by the Yellow Emperor to govern wandering ghosts, and therefore dwelt on a high mountain shaded by a huge peach tree, watching over ghosts. Any ghosts who violated the rules of conduct would be tied up and thrown into the valley to feed tigers; hence the fear of the ghosts for peach wood, tigers and the two guardian gods. The belief was thus established that these were gods could also protect the family from ghostly visitations; these guardians were put at the gates in their peach wood forms and later their names and special charms were inscribed on household gates to function as protective gods for the residents within (Wang Chong, 1954:221).

After the Tang dynasty, the two guardian gods were replaced in popular religion by two generals of the second Tang emperor Li Shimin (r.626–649), one named Qin Qiong, and the other Yuchi Jingde. The legend goes that the emperor fell ill as a result of invasion by dreadful ghosts; two of his generals then volunteered to guard his living quarters in the night. No ghosts dared to venture forth from that moment; the emperor thus ordered that pictures of these two generals be hung at the entrance to the imperial quarters, which achieved the same deterrent effect. Popularized in literature, these two generals became the archetypes of gate guardian gods for ordinary people, who placed their pictures at the gate to safeguard the household from evil forces and demons (Xu Che, 2008:200).

In sum, religion in China is closely bound up with the family and functions in the household in a variety of ways. In the 'family religion', the divine and the secular seamlessly combine, and the household becomes the pivot of material and spiritual lives. Religious life in the family nurtures a sense of togetherness, not only between ancestors and descendants, between household deities and individual family members, but also between material needs and spiritual pursuits, and between daily activities and ritual engagement.

Questions for discussion

1. In what sense can Chinese religion be regarded as a family religion?
2. Why is the family so central to Chinese religion?
3. How was the longing for a happy life transformed into a religious ideal for all religions in China?
4. What does the term ancestor mean to the Chinese?
5. 'Ancestor Worship is at the centre of Chinese religion.' Do you agree?
6. Why do the Chinese place such importance to household deities?

Religion and State

The state plays a much greater part in religious affairs in China than in many other countries; for most parts of its history, religion and the government were interlocked in a 'love-hate' relationship. On the one hand, major religious organizations in general enjoyed the tolerance or even support of the state, thereby gaining social recognition and influence, but were nevertheless constantly in fear of being negated or persecuted by the state. Few religious traditions in China were ever totally independent of the state. Towards the later part of imperial history, institutional religions, and folk-religions too, were firmly placed under the direction of the state to serve its needs, and were often subject to political manipulation partially as a result of the necessary extension of the Neo-Confucian total control to all ideological and social fields. On the other hand, any dynasty needed the support of and collaboration with religion to maintain social stability and order, but it was also weary of religiously motivated rebellions. Some dynastic states were established by the joint forces of military advancement and religious movements; while others were overthrown in social unrest fuelled by religious ideas and ideals. For the state, religion was always like a double-edged sword which could be both beneficial and harmful.

The more effective and efficient the government was, the less likely it would be to allow religion to have a free run in terms of initiation or expansion.

In such a cultural context, history easily repeats itself in modern times. The dereligionalized state continues to make use of religion for its own purpose; while religion balances survival and expansion within boundaries set by the state. The complicated relationship between religion and the state, both in the past and in contemporary times, has raised questions about the political dimension of Chinese religion, and challenged our perception about how to assess the state policies towards religion as well as the connection between religion and the government.

'Protection' vs. 'persecution'

On 30th October 2006, a grand sacrificial ceremony to the Divine Farmer (Yandi, the Red Emperor) was organized at his mausoleum by the provincial government of Hunan province. The Divine Farmer is believed to have lived about 5,000 years ago, and was deified for his initiating agriculture and tools, creating fire, weaving cloth and inventing herbal medicine. The Red and Yellow Emperors are regarded as the common ancestors of the Han Chinese who normally call themselves the 'descendants of the Yan and Huang' (see Figure 6.1). As an 'official' event, this ceremony was opened by the

Figure 6.1 Statues of the Red and Yellow Emperors, Zhengzhou city

Vice Chairwoman of the Standing Committee of the National People's Congress, after sacrifices were made (http://english.peopledaily.com.cn/200610/31/eng20061031_316788.html, accessed 19 June 2009).

Yearly sacrifices to the ancestors of the Chinese and the creators of Chinese civilization as well as many other cultural heroes and great thinkers such as Confucius have become one of the most prominent showcases for the government's support of religion. Such activities are intended, at least partially, to prove that the current government is the true bearer of traditional culture and supporter of religion.

In recent decades the Chinese government has also substantiated its direct involvement in religious activities in the name of protecting China's heritage and developing good traditions. As part of a co-ordinated programme to promote traditional culture and patriotism, the government has not only taken part in public sacrifices to legendary ancestors, but also spent hugely to support certain kinds of religious activities and to maintain religious places or rebuild religious buildings. For example, the construction of the 148-metre high Namaste Dagoba (*he shi ta*) for the finger bone of the Buddha at the famous Temple of the Darma Gate (*famen si*) in Shaanxi province was reported to have been financially and politically supported by the central government. High level representatives from the central and the provincial government turned a grand ceremony to celebrate its completion on 9 May 2009 into a political event rather than a merely Buddhist ceremony (http://news.qq.com/a/20090509/000690.htm, accessed 10 May, 2009). To deliver the message to the religious and the Western audience, Ye Xiaowen, the director of the State Administration of Religious Affairs, wrote in the *China Daily* (the overseas edition, 15 May 2009) that 'Namaste represents respect. Respect is needed between different civilizations, different ethnic nationalities and different countries. The completion of the Namaste Dagoba manifests the Chinese government's respect for and protection of religious faiths.'

Despite all these efforts, however, the Chinese government has not been spared criticism by Western observers. The self-proclaimed protector and supporter is often severely attacked as a suppressor and interferer. Each side produces evidence for its own justification, and neither would back down. For instance, the Chinese government announced a new set of regulations on religious affairs in November 2004, and praised the new regulations as 'a significant step forward in the protection of religious freedom'. However, for the religious freedom watchdogs in the West, 'new regulations were not issued to protect the rights and security of religious believers, but to regularize management practices, thus offering Party leaders more extensive control over all religious activity and groups' (US Commission, 2005:55–56). To Western eyes, while the Chinese leadership has 'praised the positive role of religious communities in China and articulated a desire to have religious groups promote "economic and social development", it is apparent that 'the government continues to restrict religious practice to government-approved religious associations and seeks to control the activities, growth, and leadership of both "registered" and "unregistered" religious groups' (US Commission, 2009:73). This difference, entangled with the debate on human rights, nationalist emotions and international politics, has further complicated the relationship between China and the West. Apart from political and ideological biases each holds against the other, underneath their open contradiction lie different perceptions concerning religion and the state.

Different views concerning the role of the government in religious affairs are also occasionally expressed by different groups of people within China. Some criticisms target its economic side (e.g., spending millions of yuan on such events is a waste of public money) while others are more concerned with the depth and extent to which the government is involved in activities of a religious nature, because such critics are opposed to the non-religious nature of the Communist Party (*The China Youth Daily*, 9 March 2009). In a sense, none of these criticisms are totally new and similar arguments on economic or political grounds have been repeatedly made throughout history; for example, Han Yu's (768–824) plea memorial against the emperor's will to greet the bone of the Buddha, or the Daoist influence on Emperor Wu's (r. 841–846) edict on the suppression of Buddhism (de Bary and Bloom, 1999:583–586).

From historical and contemporary perspectives it seems apparent that the idea of religion operating outside the government is alien to the majority of Chinese people. Religion has to strike a balance with the state about what it wants to do and what the state permits it to do; while the state is expected to take a paternal role in protecting and sponsoring 'right' religious activities while prohibiting or even suppressing 'wrong' religions, although it is also clear that the criteria for judging right from wrong depend to a great extent on the dominating ideology and the practical needs of the time. This balancing act, namely attempting at mutual accommodation between state and religion in China, is very different from what we are familiar with in the contemporary West.

Family, state and religion

The special relationship between the state and religion is closely linked with a historically fostered intimate relationship between the family and the state, and with the same or similar roles given to the heads of the family and the state.

The Chinese counterpart for the state is *guojia*, a phrase composed of *guo* (state) and *jia* (family, home), which indicates a vision of the state that is built upon the family. In a Chinese context, the family is a miniature state, while the state is an enlarged family; the head of the state parallels the head of the family.

The understanding that the family is the root of the state was derived from the fact that an ancient state grew up from the tribe which was in turn an association of families or clans. It was already popular to associate the state with the family in the time of Mengzi when people sought the 'root of the empire' in the state and the 'root of the state' in the family: 'the empire has its basis in the state, and the state in the family' (Lau, 1970:79). There was evidence that as a special political community of people living and operating in a certain geographical environment, the Chinese state developed its structure out of that of the family. The hierarchical nature of the family determined that one of the most important functions for the state was to exalt the social and political status of certain people and distinguish them from those of a lower status (Zhao, 2007:23). This resulted in a political patriarchy which, once formed, would in turn reinforce the paternal authority in the family and push both to the level of totalitarianism. It was indeed the case in later history that, 'bolstered by a social matrix that was essentially totalitarian, the legal power of the male and rulers approached the absolute' (Slote, 1998:37–38).

However, this totalitarianism was balanced by a moral element in Chinese politics. The same structure and function of the state and family promoted the same virtues, and the attitude of children to parents was easily transplanted to the state where the subjects were required to do the same as children did in the family. Hence, filial piety was regarded as the root of all virtues and the key to all human relationships:

> If a man in his own house and privacy be not grave, he is not filial; if in serving his ruler, he be not loyal, he is not filial; if in discharging the duties of office, he be not reverent, he is not filial; if with friends he be not sincere, he is not filial; if on the field of battle he be not brave, he is not filial. (Legge, 1885, xxviii: 226)

As an enlarged family, the head of the state was expected to act as the father, and the people were expected to be its children. This parental function of the state assumed more power for the government in controlling all social affairs including religion, and resulted in a close association between religious organizations and political authorities: 'religion and society, church and state, were never separate in China' (Chappell, 1987:1).

However, just as the state was based on family but placed itself above family, the state was both in religion and beyond religion. For the state, religion itself was a means to rule, and was intended to be part of the parameters defining and confining the authorities, rights and responsibilities of the king or emperor and the ruling class. Whatever forms religion was presented in, it was normally under the direction or control of the government. For the state, all religious doctrines (sacred books, teachings, disciplines), institutions (priesthood, organizations, temples) and activities (worships, ceremonies, events) were no more than social operations, and had to be constantly checked, watched and supervised.

In principle, political control of these aspects would start as soon as a strong government was established. Religious attachment to the state was therefore part of an overall ruling strategy. There was a personal element in favouring or disfavouring a particular religion or religious activity, and the belief or preference of the emperor was behind the alteration of particular religions' influence in political and economic fields, one's rising often at the expense of another. However, in general terms, religious policies were not totally determined by personal favour or disfavour; religion was one of the political instruments, and priority in consideration regarding religious policies was given to the stability and order of the state. The dynastic government was well aware that religion was part and parcel of social life, and that any rushed decision against one religion or promotion of another could have a catastrophic consequence for the state. Therefore, although there were persecutions and depressions of religion in history, in general 'the overall attitude of Chinese government to religion through the centuries was that of cautious control and careful tolerance' (Pas, 1989:3).

In such a highly centralized political country as China, religion had little chance to become independent of the state. Usually, the only way a religion could survive and expand was by attaching itself to various political forces, above all to the government. In exchange for partially giving up its independence and lending its support to the government, a particular religion could gain privileges bestowed by the state, which would normally include nominal or real assistance or support from the central government. However, this mutually beneficial relationship could not be achieved unless religion was made to accommodate itself to the needs of the state. An obvious example for this was the transformation of Buddhism from its original Indian form to that of a specifically Chinese form. In India, Buddhists considered themselves a community beyond the authority of secular rulers, renouncing any involvement in and attachment to family, society and the state. Not only did Buddhist monks feel that they were under no obligation to pay homage to the ruler, but it also appears that they regarded the king in an unfavourable light, unworthy of reverence. Although for a while and to different degrees Buddhist monks in China also claimed to be beyond the direction of the human ruler, most of them gradually lost their independence from the state, and by the time of the Northern Wei dynasty (386–534), Buddhist monks were no longer an independent community; the Chief of Monks in the imperial bureaucracy and the monks had to pay homage to the emperor; all monks and nuns were required to be registered, and ordination was limited by secular laws (Ch'en, 1973:66–84). Buddhists in general thus accepted that

> it was the duty of every individual people to render proper reverence to the ruler, and particularly 'Since the sovereign is able "to communicate the life-giving (power), his function is identical with that of the creative power"'. (Zürcher, 1972:233)

The highly centralized government in China parallels the highly patronized family. This inevitably affected the relation between the state and religion. All religionists were expected to accommodate themselves to the needs of the state, in the same way as children to their father; indeed, a clergy or priesthood never existed as a distinct social group in China (Zürcher, 1972:254; H. Maspero, 1981:163). On the other hand, by assuming a parental role for religion, the state also bore greater responsibility for religion: guiding, supporting, nourishing and protecting.

State and state religion

Throughout most of Chinese history, religion and state were integrated in the form of a state religion in which the state was religious and religion was part of the government. Different from medieval Europe where the Christian Church assumed the role of government managing secular cities in the name of God's city in Heaven, state religion in China was to add religious elements to secular administration, and to make use of religion to legitimatize the dynastic rule. State religion was centred on ancestral worship and the worship of Heaven, Earth and other spiritual powers, which were believed to be essential to the state and to the social order and harmony. In its extreme form, the king or emperor was not only the head of the state, but also the head priest who worshipped ancestors, Heaven and Earth, on behalf of his subjects. Religious rituals and sacrifices were conducted to gain blessing and protection from spiritual powers for the continuity of the state, or at least in words, for the benefit of all the people. Since the ruler assumed the role of the father for his family, his religious responsibility was also parental or more specifically paternal.

These old beliefs and practices were encouraged and furthered by Confucians when they came to the centre stage of the state, and worship of Confucius was later added to the worship of ancestors and Heaven, and became one of the three pillar sacrifices essential for any dynastic government. Although there are still debates concerning the religious nature of Confucianism, in its historical form it would be hard to deny the fact that Confucianism was part of the state religion. Confucians promoted *li* (rites, rituals, propriety) and *yue* (ceremonial music) as the means for regaining social stability, and applied religiously motivated virtues to civil administration in order to establish proper order and harmony in the family and state. They developed the traditional faith in the Mandate of Heaven and took it as the only means to legitimize the dynastic rule. Their initial understanding of natural and social order was changed in due time to suit the hierarchal order required by the state, and in this sense they fulfilled the purpose of being a mediator between the 'forces of nature' and the 'lives of the people' (Thompson, 1996:67). By transforming old traditions, Confucians formed a dual checking system that warranted the authority of the government: placing the ruled classes in a so-called natural order that the state was above the masses, and the humble must follow the noble; while providing the ruling class with a theological justification, but at the same time, requiring them to be worthy of the Mandate of Heaven. They argued that to be qualified for the mandate, the ruler must be virtuous and wise, and be the exemplar for his people to follow. This highly moralized religio-political system was effective in reinforcing and strengthening the power and authority of the central government, and laid down the foundation on which the central governments handled religious affairs.

However, we must not exaggerate the Confucian remaking of the state religion. In fact, many beliefs and practices central to state religion were older than Confucianism. Williams observed at the beginning of the twentieth century that all the deities except for Confucius who received official worship of the first and second ranks in the Qing dynasty were already worshipped during the Shang and Zhou times. Apart from those deities who were especially connected to the Beijing region, most deities receiving third-rank sacrifices had been popular by the Han dynasty (Williams, 1913:14).

In one sense this was not to the point. The contribution Confucianism made to state religion was not in the external objects of worship, nor in the form of sacrifices, but in its inner spirituality. Confucians never claimed to be independent of the past or to be 'innovators'; rather they saw themselves as the 'transmitters' or shapers of the glory tradition (Lau, 1979:86). Confucianism and the older tradition cannot be totally separated from each other; Confucians consciously attached themselves to historical beliefs and practices, but at the same time delicately reshaped them and incorporated them into their own system. While championing a humanistic government, Confucius did not deny the existence of spirits; what distinguished him was to give higher values to the personal experience of sacrifices, taking reverence as central to all religious and non-religious rituals. For him, human submission to spiritual powers was the core of an ideal person, the gentleman: 'The gentleman stands in awe of three things. He is in awe of the Decree of Heaven. He is in awe of great men. He is in awe of the words of the sages' (Lau, 1979:140).

Without its own 'body', the Confucian spirituality had to be substantialized in order to have a lasting effect on the state. This was done through the civil service examination system, by which Confucians were selected as government officials and Confucian doctrines became official guidelines for all aspects of personal and social life. In this way, Confucianism came to represent the state religion both internally and externally, and the relation between the state and religion was eventually turned to that between Confucianism and other religious organizations and practices. As we have already seen in Chapter 3, the intercommunication and intertransformation between the so-called three teachings (*san jiao*), Confucianism, Daoism and Buddhism, was the heart of religious history in China. Their interacting was important not only for supplying fresh ideas and reshaping common senses, but also for reducing antagonism between conflicting ideologies or religious teachings. As the spokesman of the state, Confucianism did not necessarily contradict other faiths; rather, most Confucian scholars themselves were committed to Buddhist and Daoist beliefs and were keenly engaged in popular practices such as *fengshui* and divination. Radical or rational Confucian scholars might have denied any association with such beliefs, but their families were pious believers and would pray for the blessing and mercy of Buddhas, immortals or other gods and goddesses on behalf of their sons, husbands or brothers. The direct and indirect penetration of religious faiths in Confucian scholars/officials enabled these faiths to be fully represented in the political ideology of the state.

The reason why Confucianism could be fully integrated with the state religion was that, apart from its 'members', Confucianism did not have its own exterior infrastructure such as priesthood and congregational assemblies. In this regard, Confucianism was like a huge vine, energetic and inspiring, but having to be supported to climb high. The trunk that enabled Confucianism to rise and function in a wider society was the political structure of the state and the government bureaucracy, through which Confucian scholars changed their hats to be members of the 'priesthood' and established their 'hierarchy' throughout different levels of the administration. In this way, Confucianism was fully integrated into the government and Confucian doctrines into the religion of the state.

This, however, has raised a question about the nature of the state religion in China. Did the integration of Confucianism with the state produce a political regime that totally unified government and religion? There are two kinds of the religio-state regime; one may be called 'religiocracy' in which religion overpowers the secular state, and the other may be called the 'religio-political regime' by which the state incorporates religious elements as administrative means. It is apparent that the state religion in China belonged to the second category. Dynastic governments in China were mostly religious because their foundation was established on the mandate of Heaven and because they took religious sacrifices as an effective approach to social and political problems. However, this does not mean that the state was already transformed into a religious organization; rather it only indicates a highly harmonious unity reached between political goal and religious means, in which the state made full use of religious tools and spiritual powers to facilitate an effective administration.

The Confucian nature of the state resisted any attempt to fully religionize the government, and there was hardly any era in the 2000-year history in which the state yielded all its responsibilities to a particular religious organization. During the southern-northern dynasties period (420–589) there were short-lived semi-Buddhist or Daoist dynasties when the emperors attempted to convert the whole country to a particular religion. While the heads of these dynasties were committed to a religious doctrine, the whole government was still under the control of civil servants rather than Buddhist monks or Daoist priests, and the state remained mostly a secular regime that was above religions.

The collapse of the last dynasty at the beginning of the twentieth century led to the abolition of the state religion and the disassociation of Confucianism from the government. Since then, the Chinese state, either the Republic or the People's Republic, has been secular in the sense that no religious requirements are in place for a particular form of government. While the Republic of China merely distanced itself from religion, the People's Republic took a hard line towards religion and has changed the 'careful control and careful tolerance' nature of the relation between state and religion. The comparative tolerance of religions in the past has been replaced by a more rigid regime that places religions under various kinds of pressure with an attempt to mobilize all religious sentiments and practices to the service of the state.

Managing religions

From an administrative perspective, religion in China is in general considered to be more an organizational activity than a purely personal faith. Whatever regime it represents, the state takes a utilitarian view toward religion, measuring its values by the consequences it has caused or will likely cause. People in general expect that religion should be managed by the state, and it sits well with this expectation that in managing religion the state places an emphasis on how to ensure religion contributes to national well-being rather than on how to guarantee the freedom with which each individual is entitled to choose his or her own faith.

There is diversity in the styles or types of managing religion; some forms of the political regime would appear to be more sympathetic and gentler toward religion, while others seem more antagonistic and harsher. The same government is more tolerant of religious activities in some circumstances, while more restrictive in others. In general, the Chinese government tends to regulate all religious orders in public domains. The state maintains authority over major religious institutions, and employs such administrative tools as granting honorific or divine titles to, and promoting or downgrading the ranks of, gods or deities or religious leaders. However, for most part of Chinese history right up until the modern era, these activities were mostly ceremonial, enabling religion to be part of a wider administrative network. They were focused on the consequential features of a religion, and were intended for that religion's organizations and activities only. In general, if a religion did not pose any threat to the state and if it were not perceived to contradict the government's policies, it would be left untrammelled. It is only in this sense that Wing-tsit Chan is right when he suggests that in history 'the government did not pass judgement on religious beliefs, interfere with religious practices, or determine religious creeds' (Chan, 1978:139).

Managing religion was part of the government as early as the Zhou dynasty. The chief source of information we have for the government of that time is the *Rites of the Zhou* (*zhou li*) or *Officials of the Zhou* (*zhou guan*), allegedly China's earliest and most complete record of official systems and rituals, but probably compiled as late as the third century BCE. It provided the blueprint of an idealized government, according to which, later dynasties established the basic structure of the state administration in six ministries (personnel, house-holds, rites, military, justice and public works) (Hucker, 1985:6). Of the six ministries, one was the Ministry of Rites (*chung guan*, 'spring officials'), headed by *Zong bo*, in charge of all kinds of rites and rituals, auspicious or inauspicious, secular or religious, such as sacrifices, funerals, pilgrimage, tributes, banquet, weddings, hunting and so forth. Of the so-called 'spring officials', there was the Director of Sorcery (*si wu*), who was 'responsible for all sorcery at court, including appeals for rain in time of drought, and various activities in response to other sorts of calamities; [and who] participated in all court ceremonies and funerals' (Hucker, 1985:459). This was probably the first officially recorded governmental post specifically for religious matters.

As part of government, all state rites and rituals were strictly regulated, and any deviation would not be tolerated, because deviation from the sanctioned ritual and ceremony was perceived to disrupt or damage the supposed harmonious relationship between spiritual powers and the state. As far as state management is concerned, religion can be divided into three aspects to which the government would apply different yet consistent sets of rules. These three aspects are state religion, religious institutions and religious creeds and practices. Traditionally in China the degree of controlling these three aspects was in a descending order: the state religion was controlled most tightly, next came religious institutions, and the least strict measures were applied to religious beliefs, creeds and practices.

The state religion was, to a great extent, politicized as part of the government. Yearly and seasonal sacrifices were conducted in exact accordance with books, especially those on the rites of the Zhou dynasty (the three books on the Rites: the *Rites of the Zhou*, the *Rites of Etiquette and Ceremonial* (*yi li*), and the *Book of Rites* (*li ji*)). Any change to an established ritual or ritual items must be officially approved; for example, in the case of Confucius, the tablets in his temple could be 'added or removed, officially by an imperial decree, but practically by the Board of Rites' (Shryock, 1966:136).

Apart from the Ministry of Rites there were other state departments or agencies with designated responsibilities for managing religious matters. In most dynastic governments, there were 'the Court of Imperial Sacrifices (*t'ai-ch'ang ssu*), which in collaboration with the Ministry of Rites, managed the host of sacrificial ceremonies that were an essential part of traditional Chinese government; . . . the Court of State Ceremonial (*hung-lu ssu*), which supervised the ritual aspects of all state functions' (Hucker, 1985:86–7). Which government department a religion was assigned to could be a matter of how this religion was seen by the state. For example, in the early years of the Tang dynasty, while Daoism was under the supervision of the Court of Imperial Clan (*zong zheng*) because it was seen as the royal family religion, Buddhism was under the supervision of the Court of State Ceremonial, a governmental organ exercising 'general supervision over foreign guests, audiences, good and evil omens, and sacrifices'. This indicates that after nearly 600 years Buddhism was still treated as a foreign religion in accordance with ceremonies accorded to foreign guests. In the year of 694, however, Empress Wu Zetian (624–705) transferred Buddhism to the Bureau of National Sacrifice, 'one of the organs in the Ministry of Rites', indicating that 'the empress no longer considered Buddhism to be a foreign religion' (Ch'en, 1964:255).

The early state management of religious matters was in general confined to the official rituals and rites. There were the directors of sacrifices in various names throughout history, and their responsibilities were to supervise all official sacrifices, such as those to royal ancestors (*ci si*), or the suburban sacrifices to Heaven and Earth (*si jiao*), and later grand sacrifices to Confucius. These positions were primarily concerned with the state religion rather than with individual religious institutions. After the arrival of Buddhism, however, various offices were set up designated to supervise or control religious institutions, in particular those of Buddhism and Daoism. The first of these offices was probably established in the year 396: 'an Office to Oversee Blessings was established, later changed to Office to Illumine the Mysteries (*chao-hsuan-ssu*), manned by officials and charged with supervision over monks and nuns'

(Ch'en, 1964:253). In the Yuan dynasty offices specifically for managing religions were established:

> 'the Office for Religious Administration (*ta-hsi tsung-yin yuan*)' and 'the Commission for the Promotion of Religion (ch'ung-fu ssu), which seems to have supervised Nestorians, Manichaeans, and other untraditional religious communities in China and had an astonishing total of 72 subordinate agencies scattered throughout the empire'. (Hucker, 1985:62)

There seemed no need for managing communal practices until the formation of Buddhist and Daoist communities. Various offices and 'Commissioners of Religion' were established during the Tang dynasty to supervise religious orders (Ch'en, 1964:255), such as taking censuses of clerical communities, compiling registries for Buddhist monks, Daoist priests and nuns, administering the examining of the candidates seeking admission into a religious order, and issuing qualification certificates. The last one was seen as an effective way to control the size of a particular religious organization. The state sanctioned examination was intended to allow those who were qualified to enter the religious order. However, this measure was manipulated in later times by the state in financial difficulties as a way to raise revenue. Ordination certificates could be purchased at a price, and this inevitably led to corruption both within government and religious orders.

Governmental positions were also assigned with wider responsibilities concerned with religious activities such as establishing religious statues, building temples, producing religious calendars, approving religious festivals, etc. For all these, religions were required to form their own administrative organs to correspond to the government's supervision. While many religious institutes and individuals attempted to retain a certain degree of freedom or to extricate themselves from that control, most of them were effectively transformed into a form of services for the state. Administrative responsibility of a major monastery or temple was normally in the hands of the abbot or master, who although being elected by the monks or priests, would have to be confirmed in the office by the government, which indicated the state's close supervision of religious institutions.

The state also tried its best to control and guide religious beliefs and practices. Ebrey has examined the four strategies of managing religious practices adopted by the government in the Song dynasty: instituting regulations to outlaw certain practices, applying the administrative apparatus to the regulating of other practices, transforming new beliefs into part of the conventional faith and setting up moral exemplars to lead the mass (Ebrey, 1993:222–229). In the case of the Goddess Mazu cult in southeast China, for example, the local and central authorities of that time no doubt played a key role in transforming it from a new cult to a popular faith: they first took patronage of it to make it 'official', and then reimposed it on local communities to make it popular (James L. Watson, 1985:292–324).

The government's patronage can be both very materialistic, such as bearing the cost of building or renovating temples, and very spiritual, such as granting titles to gods or goddesses or taking a local cult into the officially recognized 'pantheon'. This demonstrates clearly the dual purposes of the state's managing of religion. On the one hand, the state would like to have whatever supernatural assistance might be available, and on the other, by its patronage of a deity, it tacitly asserts its control over the cult and the people who follow it.

In general, the state had three tools to use in managing the power and size of a religion: to support the development of a religion by bestowing economic and political privileges on it or by depriving it of them, to use registration and ministration to monitor temple activities and believers' behaviour; and to restrict and control the size of temple and the number of religious believers. It seems that all these tools were inherited by the Republic of China and further exploited by the People's Republic of China. Immediately after 1949 when the Communist Party took power, how to manage and control religion became one of the central issues for the new authorities. In the eyes of the government, religion was dangerous because it was associated with old customs and hostile internal and external forces. At the same time, religion was something the Communists had to manage or control as part of the 'united front' that had helped them win the fight against the Nationalist Party. This tightly controlling and yet unwillingly tolerant policy lasted until the break out of the Cultural Revolution, when all religions were totally smashed at the hands of fanatic 'red guards'. Since the end of the 1970s however, the government policy towards religion has changed from 'eradicating' to 'carefully managing': the Communist Party has placed religion under the dual supervision of the Unite Front Work Department and the State Administration of Religious Affairs. Both organs have branches at provincial and county levels. Under their direction, each religion is administered by its own national associations; hence the National Associations for Buddhists, Daoists, Protestants, Catholics and Muslims which have also formed a national network through branches in provinces and counties. The management of religion has also penetrated major Buddhist and Daoist temples, the heads of which must be approved by the government and are given adequate rank, title and equivalent salaries (Jordan Paper, 1995:16). As part of the managing tools, 'religious leaders who were willing to work with the government and the CCP were appointed to advisory positions in local and central government' (Michael Dillon: 2009:103) to enhance their influence over religious institutions and believers. At the practical level, religious services and ceremonies outside approved monasteries, temples or churches are an activity that would most likely meet the disapproval of the religious administration or even be forbidden by law (Hahn, 1989:86).

Judging religions

The imperial government in China was in general tolerant of religions while taking religion as one of the administrative tools for the benefit of dynastic continuation and social stability. In this sense it tended to identify religion with the people, and how to deal with religion thus became part of its strategy about how to deal with the masses. For wise rulers, although the state had authority over the people, it also needed their support, and it could be overthrown if it did not treat them properly. It was long recognized that 'the lord is the boat; his subjects are the water. It is the water that sustains the boat, and it is the water that capsizes the boat' (Knoblock, 1988, vol.1:216).

The favour or disfavour of a king or emperor for a particular religion often led to a change of state policy towards it. However, it would also be balanced by consideration of what consequences the change of policy would produce for the dynastic rule and for the country as a whole. This was well illustrated by the attitude of the second emperor of the Tang dynasty, Taizong (r. 626–649), towards Buddhism. Taking lessons from history, Taizong did not think Buddhism was a sound religion because Buddhism had caused a number of dynasties to collapse due to depletion of economic resources and human power. Instead of Buddhism, he turned to Daoism and honoured its founder as his ancestor (Laozi was surnamed by Li, the same as the royal family). More importantly he believed Daoist *wu wei* or nonaction was the virtue on which the state could rest. Despite this, he also demonstrated his support for Buddhism and instituted a balanced policy that reflected his 'desire to use the religion for the benefit and advantage of the state', because 'political considerations dictated that the emperor should take measures to gain the support of the large body of Buddhist converts' (Ch'en, 1964:218).

Other rulers were not as skilful in managing religions as Taizong of the Tang dynasty, and often took radical measures to suppress one religion while promoting another. Their judgements of religion reflected their personal preference and the perceived merits or demerits of religions or their doctrines. One of the earliest examples of this was the First Emperor (r. 221–210 BCE) of the Qin dynasty, who took the advice of his prime minister, Li Si (?–208 BCE, one of the chief representatives of Legalist School, a rival to Confucianism), and ordered in 213 BCE the burning of books of other schools, those of Confucianism in particular. The emperor also decreed that those who dared to talk about these books, to glorify the past while criticizing the present, and to challenge his authority and policies should be executed (de Bary and Bloom, 1999:210). Approximately a hundred years later, a similar but much less dramatic decree was issued by Emperor Wu (r. 140–87 BCE) of the Han dynasty to promote Confucianism as the state orthodoxy and, to bring all other schools and ideas into line with Confucianism (Ibid., 311).

Judging 'right' and 'wrong' teachings dominated state policy towards religious schools, and at the end of the later Han dynasty (25–220 CE), Five Bushels of Rice Daoism (Heavenly Master Daoism) was branded as 'rice thieves' and the Yellow Turban Daoism was crushed under the joint force of the government and war lords in the name of attacking 'rebellious brigands'. After the spread of Buddhism during the Southern and Northern dynasties period (420–589), the judging of religions was centred on the worthy or unworthy Buddhism, the debates of which not only took place among scholars but also were sponsored by the court. Buddhism and its rivals demonstrated great skilfulness to win the debate, and used many other political tactics to manifest its value for the state. Infused with Confucian ideas, for example, newly revived Heavenly Master Daoism claimed that the Tai-wu emperor (408–452) of the Northern Wei dynasty was the 'True Ruler of Great Peace' (*Taiping zhenjun*). In return, the emperor converted to Daoism and decreed that it be the state religion. When the emperor found that Buddhist temples stored weapons and were associated with his enemy, he ordered the execution of Buddhist monks, destroyed their temples and burned Buddhist sutras. However, with the enthronement of the new emperor in the year 452 this policy changed, and consequently Buddhism regained its freedom while Daoism went into gradual decline (Pas, 1989:190).

The judging of a religion was often the prelude to the change of a religion's fortune or misfortune. Empress Wu Zetian, for example, endorsed Buddhism and considered herself 'the incarnation of Maitreya on earth': under 'the imperial patronage Buddhism flourished during the years 685–705' (Ch'en, 1964:221). The situation changed, however, during the reign of the Xuanzong emperor (685–762) who was in favour of Daoism. By instituting a network of Daoist temples throughout China and worshipping the Supreme Lord Old Master (*Taishang laojun*, Laozi), Xuanzong aimed to establish himself as the Sage Emperor, for which he 'inaugurated the Tao-chü (Taoist Examination) for recruiting students and scholars well versed in Taoist texts into civil services' (Benn, 1987:128). Favour and disfavour alternated as the state changed its judgement over Buddhism and Daoism until the Song dynasty (960–1279) when Confucianism was finally instituted as the state ideology dominating all other religions.

All these historical incidents seemed to suggest that how to judge religions was associated with the personal attitude of an emperor or empress towards religions or religious teachings, or with his or her acceptance or rejection of a particular argument for or against a particular religion. Historical records seemed also to support the view that change of religious policies was caused by the change of emperors or dynasties, and that the state's evaluation of religion in China appears to be anything but consistent.

However, if we take a closer look at state policies throughout history and in the present, it would not be too difficult for us to see that the promotion or demotion of a religion is not simply a result of personal preference, but primarily a political judgement. Underlying these policies is a concern about what this or that religion would do to the state, what consequences they can lead to and how the state should best handle them. Judged by this ultimately utilitarian criterion, all the religions that promote national interest, enhance social productivity and lead the people towards a healthy way of life are said to be good, valuable and worthy; while all the religions that are perceived as contrary to the well-being of the state, destroy the economic foundation, or deplete the wealth of the people and corrupt the mind and heart of the people, are branded as evil cults. These standards were explicitly or implicitly applied for thousands of years and are still used in contemporary times with a number of new parameters.

'Patriotic' and 'reactionary'

In a highly centralized country like China, the state has all necessary resources to control religion and is able, in most cases, to force its own agenda onto religion. Therefore, the ultimate goal of religion is defined by the state as promoting the core interests of the nation. The most valued interest of the state is considered to be political stability, or in other words the continuation of a particular regime. Those that support the state and contribute to 'peace and order' are therefore said to be 'patriotic religions'; while those who oppose the government, or obstruct the progress of the state, are branded as 'reactionary forces'. The separation of 'patriotic' religions from 'reactionary' doctrines is not an innovation of today's government. It comes from a long tradition in China which holds that great efforts must be exercised to 'stamp out evil and vain teachings', to make the state stronger, or to avoid the disintegration of the state.

One of the core values religion is required to uphold is 'unification'. It is a long-held conviction among the Chinese that unification leads to peace and order, while separation brings about chaos and war, and that a country will be surely reunited after a long time of disunity. In history we have seen many religious organizations that served the country in resisting invasion by border peoples being praised as 'patriotic religions', while those who assisted hostile forces to overpower their own country were condemned as 'treason thieves'. To gain the support or favour of the state, all religions would claim that they were truly peace-loving, ready to protect the state from being divided and to promote harmony and order against disorder. A good number of Buddhist temples, for example, are even built with the name of 'the Temple of Protecting the Country' (*hu guo si*), while some Daoist scriptures or movements take the establishment of the 'grand peace' (*tai ping*) on earth as their ultimate goal.

In the People's Republic of China, the 'patriotic *verse* reactionary' dichotomy is used in a new context in which religions are brought into a unified front seeking the unification of the motherland, namely the reunification of the Mainland and Taiwan. In this way institutional religions are seen as part of the political strategy to enhance the unification forces on both sides of the Straits while fighting against various separatist tendencies. This is both the bottom line in the state's judging of religions and an opportunity a religious institution must seize to demonstrate its usefulness to the state.

'Official' vs. 'folk' religions

The long history of centralization has cultivated a widely held belief that officially sanctioned things or teachings are good, reliable and long lasting, while local products, spontaneous forces and folk beliefs are untrustworthy and short-lived. Applying this to religions, there is a contrast between 'official religions' and 'folk-religions'. The former refers to religions that have been recognized, supported, sponsored and properly supervised by the state; while the latter refers to those popular faiths, regional practices and new movements that need to be guarded against, watched over and contained.

In the past, Confucianism, Daoism and Buddhism were officially recognized religions, while in contemporary times, the 'Five Major Religions' (*wu da zongjiao*) recognized by the government are Protestant Christianity, Catholic Christianity, Buddhism, Daoism and Islam. Each religion has its own national and local monitoring bodies which work with the United Front Work Department of the Communist Party and the State Administration of Religious Affairs in supervising its activities and managing the relationship between it and the state. By law, religious followers must register with a recognized faith in order to take part in religious activities, and the places of worship, priests and heads of churches or temples in each religion have to be agreed or approved by (or at least reported to) the authorities at a relevant level.

This purposely made division has serious consequences for the evaluation of religions. It tends to value some religious believers as 'normal' while humiliating others as 'abnormal'. While the authorities overseeing religions and their adherents are powerful and have broadly achieved their ends, some people do not want to register with officially recognized institutions, or do not want to publicly proclaim their faiths. In this way, the members of official religions, and those of 'underground' or 'folk' religions, are contrasted, and possibly opposed to each other. Furthermore, it has caused a huge disagreement between religious identity and religious belief and practice. The 2005 statistics reveal, for example, that only 4.2 per cent of the interviewees in Beijing claimed to be Buddhists, but 15 per cent said that they enshrined statues or images of Buddhas, Bodhisattvas and other Buddhist deities (Yao and Badham, 2007:99).

More importantly, this judging criterion leads to the exclusion of 'folk-religion' from official recognition. As a major content of Chinese religion, 'folk-religion' includes two kinds of beliefs and practices, respectively described as popular faiths and secret societies. Popular faiths refer to those that are widespread throughout the Chinese populace and are deeply diffused into folklore and local customs as their way of life. They do not have nation-wide organizations, nor a systematic ideology and consistent ritual system. Faiths and practices are matters of local communities, families and individuals.

Not being officially recognized, folk-religion has a limited space to expand and can easily develop into secret societies that have a clear political agenda. While 'folk-religion' is politically 'neutral' and does not pose a serous threat to the current political order, secret societies can play an active role in organizing a competitive force against the central government. This is the reason why the state tends to have different policies toward folk-religion and secret societies; the policy toward popular faiths is more restrictive than forbidding, while toward secret societies, the state always attempts to contain, persecute and suppress.

Religion, superstition and cults

Closely associated with the 'official' and 'folk' dichotomy, the state frequently makes use of another contrast between 'religion' and 'superstition' or 'cult' to judge religious faiths. The history of this contrast goes back to the early separation of the state religion from popular practices, or the debate between the state-sponsored school of thought and other schools, and finally between Confucianism and unsupervised religions. Rational Confucians were proud of their doctrines as 'philosophical teaching' while debasing popular Daoist and Buddhist beliefs and practices as 'superstition' or 'cult'.

This reflects the state's desire to bring all religious beliefs and activities under its control. In return for accepting the supervision of the state, religions expect to receive the recognition, necessary support and proper protection from the government. Recognized by the state, they become 'normal', in contrast to superstitious cults. 'Normal' here refers to both the officially permitted and the culturally desired, while 'superstitious cult' refers to the opposite. In reality, no clear definition has ever been given to either of them, and between them there is a huge grey area.

In today's China many religious practices operate in such a grey area. For example, ancestral worship is practised widely and is therefore culturally desired. Few governments would be so stupid as to forbid it whether or not it falls in line with its ideological principles. In this sense, it is 'normally' practised by the majority of people and tacitly 'allowed' by the state, although strictly speaking it has never been officially permitted by the government. It is also culturally desired that the site of a grave or a house's location and structure or the position of furniture be chosen according to the advice of masters of *yin-yang* and *fengshui* (geomancy); in this sense it is 'normal', because so many people believe it and follow it, not because the government has permitted it.

Undefinable beliefs and practices both open the doors to religion and lend a tool to the government to use the 'normal' vs. 'superstitious' to support certain religious behaviour while restricting or forbidding others. The state stipulates that while all 'normal' religions are protected and allowed, 'abnormal' or 'superstitious' religions and cults will be persecuted and suppressed. It clearly indicates that whether a religion is regarded as normal or not depends to a great extent on whether it is perceived by the government as beneficial or dangerous to the state and the people. A good example for this is the case of *qi gong* which, as a health-building practice and spiritual path, is very popular. *Fa lun gong*, or the Practices of the Wheel of Dharma was one such practice. Established by Li Hongzhi, the *fa lun gong* is a typical synthesis of traditional beliefs and practices, Confucian, Buddhist, Daoist and others, and demonstrates all the features of a new religious movement which has successfully recruited a tremendous number of followers; many of whom were party members, government officials and reputed scholars. Through the sheer influence it gained as well as the consequences its practices caused, it was seen as a competitive force and was hence banded as a 'cult' or 'evil religion' (*xie jiao*) in 1999.

To conclude this chapter we may make a number of general points concerning religion and state in China. First, throughout history and in the present time the state makes use of administrative tools to control or manage religions. This is embedded in the nature of the Chinese state and is also the expectation of the majority of the people for a variety of reasons. In managing and judging religions, the state follows an obviously utilitarian agenda. Secondly, in correspondence with the state management, religions attempt to demonstrate their usefulness or merit to contribute to the stability, peace and harmony of the country in exchange for the state's support or tolerance. Except in certain circumstances, resistance to the state's control is mostly unsuccessful. A religion that fails to be in line with the state would likely be in a dire situation or faced with persecution and suppression. Consciously aligning themselves with the dominating political power, Chinese religions demonstrate a strong pragmatic character. Thirdly, although the state claims to judge and manage religions for the greatest benefit of the nation and the people, in the last analysis its religious policy reflects the core interest and value of the ruling group or class, and is ultimately to maintain the status quo or to strengthen its authority over the country. Lastly, while it is culturally expected that the state manage religions in one way or another, the methods that are used for this purpose must change along with the change in social conditions. China is no longer the self-enclosed empire as it was in the past and the relationship between religion and state must be dealt with in accordance with internationally agreed standards.

Questions for discussion

1. Is there any justification for the Chinese state to name itself as the protector and supporter of religions?
2. 'The state is rooted in the family.' Discuss the relationship between the state and the family in China and its effect on the relationship between the state and religion.
3. What was the state religion in imperial China? What is the special role of Confucianism in the relationship between the state and religion?
4. What strategies have been adopted by the state to control and manage religions in China? How did they work in a historical context?
5. Why is it said that the utilitarian principle has been used by the Chinese government in its dealing with religious matters?
6. How does the contrast between 'patriotic' and 'reactionary' religions become a tool to mobilize the forces for unification in contemporary Mainland China?
7. What are the consequences of the state policy of dividing religion into 'official' and 'folk'?
8. How can one judge a religious faith or practice? Does the contrast between 'normal' and 'superstitious' make it easier to regulate religious activities?

7 Religious Beliefs

A religious system is characterized primarily by its beliefs. Religious beliefs in contemporary China are of various origins, Confucian, Daoist, Buddhist as well as of other sources. While some strands can be traced to a specific indigenous or imported tradition, most have been transformed or transfigured in this syncretic culture; few can be easily classified into any of stereotypical categories some scholars favour to use to define religions in China, as we have already discussed in Chapter 1. The Chinese tendency is rather to embrace diverse beliefs without much undue discrimination or at least only with minimum modification, and then to incorporate them into a single whole, giving each an appropriate position within this whole.

The formation and spread of any popular religious belief involves a number of factors or steps. At the beginning it is normally derived doctrinally from a well-known teaching in a sacred text or through the oral teachings of a religious/philosophical master. This teaching is then grafted onto an existing belief system that can provide theoretical or theological justification. To embed a teaching or belief into minds and hearts on a mass basis, it would demand not only the efforts of a group of people who commit to this belief, but also the means and the media that deliver it to the ordinary people. In this process, any change to the transmission of a particular tradition would have an impact on the belief, and different interpretations in different ages would also have shaped or reshaped it into different forms, either by connecting it to new systems or by distancing it from certain principles. Most widely known and practised religious beliefs in contemporary China were in fact formed or became widely circulated in a much later age than that in which they were supposed rooted; or in other words, their original form or content was substantially changed in a recent past.

Literature such as drama, poems and legends derive much of their subject matter from religious texts and stories, and in turn, become one of the main sources for proliferating religious beliefs and practices. Prominent in this aspect are the four classic novels: the *Dream of the Red Chamber*, the *Romance of the Three Kingdoms*, the *Journey to the West* and the *Water Margin*, which we have already briefly mentioned in Chapter 4. There are also other popular novels specifically on religion, such as *The Investiture of the Gods* (*Fengshen yanyi*), and the *Affinity between Mirror and Flower* (*Jing hua yuan*), which are of equal importance for our understanding of Chinese beliefs. These novels or fictions developed stories and legends that had long been known in oral forms or through brief records. By giving them a literary form, however, they enhanced the readability of such stories, or reshaped their religiosity, which reflected, to a great extent, the religious expectations and circumstances of the Ming-Qing era when syncretic and moralist spirituality dominated religious and secular life.

The most obvious example for this kind of religious transformation is the belief in Guanyu (?160–219), who was one of the heroes of the 'Three Kingdoms' period, latterly one of the most popular names in Chinese history. Guanyu received posthumous honours at a very early stage in Chinese history, with a cult following gradually in a later age; eventually he became the patron god of the state military administration, and thus paralleled Confucius as the patron of civil administration (Shryock, 1966:126). His huge popularity as a nation-wide god of righteousness, brotherhood, loyalty, bravery, medicine and wealth meant that more temples were dedicated to his worship than to any other god during the Ming-Qing period. This widespread following was undoubtedly increased by the influence of the novel the *Romance of the Three Kingdoms*.

Another example which demonstrates the power of popular literature in re-creating or reshaping religious beliefs is the change of the names of gate gods. As we have already described in Chapter 5, the belief in gate gods had ancient origins, where the two guardian gods were thought to be able to destroy demon ghosts. However, the two guardian gods were later transmuted into the form of two generals who guarded the gateway entrance to protect the family against evil forces. The cult popularity of the two general-gods was undoubtedly credited, at least partly, to their story of protecting the Emperor from demonic attack as retold in the *Journey to the West* (Yu, 1977, vol. 1:233–4).

All above examples have pointed to a complex of beliefs which on the one hand, are typical of the Chinese views on life and death and, on the other hand reflect mixed sources of religious ideas and practices. Our task in this chapter is therefore to unlock the mysticism behind these beliefs, to reveal the underlying themes that have bound seemingly unrelated or even contradictory beliefs into the one system that is called 'Chinese'.

Three underlying themes

This distinctive way of life, which is termed 'Chinese religion', exhibits divergent belief forms or types, ranging from those about the universal law or principle (such as the Way), cosmic powers (such as *yin-yang* and the five elements), supernatural gods or suprahuman beings, to those concerning the so-called 'holiness in human existence' (Fingarett, 1972:1).

Common to all these forms or types is that humans, deities and personalized spiritual powers are believed to exist and function in different and yet intercommunicated realms, which are viewed as different manifestations or dimensions of Dao, the cosmic Way. It is believed that each of these realms is assigned its own place and value within the whole, and that each is in a constant interaction with all others. Distinguishable from each other, humans and non-humans, the secular and the divine, the natural and the supernatural, this world and the world beyond nevertheless cannot be totally separated. The lines that distinguish them are often arbitrary or not consciously drawn at all.

This perception of a unified world with different levels or realms of existence is rooted in the view that Dao is universal, that the various realms, however different, must follow Dao, and that different phenomena or beings are from this perspective merely different presentations of Dao's individulization. This holistic view has led to a perception that the relationship between religion, the family, and the state is extremely close as discussed in previous chapters. This is also a view which has shaped religious beliefs and spiritual practices, as we examine in this and subsequent chapters.

We are faced with two difficulties in reconstructing the spiritual world of the Chinese. First, while different spiritual powers are allocated to different territories and 'assigned' different functions, structuring them into an inclusive system can be problematic. For example, the Buddhist paradise of the West and the paradises of Daoist immortals are well represented in popular religion and literature, but there is little trace of the Confucian heaven where the spirits of ancestors are thought to reside. Again, although the Jade Emperor is addressed as *Shangdi* (the Lord on High) or *Tian di* (the Lord of Heaven), his persona actually differs from what has been described in the state religion or in the Confucian classics. Secondly, it is difficult to reach any firm conclusion about the 'theological' nature and function of these beliefs. They could be termed monotheistic, as the Chinese tend to believe that the world is ruled by a single God who administers all affairs, controls all the courses of action and determines all matters, human as well as spiritual. Equally, they could be said to be pantheistic. Apart from the supreme god of each realm (the Buddha, the Jade Emperor, *Shangdi* or Heaven, or any other forms of the supreme God), there are numerous other gods and spirits who are involved in, interfere or interact with the human world. It is even true to state that Chinese beliefs are animistic, since all beings, things and phenomena are believed to have a soul or spirit which enables them to attain human form with supernatural power through cultivating their own inner power. All these facets demonstrate again that the Chinese compound of beliefs is multi-layered or multi-dimensional; these different layers and dimensions may be in harmony or may seem to be in opposition to each other, but together they are highly functional.

This is a functional unity which few would deny. However, the question has been raised of whether or not functional effectiveness can iron out intrinsic difference between beliefs. From the perspective of a religious absolutist, Chinese beliefs would be anything but consistent. Indeed, religious absolutism has made people 'accustomed to a monotheistic definition which assumes an enormous gulf between God and His creatures' (Shryock, 1966:79). This so-called 'gulf' is well conveyed in the famous question posed by Tertullian: 'What indeed has Athens to do with Jerusalem?' (Connolly, 1999:107). Rephrased in a Chinese context, this question could be rendered as: what has the Buddhist belief in incarnation to do with Daoist immortality, or what has Confucian self-cultivation to do with the belief in household gods? There seem to be many incompatible differences between these concepts; any attempt to unify them would meet strong doctrinal resistance on each side.

On the other hand, a religiously absolutist position is never widely welcome in Chinese religion. When we look closely at this spiritual world, it is not too difficult for us to grasp an intrinsic harmony underlying all sorts of beliefs, no matter however different the concepts themselves might be. From this

Figure 7.1 Cauldron of Religious Belief (http://www.chinainfoonline.com/images/ancientrelics/TheBronzeTripodorCauldron/014.jpg)

perspective, the Chinese religious system may well be compared to a great cauldron, in which all elements of belief are 'cooked' together. This 'cauldron of religious beliefs' has three 'legs', each of them necessary to sustain and support a dynamic religious life (see Figure 7.1). These three legs thus represent the three pillars of beliefs which are powerful enough to bind seemingly unrelated or conflicting beliefs together, becoming a wellhead from whence all other spiritual beliefs spring forth. At the same time, the three pillars of belief point to three underlying themes of the Chinese beliefs, explaining the convergence and diversity of their religious lives, enabling different or even opposite beliefs to co-exist and co-function to form a structured system. These are three themes which act as a key for us to unlock the secrets of Chinese religion.

The first underlying theme is that while the universe is divided into the human and the non-human realm, all realms are controlled by the universal power, and follow the same rule or law. In philosophical terms, this power or law is represented by Dao, while in religious terms, it is manifested as the spiritual ultimate that dominates and governs the spiritual and secular world.

Different names are given to this ultimate in different religious traditions; among them, the most popular names are undoubtedly Shangdi and Heaven (*tian*) in the state religion or Confucianism; the Supreme Lord Old Master (*taishang laojun*) or the Three Heavenly Worthies (*tian zun*) in Daoist religion; the Jade Emperor (*Yu huang*) in Daoism and popular religion; and Buddha *Tathagata* (*Sakyamuni*) or Buddha *Maitreya* or Buddha *Amitabha* in Buddhism and popular religion.

Apart from in Confucianism, the ultimate power is personified as a supreme deity in all other religious doctrines or belief systems, residing in a special realm. Whatever names they are given, these gods represent the supreme power of the universe, closely watching over the human world and issuing final judgements upon divine and secular affairs. It seems to be the case that different sovereign gods live or operate in parallel realms with supplementary or overlapping rather than exclusive functions; there is a visible yet ambiguous division of authority between them, but they also frequently collaborate with each other to deal with a complicated situation or make a tough decision. This is clearly revealed in the story of the Monkey before his conversion to Buddhism; here Sakyamuni (the Venerable One from the Western Region of Ultimate Bliss and the Buddhist Patriarch), the Supreme Lord (Laozi of the *Tushita* Palace at the uppermost of the 33 Heavens) and the Jade Emperor of the Heavenly Court came together to subdue the rebellious monkey (Yu, 1977, vol. 1:166–79).

The second theme is that although totally controlled by spiritual powers, humans are in the meantime capable of knowing (or having access to) the supreme or ultimate power. For Chinese intellectuals, although Dao is invisible and inaudible, yet humans have been endowed with an ability to see it; those with a highly developed faculty of intelligence and wisdom would be able to attain and practise the spiritual discipline needed to reach that level. Dao is from this perspective not only universal but also particular: it is not simply the Way under which the universe operates, but also a way for an individual to follow for spiritual development. Dao itself is 'one', but paths to this oneness can be different. This is a belief which makes it possible for humans to reach perfection through their own spiritual efforts. By embracing Dao and practising particular spiritual disciplines, a Confucian can attain the level of a sage, a Daoist the level of immortal, and a Buddhist the level of a buddha. In popular religion, all these strands interweave; all paths can be travelled by individual humans in seeking the realm of the gods. Therefore, it has become an embedded principle of Chinese religion that everybody has the potential to become a deity, god or goddess by following either Confucian, Daoist or Buddhist teaching, and by being faithful, filial, kind, righteous, quiet, contemplating, by following a pure, simple diet, and by refraining from committing any immoral sin, such as lying, stealing, taking innocent lives, ill-treating family members, committing adultery, or being intoxicated. For ordinary Chinese, part of the spiritual discipline followed would be to visualize immortals or spirits, worship tangible statues of gods, devoting themselves to deities or immortals by humble submission in the form of burning incense, reverential bowing, donating money, and offering sacrifices. These widely practised rites reflect a deeply embedded belief that direct contact and offerings would draw down blessing, protection and even salvation from supreme or lesser gods, as a reward for sincere prayer and a virtuous life.

The third theme is concerned with the spirits of living creature and natural existences. Dao is thought to not only body forth in humans but also to permeate the entire world; all existences and phenomena are therefore nothing but its embodiment or presentation. In the same way as humans can attain the level of deity by cultivating Dao, so all natural bodies, phenomena, plants, animals are believed to be capable of absorbing heavenly and earthly essences to become deities. The spiritual environment for the Chinese is thus highly animistic; all existences are believed to possess a soul or spirit or an inner power that can be cultivated to manifest as spiritual beings. Celestial bodies such as the sun, the moon, the five planets (Mercury, Venus, Mars, Jupiter and Saturn), and the 28 star constellations are believed to be gods/goddesses themselves, for example, or the sites where these gods or goddesses reside; climate phenomena such as wind, thunder, lightning, rain are in the same way believed to be controlled or carried out by gods or goddesses. There are also a huge number of terrestrial deities, such as the site or earth god (*tu di*); the town god (*cheng huang*, the prime god in a town or city where a temple would be dedicated to him, as shown in Figure 7.2); gods of the four directions (*si fang shen*); gods of earth and grains (*she ji*); goddesses or gods of rivers (*he shen*); gods of mountains or hills (*shan shen*); finally there are animal spirits, tree gods and flower goddesses. Others are not easily classifiable either as celestial or terrestrial deities, such as the god for each of the 60 years which form a cycle, the dragon kings of the four seas or the ten kings of hell.

These three underlying themes are profoundly interrelated, and together form a basic 'structure' for the religious beliefs under study. To use the word 'structure' to capture the systematic features of beliefs is not to imply that these are rigidly fixed, however. Rather the three facets of belief interpenetrate each

Figure 7.2 Temple of Town God in the ancient town of Pinyao

other, just as the three categories of deities are mutually interchangeable or at least mutually related. Fluidity rather than rigidity thus characterizes the world of Chinese beliefs and deities. Each of the religious dimensions is headed by an ultimate god and flanked by human and natural gods or goddesses; in all realms, gods and humans may transmute from one form or substance to another. The ultimate god could have been transfigured from a sage; a human could have become a deity who watches over natural phenomena or who has specific terrestrial responsibilities; a nature deity could also have become a human god for local areas. Between realms boundaries are not stressed other than superficially, and are indeed frequently blurred deliberately. Instead of separation and opposition, characteristic of their relationship are mutuality and interchangeablity, which together facilitate a religiosity that seeks meaning and value in the interrelationship between the divine and the human, between the godly realm and the secular sphere, and between the divine will and earthly desires.

Belief in ultimate Gods

Chinese belief in a spiritual ultimate goes back to the earliest records; it has since passed through a long, complex evolving process, from an exclusive god as proscribed by the state religion to a universal god that is believed and worshipped by all people. A rich diversity is present in this belief; we have already seen many names that are given to this spiritual ultimate, each carrying a different doctrinal content and practical meaning for religious life.

The first spiritual ultimate that has so far been confirmed in history is *Di* or *Shangdi* who was believed by the Shang people to be the controlling god: 'That Di was virtually the only Power who could directly order (*ling*) rain or thunder, as well as the only Power who had the winds under his control, sets him apart from all the other Powers, natural, predynastic, or ancestral' (de Bary and Bloom, 1999:11). In contemporary scholarship there are different opinions about the nature of this god. For some *Shangdi* is a creator god (Küng and Ching, 1989:16), or at least the creator of myriads of things (Ge Zhaoguang, 2001:21), but for others, *Shangdi* was only a human god who had a close relationship with the ancestors of the Shang royal house; or on the contrary, it was a nature god beyond human social world (Chen, 1956:580). In fact *Shangdi* was both, commending the human as well as the natural world, as 'Di stood at the peak of the ultra-human, ultra-natural hierarchy, giving orders, which no ancestor could do, to the various natural phenomena, and responding to the intercessions of the Shang ancestors who were acting on behalf of their descendants below' (de Bary and Bloom, 1999:11). Despite this contrary view, evidence shows that *Shangdi* was probably more transcendental than immanent, since he could be approached only through the royal ancestors who were believed to reside besides the seat of *Shangdi*.

The supreme god of the Shang dynasty was then overshadowed by the high god of the Zhou dynasty, *Tian* or Heaven. The relation between the Lord on High and Heaven itself is anything but clear, although some scholars have confirmed that the character for Heaven in the oracle bones is identifiable with that for the Lord (*di*) (Chen Lai, 1996:165). Compared with a transcendental Lord on High, however, Heaven itself as embodied in the high god was more concerned with the good or bad fortune of the people below; heavenly principles determined not only the course of natural operations but also the pattern of human behaviours (Eno, 1990:4). Heaven has a moral will to reward good deeds and punish evil, as said in the *Book of History*: 'Heaven gives charges to those who have virtue, . . . Heaven punishes those who have guilt' (Karlgren, 1950:9). Gradually Heaven was associated with the people; whether or not Heaven supported a government depends whether or not the government was supported by its own people; 'Heaven hears and sees as our people hear and see; Heaven brightly approves and displays its terrors as our people brightly approve and would fear' (Waltham, 1972:28).

In later times, the meaning of Heaven was expanded in its interpretation by rationalists and religionists. For rational intellectuals, for example, Heaven is a general name for the supreme ultimate, containing multi-dimensional meanings and functions, as explained by Neo-Confucians in the Song dynasty:

> Spoken of as one Heaven is the Way (Tao) . . . Spoken of in its different aspects, it is called heaven with respect to its physical body, the Lord (Ti) with respect to its being master, negative and positive spiritual forces with respect to its operation, spirit (*shen*) with respect to its wonderful functioning, and ch'ien with respect to its nature and feelings. (Chan, 1963:570)

In a religious context, however, belief in the Lord and Heaven changed dramatically from a royal privilege to a popular faith; the high god of heaven was also transformed from a remote spiritual authority to a visible and touchable deity. An important step in this direction took place in the Song dynasty when, under the influence of Daoist religion, the emperors decreed that the Jade Emperor (*yu huang*) be given the title Lord of Heaven (*tian di*) or the Lord on High (*Shangdi*), so that he became the supreme god in heaven, equivalent to a human emperor on earth. The previous ambiguity surrounding Lord on High or Heaven was then gradually dispersed; in its place was a personal god who resides in the palace of the Northern Dipper and administers heaven (the world of gods) and earth (the world of humans). Whereas in the past when only the king or the emperor was privileged to worship the high god in an exclusive Temple or Altar of Heaven in the southern suburb of the capital (as was the case until the beginning of the twentieth century), now the Jade Emperor became the predominant cult in Daoist temples and local shrines. There are a great number of temples (*yu huang miao*) dedicated to this deity throughout China; his birthday (the 9th day of the first month according to the Chinese calendar) is celebrated as one of the biggest religious festivals. It is believed that on the 25th day of the 12th month, the Jade Emperor tours the human world, inspecting all good and evil, fortune or misfortune, to determine awards or punishments. This again becomes a celebratory festival in local communities and for ordinary people (Xu, 2008:59).

In everyday language, the Jade Emperor is also popularly called 'the God of Heaven' (*lao tian ye*) or simply Heaven (*tian*). In fact the interchangeable uses of different titles indicate how the supreme god is perceived, and how different beliefs in the high god of heaven have intertwined. It is apparent that none of these titles assumes an exclusive claim over others; rather they are simply used indiscriminately to refer to the embodiment or personification of the supreme power, who determines the course of the world and the destiny of each individual. By whatever names he is addressed (Heaven or the Jade Emperor), this god is no longer the abstract and transcendental being as described in ancient texts; nor is he confined to the state religion. He has in effect been successfully transformed into a supreme god who holds sway over human destiny, who is open to the worship of every man and woman, and who is believed to respond to human pleas.

It is believed that the God of Heaven or Jade Emperor has a concern for humans on earth and will sometimes directly intervene in what happens below, either by actually causing disasters to occur, or by sending down gods to help, namely star gods, to the human realm incarnating as extraordinary people, and to facilitate a particular course. Stories and legends about this kind of belief are numerous in novels, dramas and public performances, and have a huge influence over religious beliefs as demonstrated in the Prologue of the great novel *Water Margin* (*shui hu*):

> [The fourth emperor of the Song dynasty] was the incarnation of the Heavenly Genii Chih Chiao (Bare-footed Genii), and when he was born, he cried continuously, day and night. His father, Emperor Chen Tsung issued a proclamation offering a reward to anyone who could cure the crying infant. When it became known in Heaven the Genii T'ai Pai (Great Whiteness) [God of Venus] was sent down to earth, and metamorphosed into an old man . . . he picked up the royal infant in his arms, and whispered eight words into his ear. Immediately the royal infant stopped and the old man vanished in a gust of wind. The eight words he whispered were: 'For civil affairs there is a civil star; for military affairs a military star'. (Jackson, 1976)

These were eight words to convey to the infant that the Jade Emperor had already sent two star gods down to assist him with civil and military affairs when he became emperor. This story has illustrated a theme which runs consistently through the history of Chinese religion. Indeed, from the time of the *Book of History* and the *Book of Poetry* onwards, the king or emperor was traditionally addressed as '*tian zi*' the 'Son of Heaven', meaning quite literally that the king was perceived as the son of the highest deity. It is not therefore uncommon in history that those great heroes, distinguished statesmen, or those of extraordinary strengths or talents were said to be an incarnation of a god or star god. Confucius, for example, was once believed to be the incarnation of the Black Emperor (*xuan di*) (one of the five emperors of five colours), or of the Literature Star (*wen chang xing*) who protects scholars and blesses them with success in civil service examinations (which is the highest target for a scholar in traditional Chinese society). Although it has now become rare in contemporary China to believe that certain individuals are sent down from heaven, we still hear from time to time that a leader of some underground new religious moment claims to be the incarnation of a god or goddess. This proves that an innate belief in spiritual deities not only persists, but also can be exploited by the unscrupulous or ambitious for their own ends. Such is this belief in something 'higher' that new forms continue to evolve in seeking the connection with the spiritual ultimate.

Apart from a belief in the direct intervention of a supreme god, there is a more widespread belief in the will of Heaven (*tian yi*, or *tian ming*); this divine will not only determines the success or failure of a particular government, but will also determine each individual's life span as well as its quality, and indeed the rank and wealth to be achieved in each life time. Although invisible, the will of Heaven is believed to be the key to human success or failure, as was believed by Confucius and his disciples 2,500 years ago. The claim was that all achievements in life such as wealth and honours depend on Heaven (Lau, 1979:113); this is a belief which still persists for a considerable part of the contemporary Chinese population, as indicated by the statistics of 2005. As many as 45.4 per cent of rural interviewees and 43.2 per cent of urban interviewees reported an experience of the view that riches and rank were predetermined by the Will of Heaven (Yao and Badham, 2007:140).

The Chinese pantheon

The Chinese belief in a supreme deity is closely associated with a belief in a pantheistic order. For supreme authorities to be executed, it is believed, the supreme deity (whatever name he is given) will of necessity command assistance from lesser gods and deities. These are gods which together comprise the Chinese pantheon, a hierarchic spiritual pyramid with the supreme deity at its pinnacle. This is a complex pantheon which in Chapter 5 is divided into five categories according to their functions; namely: ancestors, household deities, heavenly and earthly gods, communal gods and 'trade' patron saints. In terms of their nature and origin, however, it is more appropriate to group them into three interrelated dominions: natural gods, spirits of living beings and things and human deities.

Natural gods

By definition, gods of nature have their domain in nature itself and derive from transfigured natural bodies or phenomena, mostly in human form, but possibly in other forms, such as the god of thunder (*lei gong*), who more closely resembles a monkey than a human. The Chinese natural world is perceived to have three main domains; the gods are thus divided into three subgroups:

- gods of celestial bodies (planets, stars…),
- gods of climate phenomena (wind, thunder, lightning . . .),
- gods of terrestrial forms (mountains, rivers . . .).

Belief in natural gods has a long history, and is deeply rooted in ancient nature worship. In the Shang era (as we see from the oracle bone inscriptions) there was a prevailing belief in natural deities such as the god of wind, the god of cloud, the sun god, and gods and goddesses of other conspicuous stars and constellations, who were either the messengers of the Lord or his persecutors (Tung, 1952:12–21). One of the oldest cults dedicated to natural divinities was for *she ji*, the gods of earth and grains. The prominence of this belief reflected the fact that the Chinese were a people of agriculture and that earth and grains were the most important elements to them for life. It is confirmed that the cult was already predominant and well established at least in the Zhou period, and that it continued to flourish throughout the imperial era. However, the belief and practice concerning the gods of earth and grains evolved later along two pathways: on the one hand, this was a belief system fully integrated into the state religion, and gods became one of the symbols for state sovereignty so that only the king or emperor had merited the privilege of worshipping them; on the other hand, gods of grains and earth gradually merged with the belief in the god of earth (*tudi*) in folk-religion; these deities thus transmuted more and more into patron gods of local communities (Yang, 1961:97).

In a Chinese context, gods and natural bodies are not distinguished from each other in clear terms; their qualitative difference seems not to have ever been emphasized. Rather, the disparity between them is said to be more of a quantitative than a qualitative nature. In terms of religious doctrines, the Chinese view of natural gods, like that of all other sorts of spirits and deities, is associated with their understanding of '*qi*', the cosmic power that gives life to all things. Natural phenomena are therefore believed to be the manifestations of '*qi*'. This concept of *qi* thus provides nature worship with a doctrinal explanation. In this way, all natural bodies are believed to be able to attain supernatural attributes by manifesting their cosmic power and in universal 'oneness'.

It is apparent that all religious traditions or groups in China hold some kind of animistic view concerning natural bodies. A considerable number of gods of nature are thus said to be of a human origin, such as the Moon Goddess, *Chang-e*, who is said to be the wife of the great archer *Hou Yi*. By taking the elixir of immortality given to her husband by the Queen Mother of the West (*Xi wang mu*), she rose into the sky and became the moon goddess. Many other gods of nature (despite their human form) are said to originate from natural transformation processes; according to the *Completed Record of Immortals* (*Shenxian tongjian*) of the Ming dynasty, for example, many immortals (such as the Queen Mother of the West) described in these 'records' are born of the great primordial *qi*, before the world came into being.

Animistic spirits

By definition, spirits of living beings and things have originated from animals and plants. According to the sources from which they come, they can also be divided into various subgroups:

- spirits of wild animals such as the monkey and the fox;
- spirits of domestic animals such as the dog and the ox;
- spirits of aquatic animals such as the fish and the turtle;
- gods of mythical 'animals' such as the dragon, the phoenix and the unicorn;
- spirits of trees and plants such as the peach and plum tree;
- spirits of flowers such as the narcissus and the peony.

Apart from the dragon, the phoenix and the unicorn, the spirits of animals and plants are in general assigned to a much lower level of the pantheon than gods of nature or human deities. These are mostly referred to as '*jing*' (goblins), '*ling*' (fairies) or even '*guai*' (demons) rather than '*shen*' (gods, or divine beings), with occasionally some exceptions in the cases of tree gods (*shu shen*) and flower goddesses (*hua shen*). Lower as these spirits are, they are nevertheless part of the Chinese pantheon and possess supernatural powers of different degrees. They are worshipped either because they are feared, or because they are useful for humans to reach a certain end, or because they are perceived to be beneficial in general to a local community. All these spirits may have a fully transfigured human form or a half human figure, and can demonstrate extraordinary abilities such as flying, driving wind or calling in rain. Their power depends on how much and how long they have cultivated their *qi* or whether or not they have fully attained *Dao*. Although they are bound to the order of the Jade Emperor, they can sometimes behave wickedly and cause undue disasters to the people; this behaviour would lead to severe punishment, such as being banished to a lower level of the pantheon or to the human or animal level or even being executed. If their powers were impressively manifested and made known, a shrine or shrines might be built for them by local people. However, if their power is in some way weakened, or no longer effective, the temple or shrine will be left unrepaired and neglected.

Two famous syncretic novels of the Ming-Qing period, the *Journey to the West* (*Xi You ji*) by Wu Cheng-en (1505–1580) and the *Affinity between Mirror and Flower* (*Jinghua yuan*) by Li Ruzhen (1763–1830) provide us with the most colourful illustration of the Chinese belief in the spirits of animals, trees and flowers. A central theme running through the *Journey to the West* is the battles between 'good' spirits of animals (Monkey transformed from a stone, Pig and Sandy who incarnated from heavenly gods) and the evil spirits (the bear, elephant, wolf, the old plum tree, the flower and so on). *The Affinity between Mirror and Flower* is more of a Daoist nature, starting with the story that the supreme flower goddess and her 99 fellow goddesses were exiled to the human realm by the Jade Emperor for allowing flowers to blossom against seasons under the pressure of the infamous empress (Wu Zetian, 624–705), and they were to experience hardship before being allowed to return to the immortal realm. These novels reflect the two sides of the Chinese belief in the spirits of living things and beings: one is negative, and the other positive. On the negative side, the spirits are believed to be demons or personifications of evil forces who cause hurt to humans to benefit themselves. On the positive side, however, they are viewed as good companions for humans, and compassionately respond to human suffering.

It is a common animistic belief that having absorbed the essence of Heaven and Earth for a long enough period of time, natural bodies such as rocks, and animals, plants, flowers and so on would gain a spiritual life and then incarnate to the human world. No longer a spirit, the incarnated would experience all the happiness and sorrow of a human. The most famous example of this is the story of the hero and heroine of *The Dream of the Red Chamber* who are said to be the incarnations of the Stone and the Crimson Pearl Flower from the Fairy World. Watered with sweet dew each day in the spirit world, the Crimson Pearl Flower came to life and assumed the form of a beautiful girl. Owing her (spirit) life to the Stone (who dripped the sweet dew upon her), she told herself that having nothing to give him in return, 'the only way in which I could perhaps repay him would be with the tears shed during the whole of a mortal life if he and I were ever to be reborn as human in the world below.' This was the beginning of what led to a great (and sad) love story between them (Hawkes, 1973:53).

Human deities

In comparison with natural and animistic gods who remain more or less stable throughout history and legend, individual human deities change in time, some enduring for centuries all over the country while others acquire only a local fame, even passing into oblivion after a short time. These deities include legendary, historical and fictional figures, who achieved the status of a deity or god in different ways and according to different traditions, as in the following three subgroups:

- various immortals of a Daoist origin such as the famous Eight Immortals (*ba xian*), the three immortals of Good Fortune, Riches and Longevity (*fu, lu, shou*);
- sages, great heroes or statesmen who attained divinity through great achievements and virtues, such as Guanyü and Mazu;
- buddhas and *bodhisattvas* of a Buddhist origin.

A number of Daoist immortals are said to have originated from nature or natural transformation; the majority of them, however, are actual or legendary historical figures who attained Dao through self-cultivation, mysterious encounters, inner or outer alchemy or magical herbs. One of the earliest collections which described these immortals was *The Biographies of Immortals* (*Shenxian zhuan*) by Ge Hong (284–343); the number included in this compilation was dwarfed by those later amassed in this field in the Ming and Qing period, however, which gathered together hagiographies, stories, legends and records concerning the lives and extraordinary experiences of as many as 700 immortals. In folk-religion, immortals (*xian*) and gods (*shen*) are not specifically distinguished from each other; natural gods, Confucian sages and Buddhist deities are sometimes also included in the category of (Daoist) 'immortals'.

Confucianism does not in general encourage the worship of gods or immortals. Nevertheless, in popular parlance, Confucian sages, wise men and heroes are also ranked as semi-gods or even deities. Confucian views of immortality are very much indebted to an early saying recorded in the *Spring and Autumn Annals*, which establishes the principle that by means of 'virtue', 'achievement' and 'words', one can achieve immortality, as Wing-tsit Chan confirms that 'Chinese belief in the immortality of influence has not changed since ancient times, and is still the conviction of educated Chinese' (Chan, 1963:13). All these three ways of achieving immortality were soon attributed to the work of the sage, who was seen as the paragon of Confucian virtues. The Confucian sage begins as an ordinary human but ultimately attains a spiritual status.

This is confirmed by the *Doctrine of the Mean*, one of the Confucian four books: being sincere (one of the important Confucian virtues), the sage can fully develop their nature, which enables them in turn to fully develop the nature of others and of all things. In this way the sage is said to be able to 'assist in the transforming and nourishing process of Heaven and Earth', and 'can thus form a trinity with Heaven and Earth' (Chan, 1963:108). With such a spiritual power, it is natural that Confucian sages and wise men were revered and worshipped in history as special deities. Gradually sacrifices made in their honour were extended to all others who had done great work for humanity and contributed to the evolution and continuation of civilization and culture. These cultural heroes were treated in the same way as deities or gods in folklore and communal life, honoured either in Confucian or other kinds of temples or shrines dedicated to their worship.

Popular Mahayana Buddhism in China departs significantly from the early Theravada Buddhist teaching that gods or demons are not relevant and that only individual enlightenment or ignorance counts. Instead a huge pantheon developed, including buddhas, bodhisattvas, arats, kings of heaven and so on. Most of these are said to be of a human origin (Indian or Chinese), achieving the status of deities through reincarnation in numerous impeccable lives. Like Daoist immortals and Confucian heroes, every Buddhist deity serves a purpose, such as deliverance from a dangerous situation, rescuing suffering souls from hell into paradise or lifting good persons from mortality to eternity. Buddha Amitabha of the West Paradise, for example, is believed to appear at the words 'Glory to the Amitabha' when in danger or before death. In the same way, the Buddha of the Future, Maitreya is believed to be coming at the end of the age to save all the believers, while Bhaisajyaguru (the Buddha of Healing or Medicine) is thought to cure illnesses and provide medicine upon prayer. Bodhisattva Ksitigarbha (the King of Hell, who has his residence in Mountain *Jiuhua*) is attributed with power to soothe the pain and misery of the hell and to speed up the progress of suffering souls in their journey towards reincarnation. In particular, Bodhisattva Avalokitésvara is perhaps the most popular Buddhist deity in the Mahayana Buddhist world, worshipped widely in India, Tibet, Sri Lanka or Southeast Asia. In Chinese characters, this name transliterates as 'Guan Yin' or 'Guan Shi Yin', meaning 'listening to the sounds of the world'. From the ninth century onwards, this male deity was gradually transformed in the Chinese belief system into a popular goddess of compassion, who not only saves suffering souls regardless of class and gender, but also undertakes the multi-dimensional task of fulfilling the prayers of believers, such as granting a son to a couple, providing medicine for the sick, warding off evil or villainous attacks (Yü, 2001:1–5).

Belief in gods, spirits and deities continues to hold sway in contemporary China, albeit at a much reduced degree or within more confined areas. This continuing belief may have been strengthened by new martial art novels by Hong Kong and Taiwanese writers, which have become extremely popular among Mainland people since the 1980s; these novels convey (in an accessible way) traditional myths and legends concerning various gods and spiritual beings. In particular, the 15 novels by Jin Yong 'are considered more than just *kung fu* stories. Their pages burst with fantastic knight-errant tales of heroic swordsmen and beautiful heroines, intermingling romance, tragedy and comedy with Chinese and religious values' (*The Taipei Times*, 8 May 2007). Through these and other popular novels, mainland Chinese readers have not only learned Chinese culture, history, language, calligraphy, arts, music, traditional costumes, cuisine and martial arts, but also appreciated religious beliefs, gods or immortals which were forgotten for a long time.

In rural areas where atheistic education has been less enthusiastically pursued than in cities, beliefs and deities remain influential to an extent and have been visibly revived, although sometimes in the guise of saving traditional culture. As one example, Feng Jicai (a renowned scholar in contemporary literature and cultural studies) argues strenuously against the ideologically motivated practice of dismissing 'pictures of god' [*shen xiang*] as superstitious, insisting that 'beliefs are the spiritual pillar supporting folk life'; for him 'divine pictures externalise the spiritual pursuits and the ideal realm of ordinary people, demonstrating vividly the interrelation between humans and human views of nature' (Feng, 2009:54).

Divinity in humans

The religious belief of the Chinese is strongly fatalistic; it is generally believed that humans are subject to the will of a supreme god, or to the dictates of gods or spirits, and that human destiny is predetermined or cannot be changed purely through human effort. This fatalistic view is nevertheless balanced by the counter-affirmation that humans do have a vital role to play in managing secular as well as spiritual matters. It is believed that humans possess an innate spiritual nobility, and this 'spiritual nobility calls for persistence and effort' (Fingarette, 1972:3). It is further believed that if self-cultivation is practised along the path to *Dao*, then a state can be attained of possessing supreme spiritual qualities and capabilities.

In Chinese traditions, it has long been held that humans are not a normal species of creature; rather they are mediators of Heaven and Earth, and are thus assigned the role of completing what has been initiated. Hence, in the Daoist classic of *Daode jing*, we read of the potential greatness that humans can attain: 'Tao [Dao] is great. Heaven is great. Earth is great. And the king [humankind in a different version of the text] is also great. There are four great things in the universe, and the king [representative of humans] is one of them' (Chan, 1963:152). Further, the Confucian commentaries of the *Book of Changes* list humans as one of the Three Ultimate: 'The respective functions of the six hexagram lines embody the Way of the Three Ultimates [Heaven, Earth and the Human]' (de Bary and Bloom, 1999:321). Additionally, the Han syncretic scholar Dong Zhongshu proclaimed that: 'Heaven, Earth, and humankind are the foundation of all living things. Heaven engenders all living things, Earth nourishes them, and humankind completes them' (de Bary Bloom, 1999:299). Shao Yong (1011–77) of the Song dynasty went further and specifically deprecated rigid separation of the sage from humans. For him, 'Man, too, is a creature (like other creatures), and the sage, too, is a man (like other men) . . . But man is the most perfect of creatures, and the sage is the most perfect of men' (Fung, 1953, Vol. 2:465). Thus, scholars have throughout history confirmed and re-confirmed the unique position assigned to humans beings in the universe; it has hence gradually become an embedded belief in China that humans are one of the 'three ultimates of the world', not totally submissive to spiritual powers.

From this perspective, it follows that while under the sway of spiritual powers, humans nevertheless can actively engage with these powers, striving to change their own fate to prove the worth of their earthly life and activity. Fatalism and optimism are here juxtaposed to form a gigantic paradox; it is within this kind of paradox that various religious programmes and ideologies operate. Religious optimism about human ability to shape personal destiny makes it possible for the Chinese to grasp their real worth in the transformation of the universe, and to see their place in a human-divine alliance that enables them to surpass the constraints of the physical body and mind. While all traditions in China tend towards this alliance, Daoists in particular espouse an explicit spiritual pathway, which pushes the earthly being to the edge of eternity. For them 'the human body is conceived of as a microcosm, within which the *yin* and *yang* and the eight trigrams exist, just as they exist in the universe as a whole. The means to immortality, therefore, can wholly be found within oneself' (Fung, 1953:431).

If the 'means to immortality' are 'within oneself', then this raises the interesting question posed by Shryock, concerning how to differentiate gods from humans: 'Do gods differ from men only in quality; that is, do they possess the same attributes as men, only in higher degree?' A positive answer to this question, he acknowledges, would render 'any distinction between gods and men merely arbitrary'; in other words, humans can be safely said to possess a kind of divinity, however much lower in degree this might be. Shryock places his discussion of this fascinating distinction in the context of conceptual differences between East and West; the English world use the terms 'natural' and 'supernatural' to designate human beings and gods respectively, with the latter meaning either 'extraordinary and unusual', or 'non-mechanical' (Shryock, 1966:79–80).

The concept of 'human divinity' as understood by the Chinese could thus sound self-contradictory in a monotheistic context where the gap between the human and the divine is far beyond human ability to fill. No such an unbridgeable chasm exists in a Chinese context, however; rather the divine and the human are mutually contained. In this sense, 'human divinity' denotes that by nature humans beings contain a potential for divinity, or that they are born possessing a divine seed which (with the help of disciplined efforts) will grow into spiritual quality and thence 'immortality'.

A central principle in the beliefs of Chinese religion is therefore that this divine potential enables humans to attain a spiritual dimension; through specific ways of cultivation, they can thus transmute into immortals, sages, deities, buddhas or other kinds of spiritual beings. Divine and human entities are hence not perceived as belonging to two totally separated realms; rather they represent two levels within one existence. From this perspective, those who have cultivated themselves to the utmost or made great contribution to human welfare would be apotheosized to deities, as shown in Figure 7.3 where an ordinary human was deified as a god and received sacrifices because he helped build up a town temple when alive. Meanwhile gods or spirits who have violated moral and religious precepts would be 'downgraded' to a mortal existence. A sense of fluidity thus manifests itself along the continuum between 'human' and 'divine' in the religious world view of the Chinese.

It is belief in human potential that has opened the door for humans to enter the kingdom of godly knowledge. It is believed that either with a special endowment or through intensive spiritual discipline, certain humans can

Figure 7.3 A shrine to Lord Ji

divine the will of Heaven or decipher the hidden secret codes of the world; in particular they can know in advance the destiny or fate that is believed to have been determined for each individual at birth. This is a belief which underlies the huge popularity of fortune-telling and divination, one of the most fascinating aspects of religious life in China. With such knowledge, humans may journey further towards communication and interaction with spiritual and cosmic powers and other kinds of god or spirit. This communication with gods or the spirits of the dead forms an integral part of ritual and sacrifice, while interactive relationships between mortals and Heaven underlie the whole structure of Chinese religio-politics.

The conviction that human destiny is predetermined dominates the religious views of the Chinese. It is a popular belief that the success or failure of not only a political cause, but also all human affairs is ultimately determined by the will of Heaven. Heaven's will dictates that each of them has an allotted span (*shu*), which once used up would bring a dynasty, an individual's life or a particular event to an end. It is also believed that whether or not this allotted span can be changed or prolonged also depends on the will of Heaven or the order of the Jade Emperor. Those wise beings who have astrological knowledge can accordingly calculate individual destiny by observing his or her corresponding star in the sky. It is believed that the degree of brightness of a specific star reveals the life strength of any person; when death comes, the star of the person will fall from the sky.

While admitting this fatalism on the one hand it is equally important to note that acknowledgement of fixed destiny is only the first step; the step which follows is to change the seemingly unchangeable fate or improve it. It is for this reason that a great number of religious thinkers and believers are (in one way or another) inspired by Confucius to 'do things that are known impossible' (Chan, 1963:43); namely, to change, or attempt to change, personal destiny or lifespan. This effort is ritually called 'prayer and plea' (*qi xiang*), into which insight is provided by the *Romance of the Three Kingdoms* where Zhuge Liang (181–234), one of the most beloved and influential characters in Chinese history, is said to have tried to regain his ebbing life force through this ritual. Seriously ill, Zhuge Liang observed his star in the firmament which told him that his life was about to end. With an attempt to avert it, Zhuge Liang asked to prepare a ritual 'to invoke the seven Stars of the North', saying that 'If my master-lamp remain alight for seven days, then is my life to be prolonged.' In prayer Zhuge Liang 'humbly indicted a declaration to the Great Unknowable' hoping that Heaven 'will graciously listen and extend the number of his days' while performing the ritual by pacing 'the magic steps, the steps of "the four" and the "seven" stars of Ursa Major' at night. Unfortunately in the sixth night, his lamp of fate was extinguished by one of his generals, and he 'threw down the sword and sighed, saying "Life and death are foreordained; no prayer can alter them"' (Brewitt-Taylor, 1925: Vol.2:460).

Despite Zhuge Liang's resignation to his fate above, Chinese religionists are nevertheless encouraged to manipulate spiritual forces or gods for their own use. It is a firm belief that those who have cultivated themselves to the utmost will gain spiritual power, and will be like gods, who can rearrange cosmic forces and change certain conditions. The *Book of Changes* confirms this belief, stating that: 'The character of the great man is identical with that of Heaven and Earth; his brilliance is identical with that of the sun and the moon; his order is identical with that of the four seasons, and his good and evil fortunes are identical with those of spiritual beings' (Chan, 1963:264). Like Confucians, Daoists also teach 'how to nurture and perfect potency'; the one who has perfected his or her potency would be 'capable of making the rain fall and the sun shine ... Whenever he solicits, Nature responds (Lagerwey, 1986:7). Zhuge Liang, as described above, might not be able to change his allotted life span and extend the years of his life, but, according to the legend, he did possess the ability to 'call the winds and summon the rains' and indeed was able to 'procure a strong south-east gale for three days and three nights' in order to help the alliance to defeat the enemy (Brewitt-Taylor, 1925, Vol.1:509). Stories of this kind are manifestations of well-established religious traditions, and often illustrate the deepest meaning of these traditions.

The concept of human divinity in a Chinese context may also determine what mode of religious belief should continue and what should be brought to an end. In a sense, every religion is intended to serve the needs of humans, spiritual or material, although different traditions have different ways to do so. Some may demand total submission to a supreme God, while others may invoke spiritual power to reach this end. Ordinary Chinese people may juxtapose these traditions with a pragmatic cunning, demonstrating an utmost character of 'utilitarian' religion. The 'value' of a particular deity is judged according to his or her ability or effectiveness in meeting urgent needs, and this meeting of needs determines which god or goddess should be worshipped and how often. The perceived effectiveness of a divine being to protect or bless also determines how big a temple should be built in dedication to him or her, and indeed how high a position he or she would gain in the hierarchic pantheon.

Evidence shows that this multi-dimensional meaning of the concept of human divinity continues to be influential in contemporary China, which is confirmed, for example by a survey in 2008 by the Beijing Horizon-key company on religious beliefs and practices in 40 cities and towns, which found that 12.1 per cent of the surveyed families said they worshipped their ancestors' tablets in their homes. For the statue of Mao Zedong (1893–1976), the leader of the Chinese Communist Party till 1976, the figure is 11.5 per cent; the statue of the Buddha then follows at 9.9 per cent, with the god of wealth at 9.3 per cent and the god of earth at 8.8per cent (http://www.nfcmag.com/articles/1442, accessed on 12 June 2009). These statistics confirm that traditional religious beliefs continue to be held by about 10 per cent of the city population on the Mainland, with newly developed faith in Mao standing at the same level. The deification of Mao had already begun by the end of the 1980s, and was so powerful that it had to be suppressed in the 1990s. It was reported by Reuters on 7 December 1995 for example that a huge temple compound of 120,000 square metres dedicated to his worship at a cost of 20 million *yuan* was built by thousands of farmers in the county of Liuyang, Hunan province, the home province of Mao. 'It looks just like a Buddhist temple', it was affirmed, where local people 'burn incense, make offerings and kowtow to the image of Mao'. However, this was denounced by the local government, as 'superstitious and feudalistic', who forced such practices to be abandoned. Mao's deification illustrates again the power of folk-religion in sustaining traditional beliefs, telling us how religion has taken on a new form and yet contains the same aspiration of the human towards the divine. At the same time, there is a special irony in the easy transformation of a fiercely anti-religious figure into the object of popular worship, with all the functions a traditional god is believed to do for ordinary people.

Questions for discussion

1. By what means are traditional religious beliefs handed down and how do they continue to influence people's lives?
2. What are the 'three pillars' around which Chinese religion has evolved?
3. What is the Chinese pantheon? How do the Chinese belief that an interactive relationship is constructed between deities and humans?
4. How did the Chinese belief in nature gods develop from ancient religious ideology?
5. What roles are human deities believed to play in religious life in China?
6. How can the so-called inherent contradiction in the term of human divinity be explained?
7. What reasons have been given for the belief that humans (or certain humans) are able to influence the natural and the spiritual world?
8. What can we learn from the deification of Mao in contemporary China?

8

Religious Practices

The relationship between belief and practice is a contentious issue among scholars. Some argue that people participating in the same rituals may hold different beliefs because ritual can take place with no concern for meaning (Seligman, et al., 2008:4). It is true that people who engage in a religious practice may have different ideas and motivations for doing so. However, as the internal dimension of a religious system, beliefs must manifest themselves through external practices one way or another; and religious practices can consequently reveal, at least partially, the extent of religious commitment and externalize what is hidden within the belief system. There is an interaction between belief and practice and this interaction constitutes the dynamics of a religious tradition, deepening its understanding of the world, bringing it to face-to-face encounters with other traditions and accounting for the unity between diversity and consistency within itself. This is especially true for Chinese religion. The pragmatic nature of Chinese beliefs means that they naturally long for results and seek harmony between the internal and the external, between the finite and the infinite, or more characteristically, between humans and gods, and between the natural and the supernatural. In this search the Chinese develop their multi-dimensional practices.

Practice and spirituality

What is religious practice? Broadly speaking, all activities, mental or physical, that are motivated by a spiritual belief and are intended as a communication with, or an access to, the holy or supra-human realm are religious practices. In terms of subject, religious practices are often presented as two types: personal and communal. In addition to meditation, personal practices refer to the behaviour or conduct that expresses an individual's reverence or gratitude towards spiritual forces or powers, in whatever form these forces or powers might be, with the hope that this would help the individual to transcend his or her limitations, either physical, or mental or spiritual. Communal practices are carried out in groups and range from family/clan gatherings, village or town celebrations, religious community's congregations, to the grand ceremonies of the state. These activities reflect, on a much larger scale, the same wish as personal practices, which are intended to gain, through engaging in certain types of activities, the spiritual blessing or protection for the community in question.

In terms of process, religious practices can be divided into the organized and the unorganized. Organized practices, for example, communal celebration of a god's birthday, are arranged or co-ordinated in advance and in process by a group of seniors or religious masters who are responsible for the procedure of a special event or action, or a series of events and actions that are intended to reach the preset spiritual goal concerning deliverance or the relieving of suffering. Although the majority of religious practices are organized, there are also unorganized practices that often take place spontaneously as occasional gatherings or events. These gatherings or events are by definition not bound by any pre-set procedures, although they are consciously performed as a way to a clearly defined spiritual goal. People participate in these gatherings or events when they happen to be there or are drawn in by chance; they may or may not follow any rules, either because there are no such rules or because these rules are not clearly specified.

A visible factor distinguishing organized practices from unorganized ones is ritual. A gathering or event would appear to be an organized practice if it is enforced by the organizer to follow a set of commonly accepted rituals. Therefore an organized practice is most likely a ritual event or action, while the ritual element would be in general missing from an unorganized practice. Spontaneity characterises non-ritual practices.

Individual or communal, organized or unorganized, ritual-bound or no-ritual, all these subdivisions are meaningful only for a theoretical analysis of religious practice. In reality, the boundaries between them are seldom clearly or consciously drawn. For example, communal practice cannot be separated from individuals, and personal engagement is essential to both organized and unorganized activities. A sort of procedure is required for any religious practice, whether the people who participate in them are consciously aware of it or not.

Apart from these features, religious practice in China is also characterized by its cultural expectation. Taking place in a holistic culture, religious practice is often intermingled with other kinds of practice, such as social, political, educational and even economic. A gathering or event may be encompassed with all of them while remaining religious if it contains a spiritual commitment and employs mental or behavioural tools to facilitate the human transcending of limitations. In general, the commitment (belief) and the process (practice) together form the internal and external dimensions of the religious way of life, which is manifested as Chinese spirituality.

This spirituality is manifested through different paths, and people are encouraged to choose their own means to an immediate end, which range from driving off evil force, gaining godly blessings, to self-cultivation. Different paths require different activities. Having been commonly accepted and engaged in, these activities nevertheless diversify as different practices. The huge variety of personal practices in China can be seen from a literally exaggerated passage in the *Journey to the West*, which through the mouth of a religious Patriarch claims that there are 360 divisions of the practice. According to this Patriarch, these practices, although unable to lead to immortality, may all result in spiritual illumination. Among the divisions, four are prominent. First, there is an art division which consists of summoning immortals and working the planchette, divining by manipulating yarrow stalks and learning the secrets of pursuing good and avoiding evil. Secondly, there is a learning division composed of reading scriptures or reciting prayers, consulting priests or conjuring up saints, and this includes the practices propagated by the Confucian school, Buddhism, Daoism, the Yin-yang school, Mohism and the medicine school. Thirdly, there is a meditation division which is aimed at cultivating fasting and abstinence, quiescence and inactivity, engaging in cross-legged sitting, restraint of language and pursuing a vegetarian diet, as well as practising *yoga*, exercising standing or prostrating, entering into complete stillness and contemplating solitary confinement. Fourthly, there is an action division, which includes gathering the *yin* to nourish the *yang*, practising internal alchemy (cultivating the vital energy within the body) and external alchemy (producing immortal elixir by refining chemical elements) (Yu, 1977, vol.1:84–5).

Some of these practices may have taken on a form of secular activities, but they are in essence religious because they are part of the spiritual pursuit; namely, seeking personal enlightenment or enhancing one's spiritual as well as material well-being. They are driven by a desire to communicate with or to gain an access to the divine in order either to transform one's existential conditions or to transcend physical and spiritual limitations. One of the primary motives in communicating with or achieving a kind of relationship with the divine world is to know and change one's own future or destiny through various means or tools. From this motive, various practices develop which can be broadly described as divinatory.

In seeking spiritual and material well-being, the Chinese have furthered their perception or belief that humanity and spirits partake of the same cosmic power and that by taking a right path and practice, anybody is able to reach the infinite reality. Religious practice is therefore regarded as the bridge to link the human and the spiritual world, or as the necessary tool to facilitate the human gaining of spiritual (*shen*) power, or to obtain the grace and blessing of divine beings. Among the most commonly engaged practices, sacrifices, rites of passage and divination are of particular importance because they reflect the three key dimensions of Chinese spirituality. Sacrifices are performed to express a strong desire to seek harmony with the divine world, either through expressing gratitude towards deities, or by redeeming sins or wrong behaviours. To meet this desire, humans often prostrate themselves in front of supernatural forces or their embodiment (god statues, spiritual tablets, sacred places, etc), or offer precious things (sacrifices) to them. The rites of passage provide an individual with the necessary assistance to become socially and spiritually recognized, guiding him or her through various crucial stages in life. Divination demonstrates the possibility of human communication with the unknown or unseen forces. Through this communication, it is believed, human destiny can be known, and this foreknowledge is employed in taking up appropriate action to avoid disasters or in making a wise choice to gain good fortune.

Meanings of sacrifice

Sacrifice is perhaps the oldest way to communicate with divine beings or forces. There are three characters designated for sacrifice in classical Chinese: (1) *ji*, which refers to the sacrifice to earthly deities, shows a hand holding a piece of meat to offer to the spirit on a sacred altar; (2) *si*, which portrays a combination of a sacred altar and a human embryo, indicates human submission to heavenly spirits; and (3) *xiang*, a pictograph for the ancestral temple, refers to the sacrifice to ancestors (Yao, 2000:193). These words reveal to us that sacrifice was primarily offered to three categories of spiritual powers: heavenly gods such as the star gods or the god of wind, earthly deities such as the god of earth and the spirits of ancestors.

In an early stage, sacrifice simply involved presenting wine and grain as a thanksgiving to spiritual forces, as we read from the *Book of Poetry*: 'When our barns are full, and our stacks can be counted by tens of myriads, we proceed to make spirits and prepare grain, for offerings and sacrifice . . . Thus seeking to increase our bright happiness' (Legge, 1899:365). Gradually, out of the practice, sophisticated systems of ritual and a variety of sacrifices (personal, familial and state) developed. Later ritual texts provided detailed descriptions for each category of the deities, which were illustrated by Wang Chong (?27–100 CE) of the Latter Han era who tells us how sacrifices were prescribed in the ritual texts, how they were practised in his time and how these acts should be understood:

> Wood was burned on the great altar as a sacrifice to Heaven, a victim was buried in the great pit as a sacrifice to Earth . . . The ruler of the world sacrifices to all the spirits, the prince only as long as they are within their territories . . .
>
> . . . The emperor treats Heaven like his father and Earth like his mother. Comfortably to human customs he practises filial piety, which accounts for the sacrifices to Heaven and Earth. In the matter of Mountains and Rivers and the subsequent deities the offerings presented to them are in appreciation of their deserts. A living man distinguishing himself is rewarded, ghosts and spirits which are deserving have their sacrifices . . . The spirits of the Land and Grain are rewarded for their kindness in letting all the things grow.
>
> . . . If we love some one in our heart, we give him to eat and to drink, and if we love ghosts and spirits, we sacrifice to them. (quoted in Shryock, 81)

By the end of imperial history, many types of sacrifices had become an officially sponsored exercise of rituals and official duties. According to Williams, these rituals

> consisted in bathing, fasting, prostrations, prayers, and thanksgiving offerings of incense, lighted candles, gems, fruits, cooked food, salted vegetables and steamed bread, libations of wine, sacrifices of whole oxen, sheep and pigs, sometimes deer and other game and, on certain occasions, a burnt sacrifice of a whole bullock, accompanied by music, and posturing or dancing. (Williams, 1913:17)

In traditional China almost all religious rituals carried with them a sacrificial element, and sacrifices were highly ritualized. Sacrificial rituals thus became an essential feature of Chinese culture, not only standing at the centre of religious practice, but also becoming the cornerstone of familial, social and political life. By offering wine, food, fruits, meat etc. to ancestors, spirits or gods, sacrifices made a perfect sense for the Chinese, in agreement with their belief that gods or the spirits of the dead would need the same materials for living in the spiritual world as a living human. Of sacrificial offerings, meat is of prominence not only because it was believed that meat had special power in contacting the 'other' in the spiritual world, but also because it was assumed that the fragrance of burnt meat would rise up and be consumed by all the gods, but particularly by the spirits of ancestors. This changed significantly, however, after the spreading of Buddhist and Daoist vegetarianism, and it was accepted in folk-religion that Buddhist and Daoist deities would enjoy only the fragrant smell of incense, plus perhaps on occasion vegetarian food.

Traditionally sacrifice was offered to all divine and spiritual objects, all the powers that were perceived to affect human life. While sacrificial rituals were part of tradition and expected to be carried out routinely, there was a requirement for reverence and sincerity in the heart of the presenters and participants. Confucius placed a great emphasis on sacrificial ritual, but at the same time he went a step further to require the internal devotion and personal experience. He endorsed the saying that 'Sacrifice to the spirits as if they were present' and commented from his own experience that 'If I am not present at the sacrifice, as if there were no sacrifice' (de Bary and Bloom, 1999:48). Xunzi explained the meaning of the sacrifice to ancestors from a moral point of view: 'The sacrificial rites give expression to the feelings of remembrance and longing. They are the perfection of loyalty, good faith, love and reverence, and the flourishing of ritual deportment and refined demeanor' (de Bary and Bloom, 1999:177). In later ritual texts, two tendencies are specifically singled out as contrary to the nature of sacrifice: 'importunateness' and 'indifference', because the former is not consistent with reverence, while the latter would lead to forgetting sacrifices altogether (Legge, 1885, xxviii:210).

On the other hand, there was an apparently pragmatic dimension in sacrifice. Sacrifice was often seen as a gift or offering to spiritual forces or divine beings *in exchange of* their blessing and protection. The quality and quantity of sacrifices and the scale of the ritual were therefore determined not only by the hierarchal ranks of the gods in question in the pantheon but also by the perceived or expected spiritual and material return. The traditional three state sacrifices (to Heaven and Earth, to royal ancestors and to Confucius) were the most splendid and elaborate, involving full sacrifices of various kinds. Other official or popular sacrifices, such as those to the sun and moon, to mountain or river gods, to agricultural deities, etc., were presented with less offering in quantity and in kinds. Still less were the sacrifices to local gods, familial deities, popular immortals, trade patron gods, etc.

However different in scale and quantity, all categories of sacrifice would normally involve food, wine, meat and later, incense. There were two purposes for these offerings. First, offerings were intended to provide what the deities or the spirits of ancestors were supposed to need in the spiritual world. Secondly, they were intended as an expression of reverence for the deities in the hope that gods or spiritual forces would be pleased and would therefore give their blessing to, or dissolve their hostility towards, humans.

Although sacrifices were more or less stable throughout history, they differed when applied to different kinds of deities or spiritual forces, and these differences reflect in a subtle way what was believed by the Chinese. According to Wolf (cosmic) gods (who inhabit heaven and reside at temples) were offered uncooked (or whole) food, while ghosts (who inhabit purgatory) and ancestors (the senior members of one's own line of descent who are believed to be either in paradise or in permanent purgatory after death) were offered cooked food; sacrifices to ghosts were made outside the home and temple, while those to gods and ancestors were inside; ancestors were given an even number of incense sticks, while ghosts and gods were given an odd number of sticks (Wolf, 1974:7).

In contemporary times many of these sacrifices are already abolished or neglected in Mainland China, but evidence shows that in recent years some of them have come back either with official sponsorship or as popular practices. It seems that sacrifices are becoming important events again, for the state as well as for ordinary people, with different underlying reasons and motives. As we have described in previous chapters, yearly sacrifices (*ji*) are made to Confucius, the Red and Yellow Emperors, to other cultural heroes and in particular to ancestors. These ceremonial activities and events involve delicate offerings and are supported, or approved, or tacitly allowed by the government. Other kinds of sacrifices are made in conjunction with the celebration of secular or religious festivals popular with local people and communities. Along with the progress of material life, sacrifices to ancestors and gods have also changed, and the things that are offered as sacrifice now include new facilities and new items such as paper money, gold treasures, clothes, shoes and socks, and other gifts such as headgear and jewellery, cars, luxury villas with car park and swimming pool (http://www.sznews.com, accessed on 30 March 2009).

The intermingling of secular and religious ceremonies has also made sacrificial rituals less spiritual and more social or mundane. The atheistic ideological influence and political interference in Mainland China have significantly diluted traditional religious practices and have led many of them in the direction of secular pursuits. However, this is not new in contemporary times; it has been this way for thousands of years. The reason why the Chinese accept this way is embedded in their practical spirituality: both in history and at the present, all sacrifices are assigned with both religious and secular purposes; all sacrificial activities always combine these two aspects in an explainable way, and sometime even hide their religious content behind the communal and familial names. For example a Daoist sacrifice conducted in Zhangzhou, Fujian province in 1986 was entitled 'Jade Emperor Five-Day Offering: Peace to the Family' (Kenneth, 1989:51). Many sacrifices deliver their messages through ritual performances, while their spiritual commitment is submerged, as Watson has pointed out: 'Performance . . . took precedence over belief –it mattered little what one believed about death or the afterlife as long as the rites were performed properly' (Watson, 1988:4). In an extreme case, the spiritual purposes of sacrifice could be totally overshadowed by practical needs, and thus sacrificial rituals seem to have become a social, practical and personal rather than a religious or spiritual matter.

Thanksgiving and redeeming

The religious purpose for sacrifice is always multiple. In making offerings to spirits, sacrificial rituals are intended to pray for the blessing from supernatural powers and ancestors, to request help from them to ward off evil influence, to remember the dead who made great contributions to the state or the family and to satisfy and comfort the lonely ghosts and to salvage the suffering ghosts. Diverse and yet mutually included, these aims can be roughly divided into two kinds: thanksgiving and redeeming, although there is no clearly defined separation between these two and many practices in fact involve both.

A variety of sacrifices are intended to express gratitude toward gods or deities, in the hope that spiritual blessing will continue and godly protection will be effected. For these rites the Daoist ritual of *jiao* can be a good illustration. *Jiao* is a Daoist sacrifice, which according to Pas is 'the greatest, most splendid, elaborate, and colourful of all the ritual events taking place in a

Chinese community today'; it often lasts three or five days or even longer, in particular as 'celebrations of thanksgiving' or as 'rituals to exorcise the spirits of disease, especially of epidemics'; in general it is intended to express gratitude to spiritual forces and 'to ensure that the new cycle of time will be blessed by the highest powers above (Taoist Triad), who control the creative powers of the universe' (Pas, 1998:101–3). The *jiao* ritual often starts with 'zhai', 'fasting and purification' that are intended as an atonement for evil-doing, which is then followed by sacrificial offerings to the spirit world.

> Taking the broadest view, the difference in the results sought by the two [forms of ritual] is simply that their emphases are not the same: The *chai* [*zhai*] places its emphasis upon the prayers of the individual for blessings and the salvation of the dead; whereas the emphasis of the *Chiao* is upon the prayers of the public (i.e., the community) for the averting calamities and ensuring tranquillity.
> (Liu Chih-wan, 1974:24, quoted in Thompson, 91)

This set of sacrificial practice is more than what it literally means. It is intended to be the rites of cosmic renewal, or rites of community renewal, and has great religious and political consequences for Daoist religion, local communities and even the whole nation. In fact, as early as the Song dynasty, a number of emperors asked renowned Daoist priests 'to perform these grand rituals on their behalf or on behalf of the whole population' (Pas, 1998:68). The first chapter of the famous novel *Water Margin* is about how an emperor of the Song dynasty sent his envoy to invite Heavenly Master Zhang in the Dragon and Tiger Mountain (located in current Jiangxi province) to the capital to conduct such a grand ritual for the whole nation to expulse 'plague spirits', during which the envoy mistakenly opened the Daoist 'prison' for the 108 heavenly and earthly spirits and released them into the world.

Although the current Communist government does not ask Daoist priests to conduct *jiao* ritual on behalf of the state or the nation, they have tentatively given their approval and support since the 1990s for Daoists to do so with the purposes of protecting the country and the nation, prolonging life and delivering the spirits of the dead, terminating disasters and avoiding calamities and praying for blessings and exercising thanksgiving (http://big5.xinhuanet.com/ziliao/2003-01/21/content_699284.htm). The first grand *jiao* sacrifice in recent decades was conducted at the headquarters of the China Daoist Association, the White Clouds Temple (*bai yun guan*) in Beijing on 17–26 September 1993, with the purpose of praying for world peace and for the protection of China and Chinese people. According to reports, it was performed by famous Daoist priests not only from seven temples in seven sacred mountains in Mainland China, but also from Hong Kong and Taiwan. During the ceremony, 1,200 gods or deities were worshiped at 10 altars with the following rituals performed: burning incense for informing the spiritual world of the upcoming ceremony; opening altars for informing the spiritual world of the sacrifice locations; inviting holy water for the usage of purification; unfolding the long narrow flags for guarding the descending deities; announcement to the spirits or deities on the worship list; purification of the sacred place by holy water; invitation of the sages; audience with the divine powers; submission to the star; presenting the list of sacrifices; folding the long narrow flags, and sending off the sages (http://big5.xinhuanet.com/gate/big5/news.xinhuanet.com/ziliao/ 2003-01/21/content_699284.htm, accessed on 15 July 2009).

There are also a great variety of atonement practices of which the festival of feasting ghosts is a good example. The feast for ghosts is a popular sacrifice involving almost all religious traditions in China. With different names such as 'zhong yuan' or Mid-Origin Festival in Daoism and popular religion, and 'yulan pen jie' or Ullambana Festival in Buddhism, it is intended to redeem and salvage 'suffering', 'homeless' and 'hungry' ghosts by providing them with food and to accelerate their reincarnation through ritual power. Taking place on the 15th day of the 7th month in the Lunar calendar when it is believed the gates of hell are open so that the spirits of the dead would come out to visit their beloved ones, this festival is also intended as ancestor worship and as a ritual to release the suffering of the deceased. The feast of ghosts combines elements from Confucian filial piety, Buddhist hell and reincarnation, Daoist salvation rituals, folklore of redeeming sins and popular practices in supporting religious orders. During the festival, donation to Buddhist and Daoist temples and offerings to the spirits of ancestors and to all ghosts and souls are made in order to transmute and absolve the suffering of the souls as well as to bring good fortune to local communities (Teiser, 1988:38).

In Daoism, the major part of the ritual comprises several steps: blessing the food displayed at the place outside and inside of the temple; singing songs at the foot of a platform; invoking the magical power of the Heavenly Worthy Who Saves from Distress, informing the souls and ghosts of the food provided for them and conducting various ritual acts to assist their consumption of the food. The 'ghost festival' in Buddhism developed out of the *Ullambana Sutra* which consists of a brief discourse given by the Buddha to the monk Maudgalyāyana on the practice of filial piety. Ullambana means 'deliverance from suffering', with a special reference to the salvation of all the tormented souls in hell. According to this sutra, having discovered his mother was reborn in the realms of pain and suffering, Maudgalyāyana went to the netherworld to relieve her from sufferings. However, although his mother was starving, all food provided to her would turn to ashes before coming to her mouth. Realizing that his own power was not enough to save her, Maudgalyāyana went to the Buddha who instructed him to make offerings to the assembled members of the Buddhist Order and to request them to pray along with him. By such an offering, the Buddha told Maudgalyāyana that not only his mother but his forefathers and kith and kin would also be able to escape suffering and attain eternal bliss and salvation (Ch'en, 1973:24–25).

As a popular practice, the ghost festival occupies an important position in the religious life of the Chinese people, and draws together every social class and expresses a challenging blend values (Teiser, 1988:xii). Apart from elaborate rituals and ceremonies by Daoists and Buddhists, local people also prepare ritualistic food offerings, burning incense and papier-mâché forms of material items such as clothes, gold and other fine goods for the returning spirits of the ancestors. Elaborate meals are served with empty seats for each of the deceased in the family, treating the deceased as if they were still living. Other festivities may include buying and releasing miniature paper boats and lotus lanterns on water, which signifies taking the lost souls on-board and delivering them to the Western Paradise.

Rites of passage

Sacrifices are intended for communicating with the spirit world. Apart from them, a variety of practices are concerned with personal well-being and spiritual growth. We have already listed four categories of such practices in the first section of this chapter as those that are aimed at accessing the infinite reality. The 'rites of passage' are yet another kind of practice, which are intended not only to instil a sense of holiness in the participants but also to narrate the religious significance of each crucial change throughout a life course. These changes are biological and physical, but at the same time are also social and spiritual, and are naturally marked by elaborate social etiquette and religious ritual.

The Chinese hold a holistic view about nature and humans, and tend to equate life process with seasonal progression. Life stages are equivalent to the rhythm of cosmic changes; hence birth is likened to spring, youth to summer, maturity to autumn and old age to winter. The beginning of a life is viewed as the same as the start of spring while its end is considered to be similar to the withering of trees, plants in the deep cold, marking the completion of this cycle but also indicating the beginning of the next one. In the same way as the rituals for cosmic changes (e.g., winter and summer solstices, spring and autumn equinoxes), rites of passage for a person provide opportunities to signify the arrival of each of the new stages and to highlight the importance each of them potentially has for personal, familial and communal life. Because of the interrelation between human life and the universe, what the rites of passage celebrate is not only the crucial stages of a personal life in a familial and religious context, but also their cosmic and spiritual significance, and what they cultivate is the sense that one's destiny is closely associated with the destiny of all the people and is part of the great cosmic evolution.

There are two kinds of rites of passage: the rites for important stages in the religious order and the rites for life changes in a familial context. The rites for religious life vary from tradition to tradition. In Buddhism, for example, they include several important stages of the religious living, such as initiation (taking refuge in the Three Jewels: the Buddha, Dharma and Sangha; shaving off all hair on the head and accepting Buddhist precepts, etc.); ordination (renunciation of secular life, being given a Buddhist name etc.) and death (chanting sutras, cremation, burial ritual etc.). Each of these acts is marked by a strictly followed ceremony within the Buddhist community.

While the rites in a religious order signify and strengthen the commitment of the believers to a particular faith or tradition, rites of passage in the family reveal the connection between a person and his/her family, between one's biological life and one's (religious) destiny; they initiate and complete the essential parts of the Chinese way of life. Of all the stages in a life, four are prominently marked by particularly designated rites: birth, adulthood, marriage and death. While these four are equally important for a person, rites for marriage and ritual for death have carried with them higher social and religious values and reflected diverse influences of different religious traditions; marriage rites were formed primarily under the influence of ancient (Confucian) understanding of life and family; death rites were significantly affected by Buddhist conception of life, death, hell and reincarnation and Daoist ideas of life and death (Holm and Bowker, 1994:157). For these reasons, we will focus our attention below on these two rites to examine how they are used to strengthen people's belief and to fulfil their mission in the world.

Marriage

In a different culture, marriage may be primarily perceived as an institution for personal love, producing and nurturing offspring. However, in a traditional

Chinese context marriage has carried with it a much wider social and religious implication such as supporting older generations and continuing the ancestral linage. The socio-religious meaning of marriage is clearly stated in the *Book of Rites*:

> The ceremony of marriage was intended to be a bond of love between two (families of different) surnames, with a view, in its retrospective character, to secure the services in the ancestral temple, and in its prospective character, to secure the continuance of the family line. (Legge, 1885, xxviii: 428)

Through the rites, marriage is endorsed with special value for social and religious purposes. Marriage enables one family to be linked to another in order to maintain their social status or to expand their communal influence. It is also the way to enrich the family life, to serve the needs of the elders, and to ensure the continuation of ancestor worship. All the rites of marriage unfold around these two aspects, by which the secular and spiritual meanings of marriage become integrated.

The added values determine that marriage must not be simply taken as a personal matter; it is the concern of the whole family. Therefore making a proper arrangement for a suitable marriage would be the first step as required by the rites. In a traditional context, it was important not only that the two families be equal in social status but also that the two young persons involved be astrologically matched. The birth of a person is recorded by the two Chinese characters for each of the year, the month, the day and the hour of his or her birth, which together form the 'eight characters'. Different characters are seen as carrying a different element (*xing*), vital power (*qi*) and cosmic force (*yin* or *yang*). Two sets of the 'eight characters' would determine whether or not the two people in question would match each other, or whether one would be too strong or too weak for the other. For example, while a boy of the metal element can live a happy life with a girl of the earth element, he would be totally overcome by a girl of the fire. In present days, rather than going into too many details of the eight characters, attention is paid to the matching of different animal years in which the two people are born. The Chinese calendar is composed of 12 year cycles, each of them is associated with an animal: rat, ox, tiger, hare, dragon, snake, horse, sheep, monkey, cock, dog and pig. The future or the fortune of a person is believed to have been determined by the animal in which he or she was born. For example, a 'horse' boy and a 'cock' girl in general match each other, while a 'tiger' girl is regarded not as a good match with a 'cock' boy, because the latter could be totally overwhelmed by the former, in the same way as a tiger would swallow a cock.

A match would not be accepted unless a number of sub-rites had been carried out appropriately, which included, according to the descriptions in the *Book of Rites*, the proposal with its accompanying gift, the inquiries about the girl's name, the intimation of the approving divination, the receiving of special offerings, till the request to fix the day (Legge, 1885, vol. xxviii:428). Taking place in the hall of the ancestral temple, these rites not only signified that the proposal for marriage must spiritually be approved by ancestors, but also demonstrated the reverence and respect with which each family treated the other. After all these steps, an auspicious match was secured, and the two families were expected to arrange for wedding.

The culmination of the marriage rites was the wedding when the bride left her own family and was taken into the bridegroom's family. Before her departure, however, she was expected to say farewell to her ancestors, parents, grandparents and other relatives who might or might not accompany her to the wedding. In the wedding, several ritual actions are of great importance for the new family and for its spiritual well-being. In early China, the bride and bridegroom were to pay homage to ancestors to secure the spiritual approval of the marriage; more recent rites have added dramatic acts, which culminate in bridegroom and bride paying three kinds of homage: to Heaven and Earth, to parents and to each other. These three acts are both spiritual and social. Heaven and Earth are viewed as the fundamental powers of the universe, and paying homage to them is to acknowledge where humans come from, to obtain spiritual blessing and to show gratitude to the ultimate powers. Since the intercourse between Heaven (the male force) and Earth (the female force) is perceived as to be the origin of myriads of things and beings, paying homage to them is also symbolic of securing love and reproduction between husband and wife. Parents are the direct source of the bride and bridegroom, and paying homage to them is both to show filial piety which is extended from parents to ancestors, to thank parents for their care, nurture and love, and to make a solemn commitment that the young couple would support, respect and love them. Bride and bridegroom paying homage to each other is a symbolic act of accepting each other wholeheartedly and making a promise to treat each other with love and loyalty. Instead of the exchanging of rings to make this point in today's wedding ceremony, traditional rites employed other symbolic means; for example, the two sides 'joined in sipping [spirit] from the cups made of the same melon; thus showing that they now formed one body, were of equal rank, and pledged to mutual affection' (Legge, 1885, vol. xxviii: 429–30).

While some of the rites have been transformed in modern times and most city young people tend to opt for modern, civil or even Christian ceremonies, an increasing number of families have now returned to traditional rites, with variations in terms of proposal, gift, divination and betrothal. The companies that are specialized in arranging and organizing marriage ceremonies have a flourishing business to facilitate the social and spiritual meanings of marriage in city as well as in rural areas.

Death

In traditional ritual texts, rites for marriage are regarded as for an auspicious event, while rites for death an inauspicious event. As the last phase of a life cycle, death must be treated with reverence, sincerity and care. Traditional rites of death contain several interrelated elements: calling back the soul of the deceased, mourning, funeral and sacrifice.

Death is believed to have been caused by a separation of the soul from the body; with a hope that this separation might be only temporary, like the soul wandering around and 'forgetting' to return, a number of acts are designed to 'call it back'. Children or grandchildren or other relatives or officers of lower ranks would go up to the roof of the house, carrying his clothes and calling his name or title to 'return'. The callers face to north, the region that is believed to be of the *yin* or dark world: 'The looking for it to return from the dark region is a way of seeking for it among the spiritual beings' (Legge, 1885, xxvii:167). Under the Buddhist influence, this practice was changed accordingly so that the descendants of the dead shout three times, facing west, either to show the dead the way to the Western Paradise, or to pray that the deceased is being reborn in the paradise.

Death means the change of one's living place from the *yang* world to the *yin* world, for which spiritual permission must be obtained. It is therefore the next step to report to the relevant authorities of the underworld about this event, normally through intermediates such as the god of land (*tu di*), the god of city (*cheng huang*) or the god of the five roads (*wu dao*). Only by their permission and guidance, the soul is believed to be able to enter into the spirit world. At the same time in the family such works are being done as washing the corpse and garbing it with 'longevity clothes', lighting up 'longevity lamps'. Family members and relatives are also dressing up in mourning clothes, white garments made of coarse material, to express their sadness and to show their mourning status.

It is important that every set of the funeral rites be performed in accordance with the prescriptions set forth in the codes of rites, and with conspicuous addition of later times from Buddhist and Daoist rituals. For those families that can afford, religious service by Buddhists and Daoists would be an integral element of the rites, normally lasting from one day to several weeks, although it is ritually required for seven days in seven weeks.

Familial and religious rites are intended to assist the spirit of the deceased in the journey from this world to the other world, and in passing through smoothly and quickly various stages to reincarnation. After that, the deceased is believed to have changed their existential status in the family, from a living member to the spirit of an 'ancestor', continuing to look after his or her descendants from the spirit world, while the descendants provide him or her with offerings and sacrifices by following all traditionally ascribed rites and rituals. Further, mourning and sacrifices are not merely meant to strengthen the tie between the living and the dead, but also to function as a communal event and educational opportunity to all members of the family and the community. For these reasons, the following saying by one of Confucius' disciples has been cherished in China for thousands of years: 'Conduct the funeral of your parents with meticulous care and let not sacrifices to your remote ancestors be forgotten, and the virtue of the common people will incline towards fullness' (Lau, 1979:60).

Divination

Divination is one of the oldest religious practices across religions and traditions, although its form and medium vary significantly from culture to culture. In China, 'Starting from the late fourth millennium B.C. the Neolithic inhabitants of northern China appear to have been the first people to use animal shoulder blades for divination, by beating them and interpreting the cracks which ensued' (Küng and Ching, 1990:11). The earliest written records from oracle bone (tortoise shell and ox shoulder blade) inscriptions show that the so-called pyromancy reached its peak during the Shang dynasty (?1600–?1045 BCE). After that, a more sophisticated divination method was invented by playing yarrow stalks by following the *Book of Changes* and became popular from the Western Zhou era (?1045–771 BCE) onwards. Today many Chinese people are still obsessed with astrology, physiognomy, *fengshui*, fortune telling and all other sorts of divination which have run through history and permeated all aspects of the religious life.

Foreknowledge

Divination is a religious means by which people hope to gain foreknowledge, the knowledge enabling them to know what is to happen and to determine what action is to be taken to dissolve misfortune or to obtain good fortune. While in later times prophesying seems to be a privilege of Daoists and folk-religionists, in early China, it was Confucianism that was closely associated with seeking foreknowledge (*xian zhi* or *xian shi*). The author(s) of the *Daode jing* seemed to distrust foreknowing, as we read from this text that 'Foreknowledge is the flowery embellishment of the Way and the beginning of folly' (Lau, 1963:45). There is no term for foreknowledge in *The Analects*, but Confucius did believe that since human destiny was predetermined by Heaven, with knowledge of the Way and Destiny humans were able to know what would happen in future (Lau, 1979:66). It is said in the *Records of the Historian* that 'in his old age, Confucius developed a love for the study of the *Book of Changes*', a text closely associated with gaining foreknowledge, and 'he read it so thoroughly that the leather strap (holding the bundle of bamboo inscriptions) was worn out and replaced three times' (Lin, 1994:135).

Mengzi argued that it was the will of Heaven for some people to have foreknowledge by which they were able to take a lead: 'Heaven in giving birth to this people causes those who are first to know to awaken those who are later to know; and causes those who are first awakened to awaken those who are later to be awakened' (de Bary and Bloom, 1999:145). In the *Doctrine of the Mean*, foreknowledge is said to be the quality of 'absolute sincerity' which enables humans to know things beforehand. The sage is said to possess the ability to see and interpret omens, and can therefore predict the future:

> It is characteristic of absolute sincerity to be able to foreknow. When a nation or family is about to flourish, there are sure to be lucky omens. When a nation or family is about to perish, there are sure to be unlucky omens. These omens are revealed in divination and in the movements of the four limbs. When calamity or blessing is about to come, it can surely know beforehand if it is good, and it can also surely know beforehand if it is evil. Therefore he who has absolute sincerity is like a spirit. (Chan, 1963:108)

The commentaries of the *Book of Changes* take 'knowing of what is to come' (*zhi lai*) as the core of human activities and as a result from fully understanding the images of the book (de Bary and Bloom, 1999:322). The symbols and images contained in the text are considered the signs and revelations for future events and actions, not only reflecting the state of affairs in the human world but also revealing cosmic changes in Heaven and Earth. Understanding them, the sage is surely able to know what is to happen and to take necessary action to shun disasters.

For a while Confucianism was even identified with seeking foreknowledge and the sage was said to be distinguished from other people by his prophesying ability. On the other hand, the indulgence in foreknowledge was strongly criticized by rational Confucians. Although Xunzi did not totally reject the possibility of anticipating the future, he persisted in a moral determinism rather than prophecy, and placed responsibilities for the future on humans rather than cosmic powers: 'If you practice the Way and are not of two minds, then Heaven cannot visit calamities on you'; in contrast, 'If you turn your back on the Way and behave recklessly, then Heaven cannot bestow good fortune on you' (de Bary and Bloom, 1999:171). Wang Chong of the Latter Han debunked the apparently current notion at his time that sages had special divine (*shen*) qualities that helped them see the future: 'The Confucians talk about sages, saying that they can know a thousand years into the future . . . I say this is all empty [talk]' (Wang Chong, 1954:252).

The underlying reason for Confucians to value foreknowledge is their belief in the correspondence between the three realms of Heaven, Earth and humans. It seems for the majority of early Confucian scholars that signs in nature were intended to reveal what is to happen in human life, and human events would also have a bearing on cosmic changes. However, the Confucian foreknowledge was based on a morally refined cosmology. Their concern for human destiny led them to the cultivation of human nature instead of seeking mysterious reasons for what had happened. While later Confucians reversed the tendency to a prophetic religion, the exploration of foreknowledge laid down theoretical framework and justification for divination. The search for foreknowledge about human destiny was then combined with the Daoist understanding of human life and the Buddhist conception of causality. These concepts and understandings have been the force driving divination in China and become the main thread running through all aspects of religious practices.

Divination methods

Divination is intended to gain foreknowledge about human life and destiny and to determine human action. It can be carried out through a variety of methods. According to the *History of the Former Han Dynasty*, divination was the arts involving manipulating numbers (*shu shu*) and was supervised by historian-diviners. It lists six classes of the divinatory arts or methods. The first is astrology, which is used to arrange in order the 28 star constellations and to 'note the progression of the five planets and of the sun and moon, so as to record thereby the manifestations of fortune and misfortune' (Fung, 1952:26). The second method of divination is concerned with almanacs, which serve 'to arrange the position of the four seasons in order, to adjust the times of the equinoxes and solstice, and to note the concordance of the periods of the sun, moon and five planets, so as thereby to examine into the actualities of cold and heat, life and death' (Ibid., 27). The almanac combines calendrical and cabalistic information together to provide guidance and advice for daily activities or special events; for example, going out, doing business, personal engagement and ritual arrangements.

The third is connected with the Five Elements, which 'are the corporeal essences of the Five Constant Virtues': 'If one's personal appearance, speech, vision, hearing and thought lose their proper order, the Five Elements will fall into confusion and changes will arise in the five planets' (Ibid.). The fourth is to use the stalks of divination plant and the tortoise shell: 'For making certain of good and bad fortune, and accomplishing things requiring strenuous efforts, there is nothing better than the divination plant and tortoise shell' (Ibid.). In the *Book of Rites*, it is stated that 'Divination by the shell is called *pu*; by the stalk, *shih*. The two were the methods by which the ancient sage kings made the people believe in seasons and days, revere spiritual beings, and stand in awe of their laws and orders; the methods (also) by which they made them determine their perplexities and settle their misgivings' (Legge, 1885, xxvii:94).

The fifth method consists of miscellaneous divinations, which 'serve to keep records of the phenomena of various things and to observe the manifestation of good and evil'. Of these arts, the most popular is interpreting dreams. *The Book of Poetry* has 'records of dreams about bears, serpents, and assembled fish and banners, clear signs of (the coming of) a great man, whereby one may examine good and bad fortune' (Fung, 1952:28). The last one is the system of forms which 'deals with general statements about the influencing forces in the entire nine provinces, in order to erect a walled city, its outer wall, a house or a hut'. Divination by forms is one of the sources for a later popular divination method, *fengshui*. On a different aspect, 'the measurement and number of the bones of men and the six domestic animals . . . are examined, so as to find out whether their sound and matter are noble or mean and are of good or evil omen' (Ibid.). This was to become another popular set of divination methods to see the future through measuring and interpreting the face, head and body.

In contemporary times all these methods are still in use, although it seems that pyromancy has become very rare among diviners. Particularly important are 'consulting almanacs' (*huang li*), 'dream interpretation' (*jie meng*), 'astrology' (*xing xiang*), 'analysing Chinese characters' (*ce zi*) and 'physiognomy' (*kan xiang*). Though condemned as superstition in several decades, these methods of divination are now popular again in Mainland China, and astrological, almanac and prophetical advice are commonly presented in newspapers, magazines and internet websites. It has become increasingly common for people to consult a spiritual medium or divinatory text to help make decisions concerning an important event or situation.

The *Book of Changes*

The key word of the *Book of Changes* is '*yi*', which in Chinese means 'easy', implying that it would be easy for humans to understand complex phenomena, their interrelationship and impact on human destiny by simply following the structured composition of lines, trigrammes and hexagrammes this book has provided. It also means that the diviner would be able to penetrate the message or revelations from Heaven by referring to the oracles contained in the book.

However, the word has another, and more important, meaning, 'change'; hence the English title of the *Book of Changes*. Although the universe is in a constant state of change and continuous transformation, Dao underlying all changes and never changes. Experiencing and understanding the changes is necessary for understanding the constant Dao, by which humans can grasp their destiny. The lines, trigrammes and hexagrammes are interchangeable, representing phenomena, situations and movements, and indicating the flowing nature of life as well as the interplays of fortune and misfortune.

The *Book of Changes* was originated from a manual for the diviners, but has since become one of the most important books ever written on philosophy, politics and religion. For more than 2,000 years, it has served to tell people's future, to look for an oracle guidance in how to respond appropriately to an uncertain situation, or to ensure fortune and avoid misfortune.

The book is composed of four parts. The first and earliest part is concerned with the images of the Eight Trigrammes composed of three lines of two different kinds: *yin* (broken line) and *yang* (unbroken line). Their invention was attributed to the sage-king Fu Xi, the first of the legendary Three Sovereigns (*san huang*). The Eight Trigrammes are said to correspond to the eight most common natural phenomena, heaven, earth, mountain, lake, fire, water, wind and thunder.

The second part of the book was said to have been composed by King Wen, the founder of the Zhou dynasty, who expanded the Eight Trigrammes into sixty-four hexagrammes by putting two trigrammes together, and wrote brief notes for each of them. The full statement for each line of the sixty-four hexagrammes was attributed to the Duke of Zhou, the Son of King Wen and the exemplar politician for Confucius, which is to become the third part of the book. These three parts together become what we know as the text. The fourth part, the ten commentaries which are also known as the 'ten wings' (*shi yi*), was traditionally attributed to Confucius but was most likely to be added during the later part of the Warring State period.

Although difficult for us to identify the authorship of the book and its composition date, we can safely say its text was a product of many generations and became more or less coherent by the ninth century BCE, when

> hexagram divination had already changed from a method of consulting and influencing gods, spirits, and ancestors – the 'powerful dead' – to a method of penetrating moments of the cosmic order to learn how the way or Dao is configured and what direction it takes at such moments and to determine what one's own places is and should be in the scheme of things. (Lynn, 1994:1)

Fengshui

Fengshui is a divinatory practice, and is frequently connected with the use of the *Book of Changes*. Its increasing popularity in Mainland China can be seen from the fact that there is an Association of *Yi* Studies and *Fengshui* under which divination is the core business. According to the chairman of this association, it was established in 2005 and now has 15 branches and 200 members in the Mainland, engaging in various divinatory businesses by using the *Book of Changes* and *fengshui* such as foretelling, geomantic planning, naming (providing auspicious names for individuals and for companies), household and scenery designing. The chairman said that he had been practising *fengshui* as an occupation for more than 17 years and in his experience the Chinese in the south paid more attention to *fengshui*, while the northern people were more interested in knowing fate. He also confirmed that modern *fengshui* practices differed from the masters of the past whose focus was on time and space, while today's specialists paid attention to the details of things and applied 'scientific knowledge' in their work (http://home.163.com/news/080902/390958-1.shtml).

Fengshui in Chinese literally meant 'wind and water', the two most common presentations of the vital energy, *qi*, that influences or determines life and landscape. *Qi* has been translated as air, gas, breath, ether, energy, force, power etc., and is regarded as the essence and life energy of all things and beings including humans. When *qi* is strong, life is strong and fit; when *qi* is weak, life will be weak, ill or old. When *qi* is used up or completely disappeared, death will come. Therefore, to nourish and cultivate *qi* is fundamental for the people to live in a good and healthy life. Apart from humans, animals and plants, *qi* is also responsible for all other matters such as maintains, land, rivers, whose different shapes and forms are the result of *qi*'s movements.

Qi has genders; *qi* of the male (*yang*) is strong, positive, vitalizing, while *qi* of the female (*yin*) weak, negative, and potentially damaging to life. *Qi* is also manifested in quantity and quality; for example, where the male *qi* is strong and the female *qi* is weak there is a hill or mountain; where the female *qi* is strong and the male *qi* is weak, there is a lake. *Qi* can be still but more frequently moving, and flows along certain channels such as the veins and arteries of the body. *Qi* has its elements, and each of the five elements gives *qi* different nature and feature. Therefore *fengshui* is, in general, an art to maintain or regain harmony between humans and their environment and within human life by rearranging *qi*'s gender, quantity, quality, still or moving characters, and orders in the five elements in mutual production or mutual overcoming. It is an art to foreknow fortune or misfortune, or to improve one's fate by determining the auspicious or inauspicious settings of dwellings, for the living or for the dead.

Fengshui makes use of forms, shapes, positions and orientations to prophesy fortune or misfortune. It is an essential skill for a professional *fengshui* master to observe the configuration of the ground or building, which is often presented in symbols – animals such as dragon, tiger, tortoise, bird, fish, horse and dog; part of the body such as head, tongue, teeth, arm, leg, eye, hand; stars such as the sun, the moon, Mars, Jupiter, Venus, Mars; or things such as cart, net, carpet, spear, arrow, pen, brush and so on so forth. By explaining the implication of these symbols, a *fengshui* master highlights the effect a particular symbol or a combination of different symbols can bring to the people in a short or long period of time (Lip, 1979:44–45).

In reality, few environmental settings or buildings would naturally bring good fortune to the people; thus one of the most important duties for a *fengshui* master is to find out a way to improve the current settings or to change them into a near ideal site. In this rearranged living quarters various natural and spiritual forces are brought together in such a way that their negative effect will be reduced to minimum, while benefits to the people living in them are maximized. In a sense, this is what all religious practices in China are ultimately intended to achieve.

Questions for discussion

1. What are the characteristics of religious practices in China? How are they related to Chinese spirituality?
2. Why did the Chinese place so much emphasis on sacrifice?
3. Why is it said that thanksgiving and redeeming are two main purposes of sacrifices in China?
4. What are the rites of passage? How do the Chinese understand the rites of passage in relation to their cosmic views?
5. What is meant by divination in a Chinese context?
6. 'The sage is distinguished from other people by his foreknowledge.' Discuss.
7. What is the nature of the *Book of Changes*? Why is it said to have been a manual for divination?
8. How can *Fengshui* be fitted into the overall frame of religious practices in China?

Religion as the Way of Life

In a sense, to study religion is to engage in a spiritual journey. In our contextual discussion of Chinese religion, we have travelled along the way the Chinese perceive of, and deal with, the affairs and matters of a religious relevance and meaning. Throughout this journey, we are repeatedly reminded that religious belief and practice in China cannot be fully grasped unless we examine them in context and unless we have taken into full account their interaction and interpenetration with other aspects of life, in particular, history, culture, the family and the state.

Being a part of the overall infrastructure that is termed as Chinese culture, religion in China is characterized by an ambiguity in differentiation or classification; in other words, the difference between the secular and the religious, or between the profane and the holy which is held highly in many other cultures, seems to have been either deliberately reduced to minimum or subconsciously left unclarified. From this perspective, it is transparent that as an important dimension of life, religion in China does not exist independent of, or cannot be separated from, all other cultural dimensions. Rather it is closely related with, or is indeed part of, Chinese life, in which not only history, philosophy, education, literature, arts, medicine etc. are embedded with religious values and meanings, but religion also possesses a substantial position in personal, familial, communal, artistic, economic and political activities. All these have naturally led us to a conclusion that religion is none other than the way how the Chinese lead their life, and that the way of life is the single most important context in which religion originates, evolves and operates.

At this point some readers might wonder if any progress could be made in our search for a particular religiosity by claiming that Chinese religion is simply how the Chinese lead their life, or if our enquiry would not result in a 'tautology' by identifying religion and the way of life. It might seem apparent to these readers that any religion is a special way of life for its followers; for example, Christianity is the way of life for Christians, and Islam is the way of life for Muslims. It is true that all religious traditions contain a code of conduct, having this or that kind of influence over the lifestyle of the believers and underlying the attitudes and preferences of their followers. However, equally true it is that the relation between religion and life varies from culture to culture, both in terms of degree and of extention. Chinese religion has not only influenced the formation of the way of life in China, but is also an intrinsic part of it. In other words, the Chinese way of life would lose its essence without religious values, while Chinese religion could no longer be functional if its connection with other parts of life were totally severed.

Our examination of various aspects of religious life in China has demonstrated that Chinese religion is more than customary ritual and faith-related worship; it is part of the cultural system that governs the daily life, guides people in their clothing, eating, dwelling and travelling, and determines their attitudes, preferences and choices. Many people in China are deeply religious and are engaged with a particular religious tradition that shapes their expectations in life – their life itself is characterised by the belief and practice of that tradition. However, this does not change the fact that a more distinctive feature of religion that we attempt to examine throughout this book is associated with what is meant by the 'Chineseness' of religion. This 'Chineseness' is both in and above all religious codes and performances, because for the majority of the Han people in China, religion is not only a systematic approach to the ultimate reality, but also an important part of 'secular' life; these 'two' ways are not really separate for most people who never or seldom bother to clearly define what is the religious doctrine they abide by. It seems natural for them that 'religion' is to be *lived* rather than *followed*. From this perspective, the Chinese religiosity is not only demonstrated in rituals, sacred texts, specific religious acts or religious organizations, but is also revealed through familiar patterns of behaviour, modes of thinking and commonsense attitudes. As we have already observed, on many occasions the Chinese are thoroughly devotional or pious towards the objects of worship; but on many others they may well follow a norm or teaching without fully realizing that they are engaging in a particular tradition, or pursuing an ideal without entirely appreciating its doctrinal or theological significance.

The separation between religion and secularity is crucial for religion in many cultures. However, as far as ordinary people in China are concerned, the separation is not *prima facie* at all, nor is it important. A typical feature of Chinese religiosity lies exactly in the integration of the secular and the religious. In this integration seemingly secular activities in family and community have acquired a 'religious' meaning, because these activities are not perceived of as much different from 'typical' religious activities such as worship and devotion. For many people in China, the religious way of life may be to affiliate themselves to a particular faith, but it may also well be to cultivate their person in morality, education or even aesthetical appreciation. It seems for them to make perfect sense that transcendence can be gained through one's diligence in fulfilling personal, familial and communal responsibilities as effectively as through the worship of gods or the following of religious discipline.

The integration of the religious and the secular might tempt some readers to believe that the Chinese do not have a fully formed religiosity or that the Han Chinese are not a people of religion. We have already examined this argument in Chapter 2 and confirmed that it is a misrepresentation derived from a wrong interpretation of religion. Through the chapters of this book we have revealed that there is no lack of the divine and the pious in the life of the Chinese, and that many Chinese people are as devoted to religious ideals as the most faithful followers in other cultures or religious traditions. At the same time we have also indicated that the most distinctive feature of religious life in China lies in the seeking of religious values in non-religious activities or the attaching of multiple religious ideals to daily life. We have argued that the Chinese hold a strong conviction that the Way must not be distanced from humans; otherwise it would not be the Way at all; or in other words, it would not be worthy of human pursuing (Chan, 1963:100). Originally a Confucian idea, this conviction has penetrated all dimensions of religion and become one of the most important criteria for gauging the relevance of religious belief and practice. Understood as such, the goal of spiritual practice is often either identified with or made similar to the goal of ordinary life. On occasions when religious pursuits are distinguishable from daily activities, the majority of Chinese people still tend to see the gap between human intelligence and the divine power as bridgeable, and the position between humans and gods or spirits (*shen*) as exchangeable.

All these tendencies and convictions have revealed to us an anthropocentric religiosity, in which the gravity centre is located in humanity, and religion is equated with or closely associated to the way of life. As the way of life, Chinese religion is culturally inscribed with three characteristics which can be roughly described by three ready-for-use terms, syncretic, pragmatic and utilitarian, although we are clearly aware that these three English words are embedded in Western philosophy and might not be totally appropriate for the typical features of religion in China.

First, Chinese religion is a syncretic system that tends to embrace all kinds of beliefs and practices without much discrimination or with only a minimum modification. However alien a religious belief or practice might first appear to be, in the powerful syncretism of Chinese culture it will be sooner or later transformed into an element of the life, a part of the grand mechanism that operates in family, community or the state. Thus the different religious streams and strands which signify the multiplicity and divergence of religious life in China are gradually transformed into a *culturally* unified tradition. What cultural syncretism seeks to produce, however, is not a mega-unity in which all elements are simply melted together; rather it leads to a converging system in which different faiths are interlocked, co-existent and mutually complementary and are tuned to share the same ultimate concern, while still possessing their own positions and having their own values. Chinese religion thus demonstrates all the features of a syncretic system, in which divergence is to be understood only in terms of convergence, and commonality cannot be fully appreciated unless within a particular context.

Syncretism is not only characteristic of Chinese religion as a whole, but is also the basic attitude each religious tradition holds towards other traditions. This is the underlying reason why Confucianism, Daoism, Buddhism and others can easily open themselves up to 'absorb' useful teachings from one another or apply the 'borrowed' tenets in their own way at particular times. Syncretism is thus the only pathway available to new religious movements to originate and develop. These movements are both old and new. They are old because they evolve from traditional ideas and activities, and the goals they set up for themselves are not much different from the goals of the traditions that are already practised for hundreds of years. However, they are also new, in the sense that old elements from traditional beliefs and practices are reshuffled into a new structure or are reinterpreted through new hermeneutic tools.

Secondly, the Chinese approach to religious and spiritual matters is essentially pragmatic. Indeed all religious practices or activities are intended to serve this or that human need. Based on the spiritual-secular alliance, Chinese pragmatism is fully applied to religion. Religious beliefs and rituals are taken as a means to assist humans to lead a life of high standards and to ensure human efforts to have a good return either in this life or in the next. There is a popular irony in the saying 'not burning incense to the Buddha in everyday life, but hurrying to embrace his feet when urgent', and this saying has perfectly depicted the pragmatic attitude of a significant part of the Chinese population.

Under the dominance of pragmatism, rituals or rites for honouring gods are designed as a way of closing up the gap between gods and humans. Just like in human-human relations where '*guanxi*' (personal connections) are important, the Chinese are also keen to gain godly blessing by establishing an intimate human-god relation. Hence the significance of donations, burning incense, making a vow (*xu yuan*) and redeeming this vow (*huan yuan*). Religious pragmatism also explains a so-called 'bribing culture' widely practised in religious life, where offerings, either in terms of material items or spiritual promises, are made with a clear purpose to obtain blessing or to avoid punishments.

Thirdly, Chinese religion takes a utilitarian view about religious choice and evaluation. In the same way as human motives and activities are judged, gods or religious teachings are also subject to *ethical* scrutiny: there are good and bad gods, good and bad teachings, good and bad rituals, good and bad music, and so on and so forth. The criteria for distinguishing the good from the bad are based on the results they have brought about or are expected to bring about. The gods who are believed to produce the greatest benefit to the greatest number of the people are the best, and should be worshipped by the majority of the population; the spiritual powers that are expected to produce a limited number of good results for a limited number of people are good but not the ideal, while those who are assumed to generate bad results for the people will be judged to be bad or evil. At this point, the religious utilitarianism departs from secular and moral utilitarianism. In moral utilitarianism, people shun the morally undesirable or evil. However, in religious utilitarianism, although knowing that evil forces or ghosts will bring about bad results, they nevertheless posses an important position in religious life, and develop a cult involving many people who are engaged in it either out of fear or with the hope that bad results could be reversed or lessened. It seems that the majority of the Chinese population are in a constant state of balancing the pious and the opportunist, constantly calculating more and less good or bad results, by which they adjust their behaviour or orientation. For example, if in their judgment one type of conduct would bring about more benefit or less undesirable consequences, then it would be encouraged and propagated; on the contrary, if they come to the view that a particular belief would cause more pain than happiness, then they would most likely reject or condemn it.

These features are not new. They are already distinctive in history and characterize Chinese culture. In contemporary China, they are simply refreshed and further develop in new social, economic and political conditions. Chinese religion has become more than ever a part of personal and communal construction close to the life of ordinary people, from which it draws nutrition and inspiration. Thus, pious devotion to gods and promoting tourism co-exist and are both prominent in all religious sites in contemporary China, as shown in Figure 9.1. In this sense, being a Chinese itself is to be religious. At the same time, however, religion is highly secularized and commercialized. Religious orders, in particular many of Buddhist and Daoist temples, are interested in the riches of the world as much as secular organizations or groups of people. Religious rituals, blessings, texts etc. might well be merely as a means to get returns, while their sublime meaning and value may also be overshadowed in the rush to commercialize religious interests. A caution is needed here for commercializing religion: the overemphasis on material gains was one of the reasons for religions being suppressed in the past and it might well lead to a situation where religion will create a strong opposition to its best interests in the present time. How to balance the cultural side and the spiritual side of religion remains a question or challenge both for religious orders who live off

Figure 9.1 Burning incense and tourism in a Buddhist temple

the devotion and participation of the population and for ordinary people who live by the beliefs and rules these orders have prescribed.

Questions for discussion

1. Why is it said that 'religion in China is characterized by an ambiguity in differentiation or classification'?
2. How do you understand the so-called secular-divine alliance in Chinese culture? How much has it affected the Chinese way of life?
3. How do you understand syncretism in Chinese religion?
4. What is religious pragmatism in the context of Chinese culture?
5. Why is it said that religious beliefs and activities in China are subject to the evaluation of religious utilitarianism?

Appendix I: A Glossary of Chinese Characters

Pinyin or other spellings	Chinese characters	English meanings or counterparts
bailian jiao	白蓮教	White Lotus Religion, a popular sect of Buddhism established in the Song (1127–1259) but popularized in the Yuan (1260–1368), Ming (1368–1644) and Qing (1644–1911) dynasties
bai yun guan	白雲觀	The White Clouds Temple in Beijing, the headquarters for Perfect Truth Daoism, the location of the China's Association of Daoism
ba xian	八僊	Eight Immortals, the most famous immortal group in Daoist and popular religions
bei zong (chan)	北宗（禪）	The northern transmission of Chan Buddhism, allegedly started from Shenxiu (606–706)
bu he	不和	Disharmony
cai shen	財神	God of fortune, god of wealth
ce zi	測字	A divination method through analysing Chinese characters
chan	禪	Buddhist meditation
chang	常	Constant, frequent, eternal
Chang e	嫦娥	Moon Goddess, who is said to have been the wife of the great archer Hou Yi and become an immortal by taking an immortality elixir pill given to her husband by the Queen Mother of the West
chang sheng	長生	Long life, longevity, immortality
chang sheng niangniang	長生娘娘	Goddess of Eternal Life
chan zong	禪宗	School of Chan Buddhism where meditation is seen as the path to enlightenment
chao du	超度	To relieve the suffering of souls in hell and to accelerate their reincarnation
chao-hsuan-ssu	昭玄寺	Office to Illumine the Mysteries
cheng huang	城隍	The town god or the god of city
chenjia Ci	陈家祠	The Ancestral Temple of the Chen Clan
Chenshi Shuyuan	陈氏书院	The private school of the Chen clan
Chih chiao daxian	赤脚大仙	Bare-footed Genii or immortal
chou pi nang	臭皮囊	Revolting skin bag, a Buddhist term for the human body
chuang shen	床神	The god of bed
chujia	出家	To denounce the secular world and lead a religious life; living in a monastery or temple outside of one's family

Pinyin or other spellings	Chinese characters	English meanings or counterparts
ch'ung-fu ssu	崇福司	A governmental administrative body established by the Yuan dynasty for administering religious affairs
chun guan	春官	Spring officials who were in charge of the Ministry of Rites during the Zhou dynasty
ci si	祠祀	A traditional term for sacrifices to royal ancestors
dangtian	当天	Heaven God
dao	道	The Way, Nature, Reason, Logos, Natural Law, etc.
daode	道德	Morality; the Daoist School, one of the six major schools popular from the Warring State period onwards
dao jia	道家	Daoism, usually for philosophical Daoism
dao jiao	道教	Daoism, normally for religious Daoism
dao tong	道統	The transmission of the Confucian Way
da tong	大同	Grand unity or great harmony, a term for the Confucian ideal society
dawenkou	大汶口	A place famous for Dawenkou culture (4300–2500 BCE)
da zong	大宗	The grand clan, the lineal ancestor
de	德	Virtue, power
de dao	得道	Obtaining the way, becoming an immortal
di	帝	Supreme God, a posthumous title to honour royal ancestors, the emperor
ding ming	定名	Definite name
di zhu/dizhu	地主	Master of the Site, a god in popular religion
di zi	弟子	Disciple, student
fa	法	Law, the School of Law or Legalism, one of the six major schools popular in the Warring State period
falungong	法輪功	The Practices of the Wheel of Dharma, a syncretic *qigong* practice headed by Li Hongzhi
famen si	法門寺	Temple of the Dharma Gate, located in Shaanxi province which is claimed to hold the finger bone of the Buddha
fangshi	方士	Prescription-masters in the Qin and Han period who travelled around to heal the sick by using formulae, charms and rituals as well as herb medicine and to seek the way to immortality
fengshui	風水	Water and wind, geomancy, a cosmic theory and practice used to determine good or bad fortune for human buildings or graves
fo	佛	The Buddha, a buddha
fo mu	佛母	Mother of the Buddha
fo zu	佛祖	The founder of Buddhism, the Buddha
fu, lu and shou	福禄寿	God of Good Fortune, God of Riches and God of Longevity
fuzi zhi dao	夫子之道	The Way of Confucius
guai	怪	Demon, monster, evil beings, strange powers
guandi	關帝	Lord Guan, the deified general of the Three Kingdoms period, regarded as the patron god for state military administration
guang xiao si	光孝寺	Temple of Glorifying Filial Piety
guan xi	關系	Personal relations, favourable connections

(Continued)

Pinyin or other spellings	Chinese characters	English meanings or counterparts
guanyin/ guan shi yin	觀音/觀世音	The *Avalokitésvara* bodhisattva, the Goddess of Compassion, popular in Buddhism, Daoism and folk religion
gui	鬼	The earthly soul, evil forces, the spirit of the dead
guo	國	State, country
Guodian	郭店	A place where bamboo stripes of Confucian and Daoist texts dated to 300 BCE were excavated in the 1990s
guojia	國家	State, country
gu shen	谷神	The spirit of the valley, a term used in the *Daode jing* to refer to the Way
hanshi	寒食	A religious festival for offering sacrifices to the dead
he	和	Harmony
he	荷	Lotus flower
he shen	河神	Goddess or god of a river
he shi ta	合十塔	The Namaste Pagoda, a newly established pagoda in the Temple of the Dharma Gate in Shaanxi province
hong qiang hui	红槍會	Society of Red Spears, a secret society popular in the 1920s
hou yi	后羿	The great archer in Chinese myth, who is said to shot down nine out of ten suns
hua	化	Transformation and education (of individuals and society)
huang li	黃歷	Almanacs
huan yuan	还愿	Redeeming a vow (to a god or Buddha), fulfilling one's promises to gods, donating what has been promised to a god or temple
hua shen	花神	Flower goddess, goddess of flower
huayan	華嚴	A Chinese Buddhist school taking the *Huayan sutra* as the highest teaching by the Buddha
hu guo si	護國寺	Temple of Protecting the Country
hun	魂	Spirit, part of the human spirit coming from Heaven
hung-lu ssu	鴻臚寺	The Court of State Ceremonial, a governmental branch in charge of national and foreign affairs in the Tang dynasty
hu zhu	户主	The head god of the household, the head of the household
ji	祭	Sacrifices, sacrifice to earthly deities
jia	家	Family, home, household, a philosophical and religious sect
jia jiao	家教	The family code, the tradition or principle of a family
jia li	家禮	Family rituals, family rites, family codes of conduct
jiao	教	Teaching, doctrine, education, a religious sect or school
Jiao/ Chiao	醮	Daoist sacrifice ritual, cosmic renewal rites
jiaohua	教化	To educate and transform
jia tang	家堂	The patriarchal god in the household
jia zhu	家主	The head god of the household, the head of the family
jidu jiao	基督教	The teaching of the Christ, Protestantism
jie meng	解夢	Dream interpretation
jing	精	Goblins, spirits, the essence of human body
jing shen	井神	The god of well
jingtu zong	净土宗	Pure Land Buddhism, a Buddhist School based upon Pure Land Sutras

Pinyin or other spellings	Chinese characters	English meanings or counterparts
jing zuo	静坐	Quiet sitting, a method of meditation
jin wen	今文	The new text school
jiu	久	Eternal, long time
Jiuhua	九華	The famous mountain where Bodhisattva Ksitigarbha (the King of Hell) resides
junzi	君子	Gentleman, superior person, (Confucian) ideal man
kan xiang	看相	Physiognomy
Ke	剋	Conquest, control, overcome
kung fu	功夫	Martial arts, moral efforts
lao tian ye	老天爷	A popular name for Heaven, or Lord of Heaven or the Jade Emperor
lei gong	雷公	God of thunder
li	禮	Rites, ceremonies, moral codes and rules of propriety
li	理	Principle, reason
ling	令	Directly order
ling	靈	Fairies, the numinous
lingbao	靈宝	Numinous Treasures, a Daoist sect based on the *Scripture of Numinous Treasure* or *the Classic of the Sacred Jewel*
Liuyang	瀏陽	A county of Hunan province where the cult of Mao developed in the 1990s
longshan	龍山	A place located in Shandong province where Longshan culture was first discovered
long wang	龍王	Dragon king, king of dragon
lu	鲁	The home state of Confucius, located in current Shandong province
Mazu	媽祖	Protector goddess of seafaring people and the most popular Goddess in Southeast China and Taiwan, the Empress of Heaven (tian hou)
men guan or men shen	門官/門神	Door gods or gate guardian gods
ming	明	Light, bright, the Ming dynasty (1368–1644)
ming	名	Name, a philosophical school in the Warring State period focusing on formal logic
ming	命	Destiny, fate, mandate
minjian xinyang	民間信仰	Folk beliefs, popular faiths
minjian zongjiao	民間宗教	Folk religion, popular religion
mo	墨	Mohism, a philosophical and religious school founded by Mozi
nan zong (chan)	南宗 (禪)	The southern transmission of Chan Buddhism, initiated by Huineng (638–713)
nei dan	内丹	Internal alchemy; the inner power produced by circulating and nourishing *qi* (the vital energy)
nian jing	念經	Chanting sutras
nü jie	女戒	*Lessons for Women*, a pamphlet by Ban Zhao 班昭 (49–120), a female Han historian and scholar
pi gu	辟谷	Avoiding cereals, fasting
Po	魄	Soul, a part of the human spirit coming from earth

(Continued)

Pinyin or other spellings	Chinese characters	English meanings or counterparts
pu/bu	卜	A divination method by applying heat on tortoise shells and ox shoulder blades, pyromancy
qi	氣	Air, gas, breath, ether, energy, force, power, life energy, material power
qi gong	氣功	An exercise for strengthening one's vital energy by breath control and meditation
qingming	清明	Pure bright, a festival of ancestral worship, 'cleaning the tomb', dated 5 April
qi xiang	祇禳	A Daoist ritual composed of prayer and plea for the blessing from gods or spiritual powers
quan zhen	全真	Perfect Truth, a Daoist sect established by Wang Zhe (1112–1179), featured by syncreticism, rituals and moral asceticism
ren	人	Human, a person, people, humankind
ren	仁	Humaneness, benevolence, humanity
ren zhe shou	仁者壽	The virtuous and benevolent will be able to live a long life
ru	儒	Confucians, Confucianism, a group of people proficient in ritual and education in early China
ru jia	儒家	Confucianism, a philosophical school
ru jiao	儒教	Confucianism, the religious tradition of Confucianism, the teaching or religion of Confucian scholars
san dai	三代	The three Dynasties in early China: Xia, Shang and Zhou dynasties
san huang	三皇	The Three Sovereigns in myth or legends, normally referring to Fuxi, the Divine Farmer and the Yellow Emperor
san jiao	三教	The Three religions: Confucianism, Daoism and Buddhism
sanxingdui	三星堆	A place in south-west China where Sanxingdui culture (2800–800 BCE) has been discovered
shangqing	上清	Supreme Purity, Highest Clarity, a Daoist sect elaborated and expanded by Tao Hongjing (456–563)
shang-ti/ Shangdi	上帝	Lord on High, Supreme God
shan shen	山神	God of mountain or hill
she ji/ sheji	社稷	Gods of earth and grains
shen	神	God; spirit, heavenly spirit, the mysterious, divine being
shen dao	神道	Divine way, mysterious way
sheng	生	Production, to produce, begetting; giving birth to
sheng	聖	Sagehood, the sage
Shennong/ shen nung	神農	The divine farmer, the patron god of agriculture and medicine, also known as Yandi (the Red Emperor), who is believed to be one of the two common ancestors for all Han Chinese people
shen xiang	神象	Pictures of gods
shen zhu	神主	The chief spirit in popular religion, the ancestor worshipped in the ancestral temple, ancestors' tablets in the ancestral temple or shrine
shi	示	A radical symbolizing the sacred or divine, a pictograph for a sacred stone or human made altar
shi bo	師伯	One's master's elder learning brother

Pinyin or other spellings	Chinese characters	English meanings or counterparts
shi di	師弟	A younger male disciple who studies under the same master
shi fu	師父	The master, supervisor
Shih/shi	著	Divination by the stalk, in conjunction with the *Book of Changes*
shi jing	詩經	*Book of Poetry, Classic of Poetry, Book of Songs*, one of the Confucian classics
shi mei	師妹	A younger female disciple who studies under the same master
shi nian	師娘	Teacher + mother: the wife of one's master
shi shu	師叔	One's master's younger learning brother
shi xiong	師兄	An elder learning brother, a male elder classmate who studies under the same master
shi xiong mei	師兄妹	Male and female disciples under the same master
shi zu	師祖	The founder of the (religious or learning) school, teacher and ancestor: the master of one's master or supervisor
shou yi	守一	Preserving the One, to keep consistency
shu	数	Count, numbers
Shu	蜀	A short name for Sichuan province in south-west China where a culture parallel to the Shang culture has been excavated
shu shen	树神	Tree god, the god of tree
shu shu	術数	Divination, divination methods, manipulating numbers
si	祀	Offerings, sacrifice (to heavenly spirits)
si fang shen	四方神	Gods of the four directions
si jiao	司郊	Suburban sacrifices to Heaven and Earth
si wu	司巫	Director of sorcery, an administrative official in charge of religious affairs in early China
songzi Guanyin	送子觀音	The son giver bodhisattva
songzi niangniang	送子娘娘	The Goddess who responds to the prayer for sons, a goddess in Daoist and folk religion
su wang	素王	The uncrowned king, Confucius
ta-hsi tsung-yin yuan	大禧宗埋院	The Office for Religious Administration in the Yuan dynasty
t'ai-ch'ang ssu	太常寺	The Court of Imperial Sacrifices
tai chu you dao	太初有道	In the very beginning there was the Dao
taiji	太極	The Supreme Ultimate, a popular exercise in China
t'ai pai	太白	Great Whiteness, God of Venus
tai ping	太平	Grand peace, a Daoist utopia of harmonious society
taiping zhenjun	太平真君	True Ruler of Grand Peace
taishang laojun	太上老君	Lord Lao the Most High; Supreme Old Master; Very High Old Lord; the deified Laozi
taiwei/tai wei	太微	A name of a Daoist Immortal, a star god
taiyi shengshui	太一生水	The ultimate One who gives birth to water
tao	道	The Way
tao-chü	道舉	National civil service examination by Daoist scriptures (in the Tang dynasty)
tian	天	Heaven, sky
tian di	天帝	Lord of Heaven

(Continued)

Pinyin or other spellings	Chinese characters	English meanings or counterparts
tian ming	天命	The Mandate of Heaven
tian shi	天師	Heavenly Master; Celestial Master
tian shi dao	天師道	The Way of Heavenly Masters, a major Daoist school developed from the Five Bushels of Rice Daoim in the Latter Han dynasty
tian tai	天臺	An important Chinese Buddhist sect, also called the Lotus School for its emphasis on the *Lotus Sutra*, founded by Zhi Yi (538–597)
tian yi	天意	The will of Heaven
tian zi	天子	The Son of Heaven, a title for the king or emperor
tianzhu jiao	天主教	The Teachings of the Lord of Heaven, Catholicism
tian zun	天尊	Heavenly Worthies, the original gods or powers in Daoism
tu di	土地	The god of earth, god of soil, gods of site
wai dan	外丹	External alchemy, immortality elixirs made from cinnabar and other chemical elements
wei he	違和	Contrary to harmony, becoming ill
wen	文	Culture, gentleness, the civilized
wen chang	文昌	The stellar god of literature
wen chang xing	文昌星	The literature star, God of Literature
wenhua	文化	Culture
wu chang	五常	Five Cardinal Virtues: benevolence, righteousness, propriety, wisdom and trustfulness; Five constant relationships: father-son, husband-wife, ruler-subject, elder-younger brothers, friend-friend
wu dao	五道	God of the five roads
wu da zongjiao	五大宗教	Five major religions in contemporary Mainland China: Daoism, Buddhism, Catholicism, Protestantism and Islam
wu di	五帝	Five Emperors, Five Gods
wu jie	五戒	Five essential Commandments of Buddhism: not kill, not steal, not commit adultery, not lie, and not drink alcohol
wusheng laomu	无生老母	Eternal Mother
wu wei	无為	Non-action, no striving
wu xing	五行	Five elements, five agents, five principles, five powers, five movers, or five phases, five activities, referring to five most important forces of the universe: water, wood, metal, fire and earth
xian	仙, 僊	Immortals, gods
xiang	享	Sacrifices to ancestors
xiantian jiao	先天教	The Formerly Heaven Religion
xian zhi/xian shi	先知、先識	Foreknowledge, foreknowing
xiao	孝	Filial piety, filiality
xiao zong	小宗	The collateral ancestor line
xie jiao	邪教	Cult, evil religion, heretical teaching
xin	心	Heart/mind
xing	性	Nature, human nature

Pinyin or other spellings	Chinese characters	English meanings or counterparts
xing xiang	星象	Astrology
xin zhai	心齋	The fasting of the heart/mind
xi wang mu	西王母	Queen Mother of the West
xuan di	玄帝	The Black Emperor, one of the five gods
xuan pin	玄牝	Mystical female
xuan xue	玄學	Dark learning, mystical learning, neo-Daoism
xuanzong (685–762)	玄宗	The title for the Tang Emperor, Li Longji 李隆基 (r. 712–756), which indicates his favour of Daoism
xue	學	Learning, study
xu wei	虛位	An empty position
xu yuan	許願	Making a vow to a god or spiritual power in exchange of godly blessing or protection
yandi	炎帝	The Red Emperor, the Divine Farmer, who together with the Yellow Emperor are believed to be the common ancestors of the Han Chinese
yang qi	養氣	Nourishing one's vital power
yangshao	仰韶	A place in Henan province where Yangshao culture (5000–3000BCE) is first found
yao	尧	A Confucian legendary sage king
ya sheng	亞聖	The second sage of the Confucian tradition
yi	一	The One, another name for Dao; the source and origin of the universe
yi	易	Easy, change or constant transformation; the *Book of Changes*
yi guan dao	一貫道	The Pervading Way, a popular Daoist religious school formed at the end of the Qing dynasty, still influential in Taiwan
yi he tuan	義和團	Boxer Rising (1898–1900) movement, Harmonious Fists, a religio-political movement against foreign powers
yi li	儀禮	*The Rites of Etiquette and Ceremonial*, one of the ritual texts from early China, one of the thirteen classics in Confucianism
yin	音	Tones, sounds
yin-yang	陰陽	Two opposite and complementary elements or forces of the universe, school of yin-yang is one of the six major schools in ancient China
yu	禹	A Confucian ancient sage king and the supposed founder of the Xia dynasty
yuan	元	The beginning; the origin, a monetary unit
yue	樂	Music
yu huang	玉皇	The Jade Emperor, the Lord of Heaven
yu huang miao	玉皇廟	Temple of the Jade Emperor
yulan pen jie	盂蘭盆節	Buddhist Ullambana Festival (on the 15th day of the 7th month) for releasing suffering souls
zaijia	在家	Staying home, to live a religious life through secular familial activities rather than a monastery life
zaojun	竈君	Kitchen God, God of Stove, gods of hearth
zao shen	竈神	The kitchen gods

(Continued)

Pinyin or other spellings	Chinese characters	English meanings or counterparts
zao wang nai	竈王奶	Lady of Kitchen
zao wang ye	竈王爷	Lord of Kitchen
zhai/chai	齋	Fasting and purification
zheng yi	正一	Way of the Complete Orthodox (Orthodox One), another name for the Heavenly Master Daoism
zhengzhou	鄭州	The capital city of Henan province
zhen kong dao	真空道	Way of True Emptiness, a Daoist school
zhen ren	真人	True persons, complete person, a Daoist term for ideal humans or immortals
zhi lai	知來	Knowing of what is to come, foreknowing the future
zhisheng xianshi	至聖先师	Supreme Sage and Former Teacher, Confucius
zhong yuan	中元	The mid-origin festival of Daoism and popular religion (15th day of the 7th month) for worshipping ancestors and releasing the suffering souls
zhongyuan wenhua	中原文化	The culture of the central region
zhou guan	周官	Officials of the Zhou dynasty, *the Rites of the Zhou*
zhuan xü	顓頊	A legendary Sage King in the third millennia BCE, alleged to have first introduced the state control of religion
zong	宗	Clan ancestor, schools or sects
zong bo	宗伯	Head of the Ministry of Rites during the Zhou dynasty
zong ci	宗祠	The clan ancestral temple
Zongjiao	宗教	Religion, ancestral teaching; pious doctrine
zong zheng	宗正	*the Court of the Imperial Clan*, a state office in charge of affairs relating to the royal family members and clan
zong zu	宗族	Clan, a group of families from the same ancestors
zu	祖	Ancestor
zu miao	祖廟	The ancestral temple, the temple of ancestors

Appendix II: A Glossary of Chinese Names and Texts

Pinyin or other spellings	Chinese characters	English meanings
Ban Gu	班固 (32–92 CE)	A Han historian, the main author of the *History of the Former Han Dynasty* (Hanshu)
Ban zhao	班昭 (?48–?112)	A female *literata* of the Later Han dynasty, author of *Lessons for Women* (*nü jie*)
baopuzi	抱朴子	*The Master who has Embraced Simplicity*, a Daoist book by Ge Hong (284–364)
Chen Tsung	真宗 (1048–1085)	The sixth emperor of the Song dynasty (r. 1067–1085)
Dao An	道安 (312–385)	A Buddhist master, renowned for his translation of Buddhist scriptures; his interpretation of Buddhist doctrines influenced a number of Buddhist schools
daode jing	道德經	The *Book of the Way and its Power*, an essential Daoist Classic, traditionally alleged to have been composed by Laozi
Dao Yuan	道原 (?–?)	A Buddhist monk and scholar, the editor of *Jingde Chuandeng lu* or *The Records of the Lamp*, probably in the tenth century
Dong Zhongshu	董仲舒 (179–104 BCE)	The most important Han Confucian who played an essential role in setting up Confucianism as the state orthodoxy during the reign of Emperor Wu (r. 141–87 BCE)
Fanwang	梵网	A Buddhist sutra enhancing filial piety
Fei Xiaotong	费孝通 (1910–2005)	A prominent anthropologist and sociologist in modern China
Feng Jicai	冯骥才 (1942–)	A renowned scholar in contemporary Chinese literature and cultural studies
fengshen yanyi	封神演義	*Investiture of the Gods*, a famous novel by Chen Zhonglin of the Ming dynasty
Fu Xi/Fu Hsi	伏羲	A legendary or mythic figure in early China, the patron god of hunting and husbandry, believed to live around 2852 BCE
Ge Hong	葛洪 (283–343)	A significant Daoist theorist and immortality practitioner, the author of the book *Baopuzi* (*The Master who has Embraced Simplicity*), compiled around 320 CE
Guan Yin	關尹 (?–?)	A short name of Guanling Yinxi (Yinxi the Official of the Gate), who is believed to be the one who asked Laozi for *Daodejing*

(Continued)

Pinyin or other spellings	Chinese characters	English meanings
Guanyu/Guan Yu	關羽 (?160–219)	A warrior of the Three Kingdoms period, later Lord Guan, the nationwide supreme god of righteousness, brotherhood, loyalty, bravery, medicine, wealth, etc.
Guo Moruo	郭沫若 (1892–1978)	A distinguished modern Chinese scholar on history, culture and literature
guoyü	國語	*Sayings of the States*, an early historical account for the Spring and Autumn (771–479 BCE) and the Warring States periods (479–221 BCE)
Hanshan	寒山 (691–793)	A Buddhist monk poet, later becoming one of the two gods of harmony in folk-religion
han shu	漢書	*The History of the Former Han Dynasty*
hong lou meng	紅樓夢	The *Dream of the Red Chamber* by Cao Xueqin (?1724–?1764)
huang ting jing	黃廳經	*The Yellow Court Scripture*, the most important scripture for the Shang qing Daoist sect and the school of Internal Alchemy
Hui yuan	慧遠 (334–416)	A Buddhist monk and scholar who played a key role in the acculturation of Buddhism in China, later regarded as the first patriarch of Pure Land Buddhism
jingde chuandeng lu	景德傳燈錄	*The Records of the Lamp*, a collection of Buddhist biographies by Dao Yuan, first published in the year of 1006
jing hua yuan	鏡花緣	*Affinity between Mirror and Flower*, a novel by Li Ruzhen (李汝珍, 1763–1830)
Jin Yong	金庸 (1924–)	Original name Zha Liangyong 查良鏞, a famous Hong Kong martial-art novel writer
Kong fuzi	孔夫子 (551–479 BCE)	Master Kong, a venerable name for Confucius, the founder of Confucianism
Kou Qianzhi	寇謙之 (365–448)	A Daoist reformer, responsible for the revival of the Heavenly Master tradition in north China
Laozi	老子 (?600–?470 BCE)	Old master, Supreme Lord, a venerable name for the supposed author or compiler of *Daode jing*
laozi xianger zhu	老子想爾注	The first commentary on *Daode jing*, allegedly by Zhang daoling (34–156) or his grandson Zhanglu (?–216)
Li	李	The surname of Laozi and the Tang royal family
Li Hongzhi	李洪志 (1951–)	Founder of Falungong (the Practices of the Wheel of Dharma)
li ji/li ki	禮記	*The Book of Rites*
Li Ruzhen	李汝珍 (?1763–1830)	Author of *Affinity between Mirror and Flower* (*Jinghua yuan*)
Li Shimin	李世民 (599–649)	The second emperor of the Tang dynasty who ruled China from 626 to 649
Li Si	李斯 (?–208 BCE)	Prime minister of the First Emperor of the Qin dynasty, one of the chief representatives of the Legalist School
Liu Xiang	劉劉向 (?77–6 BCE)	A famous Han scholar in the study of ancient Chinese classics, responsible for editing or compiling a number of classical texts

Pinyin or other spellings	Chinese characters	English meanings
lun liu jia zhi yaozhi	論六家之要旨	*On Essentials of the Six Orientations*, a book written by Sima Tan 司馬談 (?–110 BCE) of the Han dynasty
lunyu	論語	*The Analects*, a short book recording the words and acts of Confucius and conversations between him and his disciples
Luo Qing	罗清 (1424–1527)	The founder of the *Wu-Wei* (Nonaction) Religion, one of the biggest branches of the White Lotus Religion during the Ming-Qing dynasties
Lu Xiujing	陸修靜 (406–477)	A Daoist master, promoting the *Lingbao* Daoist sect, a tradition developed under the influence of Buddhist devotion to bodhisattvas, and emphasized the ritual and worship of heavenly deities
Mao Zedong	毛泽东 (1893–1976)	The communist leader and the founder of the People's Republic of China
Mengzi	孟子 (?372–?289 BCE)	The second sage of the Confucian tradition; the representative of the Zi Si-Mengzi school that promotes the goodness of human heart/mind
Mo	墨	Moism or Mohism, one of the philosophical and religious schools, best known for its propagation of universal love
Modi	墨翟 (470–391 BCE)	The founder of Mohism; also addressed as Mozi, Master Mo.
Nüwa	女娲	A myth figure, who is believed to have repaired the sky and created humankind by earth
Qin Qiong	秦瓊 (?–638)	A famous general under the Emperor Li Shimin of the Tang dynasty, later one of the gate guardian gods in folk-religion
san guo yanyi	三國演義	*Romance of the Three Kingdoms* by Luo Guanzhong (1330?–1400?)
shang shu	尚書	The *Book of History*, the Book of Documents
Shao Yong	邵雍 (1011–1077)	A Confucian scholar of the Song dynasty
Shen shu and Yu Lu	神荼, 郁垒	The two brothers who were believed to be able to protect the household from demons and were taken as the gate guardian gods in early China
shenxian tongjian	神仙通鑑	*A Completed Record of Immortals*, compiled around 1700 by Zhang Jizong (1679–1715)
shenxian zhuan	神仙傳	*The Biographies of Immortals*, by Ge Hong (283–343)
Shide	拾得 (?–?).	A famous Buddhist monk poet of the Tang Dynasty; later one of the two gods of harmony
Shi yi	十翼	The ten commentaries on the text of the *Book of Changes* which are traditionally attributed to Confucius
Shui hu	水滸	*Water Margin* by Shi Nai-an (1296–1372), one of the four famous Chinese classical novels
Shun	舜	A Confucian sage king, succeeding the sage king Yao; famous for his virtue of filial piety
Sima Qian	司馬遷 (?145–?86 BCE)	Author of the *Records of the Historian*
Sima Tan	司馬談 (?–110 BCE)	Father of the author of the *Records of the Historian*, Sima Qian, and the author of *Essentials of the Six Orientations*

(Continued)

Pinyin or other spellings	Chinese characters	English meanings
Sun Chuo	孫綽 (314–371)	The author of *Yü Dao Lun* (*A Discourse on Illustrating the Way*)
tai ping jing	太平經	*The Scripture of Grand Peace*
Tai-wu	太武 (408–452)	The third emperor of the Northern Wei dynasty, Tuoba Tao 拓跋燾 (r. 423–252)
Taizong of the Tang	唐太宗 (599–649)	Li Shimin (李世民, r. 626–649), the second emperor of the Tang dynasty
Tang Saier	唐賽尔 (?–?)	A leader of the White Lotus sect during the Ming Dyansty who claimed to be the 'Mother of the Buddha' (*fo mu*) in 1420
Tang Sanzang	唐三藏 (602–664)	An honourable name for Xuanzang (玄奘), a famous Buddhist Monk of the Tang dynasty who went to India to learn Buddhism; the hero of the popular novel, the *Journey to the West*
Wang Chong	王充 (27–?97)	A famous Han scholar and the author of *Lun Heng*
Wang Yangming	王陽明 (1472–1529)	A Ming Confucian scholar and politician, one of the famous representatives of Idealistic Confucianism who propagated the idea of the unity between knowledge and action
Wu Cheng-en	吳承恩 (1505–1580)	A Ming novelist, possible author of one of the four great classical Chinese novels, the *Journey to the West*
Wu Zetian	武則天 (624–705)	Empress Wu, who was the Queen of the third Tang emperor Gaozong (655–683) and the Queen Mother of emperors Zhongzong and Ruizong (683–690); she established her own dynasty, Dazhou (690–705)
xiao jing	孝經	*Classic of Filial Piety*
xi you ji	西游記	*Journey to the West,* by Wu Cheng-en
Xuan zang	玄奘 (?602–664)	The Buddhist monk pilgrim to India during the Tang dynasty (618–906) to fetch the *Tripitaka* Sutras
xuehai	学海	A title of an academic journal in Chinese
Xunzi	荀子 (?313–?238 BCE)	The most sophisticated and influential thinker during the late Warring States period
Yandi	炎帝	The Red Emperor, Divine Farmer, who together with the Yellow Emperor are believed to be the common ancestors of the Han Chinese
Yang Zhu	楊朱 (?370–?319 BCE)	An early Daoist philosopher advocating the preservation of one's person or an egoist doctrine
Ye Xiaowen	叶小文 (1950–)	The director of the State Administration of Religious Affairs of China between 1995 and 2009
Yin Xi	尹喜 (?–545? BCE)	The pass-keeper who requested Laozi to write the 5,000 character text, *Daode jing*, before his retreating from the world
Youxuan zi	有玄子 (?–?)	A Daoist practitioner, the supposed author of the earliest extant ledger of merits and demerits (dated 1171) that served as a model for later morality books
Yuchi Jingde	尉遲敬德 (585–658)	A famous Tang general who later become one of the gate guardian gods in Chinese popular religion

Pinyin or other spellings	Chinese characters	English meanings
yü dao lun	喻道論	*A Discourse on Illustrating the Way*, by Sun chuo 孙绰 (314–171)
Zengzi	曾子 (505–436)	The venerable name for Zengshen曾参, one of the 72 famous disciples of Confucius, renowned for filial piety and traditionally credited with the authorship of the *Great Learning* (da xue)
Zhang Daoling	张道陵 (34–156)	Also Zhang Ling, regarded as the founder of Heavenly Master Daoism, and the first Heavenly Master; the initiator of the Way of Five Bushels of Rice
Zhang Heng	张恆 (?–?)	The son of Zhang Daoling, who inherited his father's mission through the Way of Five Bushels of Rice religion
Zhang Jue	张角 (?–184)	One of the leaders of the Yellow Turbans Movement, a military movement based on religious Daoism
Zhang Lu	张鲁 (?–216)	The grandson of Zhang Daoling and son of Zhang Heng, who further developed their teachings and organized Daoist communities into religious-military units, and headed a small kingdom for a short period of time
Zhang Zai	张载 (1020–1077)	A prominent Neo-Confucian scholar of the Song Dynasty
zhou li	周禮	*Rites of the Zhou*, the earliest and most complete record of official systems and rituals in China
zhouyi cantong qi	周易參同契	A *Collection of Daoist Commentaries on the Book of Changes* which is generally considered to be the earliest work on alchemical techniques
Zhuangzi	庄子 (?399–?295 BCE)	An important early Daoist philosopher, believed to be the author of the *Book of Zhangzi*
Zhuge Liang	诸葛亮 (181–234)	One of the most beloved and influential characters in Chinese history and the strategist for one of the three kingdoms
Zhu Xi	朱熹 (1130–1200)	The editor of the famous Four Books and the most important representative of rationalistic Confucianism
Zhu Yuanzhang	朱元璋 (1328–1398)	The founder of the Ming dynasty (r. 1368–1398), who rose from the Red Turban movement, and named his dynasty the Ming (Light) to align himself with the widespread principles of the significant 'Religion of Light'
zhuzi jiali	朱子家禮	*Family Codes of Master Zhu*, a book for family rituals by Zhu Xi (1130–1200)

Bibliography

Adler, Joseph, *Chinese Religion*, London and New York: Routledge, 2002.

Allan, Sarah, 'Erlitou and the foundation of Chinese Civilization: Toward a New Paradigm' *The Journal of Asian Studies*, 2007, Volume 66, Issue 2: 461–496.

Benn, Charles, Religious Aspects of Emperor Hsüan-tsung's Taoist Ideology, in Chappell, David W. (ed.), *Buddhist and Taoist Practice in Medieval Chinese Society: Buddhist and Taoist Studies II*, Honululu: University of Hawaii Press, 1987, pp. 127–145.

Berthrong, John, H, *Transformations of the Confucian Way*, Boulder, CO: Westview Press, 1998.

Bilsky, Lester James, *The State Religion in Ancient China*, Taipei: The Chinese Association for Folklore, 1975.

Bol, Peter K, '*This Culture of Ours' – Intellectual Transitions in T'ang and Sung China*, Stanford: Stanford University Press, 1992.

Bowker, John, *World Religions: The Great Faiths Explored and Explained*, London: Dorling Kindersley, 1997.

Bowker, John. (ed.), *Cambridge Illustrated History of Religion*, Cambridge: Cambridge University Press, 2002.

Brewitt-Taylor, C. H. (tr.), *San Kuo or Romance of the Three Kingdoms*, volumes I and II, Shanghai, Hongkong, Singapore: Kelly & Walsh, Limited, 1925.

Bu Gong, *Wenming qiyuan de zhongguo moshi* 文明起源的中国模式, Beijing: Kexue chubanshe, 2007.

Bush, Richard, *Religion in China*, Niles, IL: Argus Communications, 1977.

Chan, Wing-tsit. (tr. And Comp.), *A Source Book in Chinese Philosophy*, Princeton: Princeton University Press, 1963.

—*Religious Trends in Modern China*, New York: Octagon Books, 1978.

Chappell, David W. (ed.), *Buddhist and Taoist Practice in Medieval Chinese Society: Buddhist and Taoist Studies II*, Honululu: University of Hawaii Press, 1987.

Ch'en, Kenneth, *Buddhism in China: A Historical Survey*, Princeton: Princeton University Press, 1964. *The Chinese Transformation of Buddhism*, Princeton: Princeton University press, 1973.

Chen, Guying, *Daojia Wenhua Yanjiu* 道家文化研究 (volume 18)：郭店楚简专号, Beijing: Sanlian chubanshe, 1999.

Chen, Lai: *Gudai zongjiao yu lunli – rujia sixiang de genyuan*古代宗教与伦理--儒家思想的根源, Beijing: Sanlian chubanshe, 1996.

Chen, Mengjia, *Yinxu Buci Zongshu* 殷墟卜辞综述, Beijing: Kexue chubanshe, 1956.

The China Youth Daily, 9 March 2009.

Ching, Julia, *Chinese Religions*, Maryknoll and New York: Orbis Books, 1993.

—*Mysticism and Kingship in China—The Heart of Chinese Wisdom*, Cambridge: Cambridge University Press, 1997.

Concise Oxford Dictionary, Oxford: Oxford University Press, 2008, the 11th revised edition.

Connolly, Peter (ed.), *Approaches to the Study of Religion*, London and New York: Cassell, 1999.

Dao Yuan, *Jingde chuandeng lu*, Taipei: Zhenshanmei Publishing House, 1970.

Dawson, Raymond, *The Chinese Experience*, London: Weidenfeld and Nicolson, 1978.

de Bary, Wm. Theodore and Bloom, Irene (ed.), *Sources of Chinese Tradition*, second edition, Vol. 1, New York: Columbia University Press, 1999.

de Bary, Wm. Theodore, Chan, Wing-tstit and Watson,Burton, *Sources of Chinese Tradition* Vol. 1 (Introduction to oriental Civilization), New York: Columbia University Press,1960

De Groot, J. J. M, *The Religious System of China*, Vol. 1, reprint, Taibei: Xin wenfeng, 1976.

Dillon, Michael, *Contemporary China*, London and New York: Routledge, 2009.

Dudbridge, Glen, *Religious Experience and Lay Society in Tang China*, Cambridge: Cambridge University Press, 2002

Durkheim, Emile, *The Elementary form of Religious Life*, Oxford: Oxford University Press, 1961, reprinted in 2008.

Ebrey, Patricia Buckley, 'The Response of the Sung State to Popular Funeral Practices', in Patricia Buckley Ebrey and Peter, N. Gregory (eds), *Religion and Society in T'ang and Sung China*, Honolulu: University of Hawaii Press, 1993, pp. 209–239.

Ebrey, Patricia Buckley and Gregory, Peter N. (eds), *Religion and Society in T'ang and Sung China*, Honolulu: University of Hawaii Press, 1993.

Eno, Robert, *The Confucian Creation of Heaven – Philosophical and the Defense of Ritual Mastery*, Albany: State University of New York Press, 1990.

Fan Yi, Sanxingdui xunmeng 三星堆寻梦, Chengdu: Sichuan minzu chubanshe, 1998.

Fang Litian: *Fojiao yu zhongguo wenhua* 佛教与中国文化, Beijing: zhonghua shujü, 2008.

Fei Xiaotong, 'jiating jiegou biandong zhong de laonian shanyang wenti' 家庭结构变动中的老年赡养问题, in *zhongguo jiating yanjiu* 中国家庭研究, Shanghai: Shanghai shehui kexue chubanshe, 2006, pp. 3–15.

Feifel, E. (tr.), Pao P'u Tzû, *Monumenta Serica*, Vol. VI, 1941.

Feng Jicai, Nianhua de faxian 年画的发现, in Shou Huo 收获 (*Harvest – A Literary Bimonthly*), No.1, 2009, pp. 53–62.

Feuchtwang, Stephan, 'Domestic and Communal Worship in Taiwan', in Arthur P. Wolf (ed.), *Religion and Ritual in Chinese Society*, Stanford University Press, California, 1974, pp. 105–129.

—*The Imperial Metaphor: Popular Religion in* China, New York and London: Routledge, 1992.

Fingarette, Herbert, *Confucius – The Secular as Sacred*, New York and London: Harper Torchbook, 1972.

Flood, Gavin, *Beyond Phenomenology: Rethinking the Study of Religion*, London and New York: Cassell, 1999.

Fowler, Jeaneane, *An Introduction to the Philosophy and Religion of Taoism: Pathways to Immortality*, Brighton and Portland: Sussex Academic Press, 2005.

Freedman, Maurice, 'On the Sociological Study of Chinese Religion', in Arthur P. Wolf (ed.), *Religion and Ritual in Chinese Society*, Stanford: Stanford University Press, 1974, pp. 19–41

—*The study of Chinese Society: Essays by Maurice Freedman, selected and introduced by G. William Skinner,* Stanford: Stanford University Press, 1979

Fung, Yu-lan, *A History of Chinese Philosophy*, vol. 1 The Period of The Philosophers (From the Beginning to Circa 100 B.C.), and vol. 2, The Period of Classical Learning (from the second century B.C. to the twentieth century A.D.), translated by Derk Bodde, Princeton: Princeton University Press, 1952, 1953.

—*A Short History of Chinese Philosophy,* New York: Macmillan, 1961.

Ge, Zhaoguang, *Zhongguo Sixiangshi* 中国思想史, volume 1, *Shanghai: Fudan daxue chubanshe,* 2001.

Geertz, Clifford, *The Interpretation of Cultures*, London: Hutchinson, 1975.

Gernet, Jacques and Verellen, Franciscus, *Buddhism in Chinese Society*, New York: Columbia University Press, 1998.

Gregory, Peter, N. and Ebrey, Patricia Buckley, The Religious and Historical Landscape, in Patricia Buckley Ebrey and Peter N. Gregory (eds), *Religion and Society in T'ang and Sung China*, Honolulu: University of Hawaii Press, 1993, pp. 1–44.

Guo Moruo郭沫若, 'Shi Bizu'释妣祖, in *Jiagu wenzi yanjiu* 甲骨文字研究, Shanghai dadong shuju 上海大东书局, 1931, chapter 1.

Hahn, Thomas H, 'New Developments concerning Buddhist and Taoist Monasteries', in Julian F. Pas (ed.), *The Turning of the Tide: Religion in China Today*, Hong Kong: Royal Asiatic Society, 1989, pp. 79–101.

Han Yu, *Han Yu Quanji* 韩愈全集, Shanghai: Shanghai guji chubanshe, 1997.

Harvey, Peter (ed.), *Buddhism*, London and New York: Continuum, 2001.

Hawkes, David (trans.), *The Story of the Stone*, vol. 1, England: Penguin Books, 1973.

He Gang: Hunan hong jiang gaomiao yizhi kaogu fajue huo zhongda faxian 湖南洪江高庙遗址考古发掘获重大发现, in *Zhongguo wenwubao* 中国文物报, 2006年1月6日.

Hinton, David (trans.), *Mencius*, Washington, D.C.: Counterpoint, 1998.

Holm, Jean and Bowker, John (ed.), *Rites of Passage*, London and New York: Pinter Publishers, 1994.

Horton, R, 'A Definition of Religion', *Journal of Royal Anthropological Institute*, 1960, vol. 90, no. 2, pp.201–226.

Hu Shih, *Independence, Convergence, and Borrowing*, Cambridge, MA: Harvard University press, 1937.

Hucker, Charles O, *A Dictionary of Official Tiles in Imperial China*, Stanford: Stanford University Press, 1985.

Jackson, J. H. (tr.), *Water Margin*, Vols. 1–2, Hong Kong: The Commercial Press, 1976.

Karlgren, Bernhard (trans.), *The Book of the Documents*, in *Bulletin of the Museum of Far Eastern Antiquities*, Stockholm, 1950.

Keightley, David N. (ed.), *The Origins of Chinese Civilization*, Berkeley: University of California Press, 1984.

Kenneth, Dean, 'Revival of Religious Practices in Fujian: A Case Study', in Julian F. Pas (ed.), *The Turning of the Tide: Religion in China Today*, Hong Kong: Royal Asiatic Society, 1989, pp. 51–78.

Kleeman, Terry F, 'The Expansion of the Wen-chang Cult', in Patricia Buckley Ebrey and Peter N. Gregory (eds), *Religion and Society in T'ang and Sung China*, Honululu: University of Hawaii Press, 1993, pp. 45–73.

Knoblock, John, *Xunzi: A Translation and Study of the Complete Works*, Vol.1 Stanford: Stanford University Press, 1988.

Kohn, Livia and Roth, Harold David, *Daoist Identity: History, Lineage and Ritual*, Honululu: University of Hawaii Press, 2002.

Küng, Hans and Julia Ching, *Christianity and Chinese Religions*, New York: Doubleday, 1990.

Lagerwey, John, *Taoist Ritual in Chinese Society and History*, London: Macmillan Publishing Company, 1986.

Language Institute at Social Science Academy of China (eds), *The Contemporary Chinese Dictionary* [*Chinese-English Edition*], Beijing: Foreign Language Teaching and Research Press, 2002.

Lau, D. C. (tr.), *Lao Tzu–Tao Te Ching*, London: Penguin Books, 1963.

—(tr.), *Confucius–The Analects*, London: Penguin Books, 1979.

—(tr.), *Mencius*, London: Penguin Books, 1970.

Legge, James, *The Sacred Books of China, The Texts of Confucianism, Part I The Shu King, The Religious Portions of the Shih King, The Hsiao King*, Oxford: The Clarendon Press, 1899.

—*The Li Ki*, in *The Sacred Books of the East* (edited by F. Max Müller), Vol, XXVII and Vol XXVIII, Oxford: Clarendon Press, 1885; Delhi: Motilal Banarsidass, 1968 reprinted.

—*The Analects* in James Legge: *The Chinese Classics*, volume 1, Taibei: SMC Publishing INC, 1991 reprint.

— *The Ch'un Ts'ew with the Tso Chuen (Zuozhuan)*, in *The Chinese Classics*, volume 5, Taibei: SMC Publishing INC, 1991, reprint.

Li Ruzhen (1763–1830), *Affinity between Mirror and Flower* (*Jinghua yuan*, 镜花缘) Taipei: Fengche tushu, 2000.

Li Xueqin, (ed.), *Zhongguo gudai wenming qiyuan* 中国古代文明起源, Shanghai: Shanghai kexue jishu wenxian chubanshe, 2007.

Lin Yutang (tr. and ed.), *The Wisdom of Confucius*, Taipei: Zhengzhong shuju, 1994.

Lip, Evelyn, *Chinese Geomancy*, Singapore, Kuala Lumpus: Times Books International, 1979.

Liu Chih-wan, 'Zhongguo Chiaoshi Shi Yi' (Analysis of the Meaning of the Chiao Sacrifice) in his book *Zhongguo minjian Xinyang Lunji (Essays on Chinese Folk Beliefs)*, Taibei: Institute of Ethnology, Academic Sinica, Monograph, no 22, 1974.

Loewe, Michael and Edward L. Shaughnessy (eds), *The Cambridge History of Ancient China*, Cambridge: Cambridge University Press, 1999.

Lü Daji and Mou Zhongjian, *Gaishuo zhongguo zongjiao yu chuantong wenhua* 概说中国宗教与传统文化, Beijing: Zhongguo shehui kexue chubanshe, 2004.

Lu Sixian, *Shenhua kaogu* 神话考古, Beijing: Wenwu chubanshe, 1995.

Lynn, Richard John (tr.), *The Classic of Changes – A New Translation of the I Ching as Interpreted by Wang Bi*, New York: Columbia University Press, New York, 1994.

Maspero, Henri, *Taoism and Chinese Religion*, Amherst: University of Massachusetts Press, 1981.

Miller, James, *Chinese Religions in Contemporary Societies*, Santa Barbara: ABC-CLIO, 2006

Mou Zhongjian, *Zhongguo zongjiao yu zhongguo wenhua:zongjiao, wenyi, minsu* 中国宗教与中国文化：宗教，文艺,民俗, Beijing: Zhongguo shehui kexue chubanshe, 2005.

Mou Zhongjian and Zhang Jian: *Zhongguo zongjiao tongshi* 中国宗教通史 (上下), Beijing: Zhongguo shehui kexue chubanshe, 2007.

Overmyer, Daniel L.(ed.), *Religion in China Today*, The China Quarterly Special Issues New Series, No.3, Cambridge University Press, 2003.

Overseas Chinese Affairs Office of the State Council, *Common Knowledge about Chinese Geography*, Beijing: Higher Education Press, 2007

Paper, Jordan D, *The Spirits are Drunk: Comparative Approaches to Chinese Religion*, New York: State University of New York Press, 1995.

Pas, Julian, F. (ed.), *The Turning of the Tide: Religion in China Today*, Oxford and New York: Oxford University Press, 1989.

—*Historical Dictionary of Taoism*, Lanham, MD and London: The Scarecrow Press, Inc, 1998.

Passmore, John, 'Philosophy', in Paul Edwards (ed.), *The Encyclopaedia of Philosophy*, New York: Macmillan, 1967, Vol. 6, pp. 217–8.

Patton, Laurie L. and Doniger, Wendy, *Myth and Method*, Charlottesville and London: The University of Virginia Press, 1996.

Qi Liang, *Zhongguo wenmin shi* 中国文明史, Guangzhou: Huacheng chubanshe, 2001.

Rawson, Jessica (ed.), *Mysteries of Ancient China: New Discoveries from the Early Dynasties*, London: British Museum Press, 1996.

Redfield, R, *Peasant Society and Culture: An Anthropological Approach to Civilization*, Chicago: The University of Chicago Press, 1956.

Ren Jie and Liang Ling, Zhongguo de zongjiao zhengce 中国的宗教政策, Beijing: Minzu chubanshe, 2006.

Robinet, Isabelle, *Taoism: Growth of a Religion*, translated by Phyllis Brooks, Stanford: Stanford University Press, 1997.

Saso, Michael, *Blue Dragon, White Tiger: Taoist Rites of Passage*, Honolulu: University of Hawaii Press, 1990.

Seligman, Adam B, Weller, Robert P. and Simon, Bennett, *Ritual and Its Consequences: An Essay on the Limits of Sincerity*, Oxford: Oxford University Press, 2008.

Sharma, Arvind (ed.), *Our Religions*, New York: HarperCollins Publishers, 1993.

Shryock, John K, *The Origin and Development of the State Cult of Confucius: An Introductory Study*, New York: Paragon Book Reprint Corp, 1966.

Sima Qian: *Shiji* 史记 (*The Book of History*), Beijing: zhonghua shuju, 1959.

Slote, Walter H, Psychocultural Dynamics within the Confucian Family: Past and Present, *Confucianism and the Family*, (ed.), Walter H. Slote and George A. DeVos, Albany: State University of New York Press, 1998.

Smart, Ninian, *The World's Religion*, 2nd edition, Cambridge: Cambridge University press, 1998.

Sommer, Deborah (ed.), *Chinese Religion: An Anthology of Sources*, New York: Oxford University Press, 1995.

Soothill, W. E, *The Three Religions of China*, Oxford: Oxford University Press, 1929.

Su Bingqi, *Zhongguo Wenming Qiyuan Xintan* 中国文明起源新探, Beijing: Sanlian chubanshe, 1999.

Tang Junyi, *Zhongguo wenhua zhi jingshen jiazhi* 中国文化之精神价值, Nanjing: Jiangsu jiaoyu chubanshe, 2005.

Teiser, Stephen F, *The Ghost Festival in Medieval China*, Princeton: Princeton University Press, 1988.

Thompson, Laurence G, *Chinese Religion: An Introduction*, Belmont, CA: Wadsworth Publishing Company, 1996 (Fifth Edition).

—*The Religious Life of Man: The Chinese Way in Religion*, Encino, CA: Dickenson Publishing Company, INC, 1973.

Tsui, Bartholomew P. M, 'Recent Development in Buddhism in Hong Kong', in Julian F. Pas (ed.), *The Turning of the Tide: Religion in China Today*, Oxford: Oxford University Press, 1989, pp. 299–312.

Tung Tso-pin, *An Interpretation of the Ancient Chinese Civilization*, Taipei: Chinese Association for the United Nations, 1952.

Twitchett, Denies and Michael Loewe: *The Cambridge History of China: Volume I The Ch'in and Han Empires, 221 B.C.-A.D. 220*, Cambridge: Cambridge University Press, 1986.

US Commission, 'Annual Report of the United States Commission on International Religious Freedom', Washington, DC: U.S. Commission on International Religious Freedom, 2005, 2009.

von Glahn, Richard, *The Sinister Way: The Divine and Demonic in Chinese Religious Culture*, Berkeley: University of California Press, 2004

Waltham, Clae, *Shu Ching: Book of History: A Modernized Edition of the Translations of James Legge*, London: George Allen & Uniwin LTD, 1972.

Wang Chong: *Lun Heng* 论衡, in *Zhuzi Jicheng Vol. 7, Beijing:* Zhonghua Shuju, 1954.

Wang, Hongyuan, *The Origins of Chinese Characters*, Beijing: Sinolingua, 1993.

Watson, Burton (tr.), *Zhuangzi: Basic Writings*, New York: Columbia University Press, 1968.

Watson, James L, 'Standardizing the Gods: The Promotion of T'ien Hou (Empress of Heaven) among the South China Coast, 960-1960', in David Johnson, Aandrew J. Nathan and Evelyn S. Rawski (eds), *Popular Culture in Late Imperial China*, Berkeley: University of California Press, 1985, 292–324.

—'The Structure of Chinese Funerary Rites: Elementary Forms, Ritual Sequence, and Primacy of Performance', in James Watson and Evelyn S. Rawski, (eds), *Death Ritual in Late Imperial and Modern China*, Berkeley and Los Angeles: University of California Press, 1988, 3–19.

Weber, Max, *The Religion of China: Confucianism and Daoism*, New York: Free Press, 1968.

Wilhelm, Richard, *I Ching or Book of Changes*, translated by Cary F. Baynes, London and New York: Penguin Books, 1989.

Williams, E. T, 'The State Religion of China during the Manchu Dynasty', *Journal of the North China Branch, Royal Asiatic Society*, Vol. XLTV, 1913, 11–45.

Wolf, Arthur P. (ed.), *Religion and Ritual in Chinese Society*, Stanford: Stanford University Press, 1974.

Xiandai Hanyu Cidian 现代汉语词典, Beijing: Shangwu yinshuguan, 2002.

Xu Che, *Zhongguo bai shenxian* 中国百神仙, Shanghai: Shanghai kexue jishu wenxian chubanshe, 2008.

Xu Zhongshu (ed.), *Jiaguwen zidian* 甲骨文字典 (*A Dictionary of Oracle Bones Inscriptions*), Chengdu: Sichuan Cishu Chubanshe, 1990.

Yang, C. K, *Religion in Chinese Society–A Study of Contemporary Social Functions of Religion and Some of Their Historical Factors*, Los Angeles: University of California Press, 1961.

Yang, Fenggang and Tamney, Joseph B, *State, Market and Religions in Chinese Societies*, Leiden, Boston: Brill Academic Pub, 2005.

Yao, Xinzhong, *Confucianism and Christianity*, Brighton and Portland: Sussex Academic Press, 1996.

—*An Introduction to Confucianism*, Cambridge: Cambridge University Press, 2000.

Yao, Xinzhong and Paul Badham, *Religious Experience in Contemporary China*, Cardiff: University of Wales Press, 2007.

Yu, Anthony C. (tr. and ed.), *The Journey to the West*, vols. 1–4, Chicago and London: The University of Chicago Press, 1977, 1980, 1983.

Yü, Chün-fang, *Kuan-yin, the Chinese Transformation of Avalokitesvara*, New York: Columbia University Press, 2001.

Yü, Yingshih, 'O Soul Come Back!' A Study in the Changing Conceptions of the Soul and Afterlife in Pre-Buddhist China, *Harvard Journal of Asiatic Studies*, vol. 47, 2001, 363–95.

Zhang Jian, *Zhongguo Zongjiao yu Zhongguo Wenhua* 中国宗教与中国文化, Beijing: Zhongguo shehui kexue chubanshe, 2005.

Zhao, Yanxia, *Father and Son in Confucianism and Christianity: A Comparative Study of Xunzi and Paul*, Brighton and Portland: Sussex Academic Press, 2007.

Zhuo Xinping, Dangdai zhongguo zongjiao yanjiu: wenti yu silu 当代中国宗教研究：问题与思路, in Jin, Ze & Qiu, Yonghui (eds): *Blue Book of Religions: Annual Report on China's Religions 2008*, Beijing: Zhongguo shehui kexue chubanshe, 2008.

Zürcher, Eric, *The Buddhist Conquest of China: The Spread and Adaptation of Buddhism in Early Medieval China*, Leiden: E. J. Brill, 1972.

Index

43624971R00137

Made in the USA
San Bernardino, CA
21 December 2016